T0320056

Consequences of Creating a Market Economy

For Eric

Consequences of Creating a Market Economy

Evidence from Household Surveys in Central Asia

Kathryn H. Anderson
Associate Professor of Economics, Vanderbilt University, US

and

Richard Pomfret
Professor of Economics, University of Adelaide, Australia

Edward Elgar
Cheltenham, UK • Northampton, MA, USA

© Kathryn Anderson and Richard Pomfret 2003

All rights reserved. No part of this publication may be reproduced, stored in a retrieval system or transmitted in any form or by any means, electronic, mechanical or photocopying, recording, or otherwise without the prior permission of the publisher.

Published by
Edward Elgar Publishing Limited
Glensanda House
Montpellier Parade
Cheltenham
Glos GL50 1UA
UK

Edward Elgar Publishing, Inc.
136 West Street
Suite 202
Northampton
Massachusetts 01060
USA

A catalogue record for this book
is available from the British Library

Library of Congress Cataloguing in Publication Data

Anderson, Kathryn H.
  Consequences of creating a market economy : evidence from household surveys
in Central Asia / Kathryn Anderson, Richard Pomfret.
   p. cm.
  Includes bibliographical references.
   1. Cost and standard of living—Asia, Central. 2. Asia, Central—Economic
conditions—1991-3. 3. Cost and standard of living—Kyrgyzstan. 4. Kyrgyzstan
—Economic conditions—1991-5. Household surveys—Asia, Central. 6.
Household surveys—Kyrgyzstan. I. Pomfret, Richard W. T. II. Title

  HD7049.22 .A54 2003
  330.958—dc21
                                                                    2002037924
  ISBN 1 84376 169 6

Printed and bound in Great Britain by MPG Books Ltd, Bodmin, Cornwall

Contents

Figures

Tables

Preface

The research reported in this book was begun in 1996, and we are grateful to many people who assisted us in obtaining and understanding the data, particularly at the World Bank and in the national statistical offices. Financial support was provided by a grant under the University of Adelaide Research Scheme. The Asian Development Bank supported travel to Central Asia in July 2001 for a related project; the ADB is not responsible for any of the opinions or findings in this book.

Several parts of the book draw upon our previously published work or papers presented at conferences. Chapters 2 and 3 are based in part on 'Economic Development Strategies in Central Asia since 1991' in *Asian Studies Review*, **25**(2), 2001, 185–200. Chapter 4 draws upon 'Poverty in Kyrgyzstan' in *Asia-Pacific Development Journal*, **6**(1), June 1999, 73-88, and 'Living Standards during Transition to a Market Economy: The Kyrgyz Republic in 1993 and 1996' in *Journal of Comparative Economics*, **26**(3), September 2000, 502–23. Chapter 5 is based upon 'Transition and Poverty in Central Asia' in *The Soviet and Post-Soviet Review*, **25**(2), 1998, 149–62, and 'Living Standards in Central Asia 1991–2001,' a paper presented at the American Economics Association conference in Atlanta, 3–6 January 2002. Chapter 6 draws on 'Gender Effects of Transition: The Kyrgyz Republic', a paper presented at the American Economics Association conference in New Orleans, 5–7 January 2001. Chapter 7 is based upon 'Development of Small and Medium Enterprises in the Kyrgyz Republic, 1993-1997' in Faculty of Economics, Split (eds) *Enterprise in Transition* (University of Split, Croatia, 2001), p. 400–401 (summary in hard copy, full text on accompanying cd-rom), 'Challenges facing Small and Medium-sized Enterprises in the Kyrgyz Republic, 1996–7' in *MOCT-MOST* (*Economic Policy in Transitional Economies*), **11**(3), 2001, 205–19, and 'Business Start-ups in the Kyrgyz Republic'. We are grateful to the editors of the above-mentioned journals for permission to re-use copyright material.

We are grateful to Robert Ackland, Nauro Campos, Jane Falkingham, Yelena Kalyuzhnova, Sheila Marnie, John Micklewright, Mike Mills, Charles Becker, J.S. Butler and Charles Scott for helpful comments and suggestions on drafts of the various papers. We are very grateful to the National Statistics Committees in the Kyrgyz Republic, Kazakhstan and Tajikistan for providing us access to their survey data and to the LSMS division of the World Bank for facilitating our access to these data.

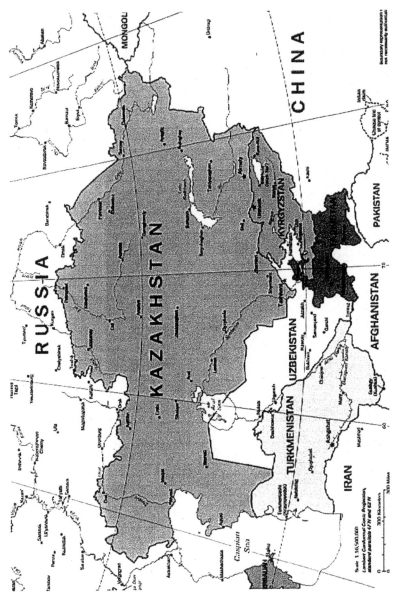

Source: http://www.centralasianews.net/map.html

Map of Central Asia

1. Introduction

This book uses rich household survey data to examine questions about household decision-making during the transition from central planning to a market-based economy. The five Central Asian successor states to the Soviet Union provide a natural experiment insofar as, from similar initial conditions when the USSR dissolved at the end of 1991, they pursued differing economic policies and experienced differing macroeconomic outcomes during the following decade. We address questions about the characteristics of gainers and losers from the introduction of market forces, including the role of education, household composition, location and gender. We also examine the characteristics of the founders of household businesses, which is important in light of the growing evidence that the emergence of new enterprises is a key distinguishing feature of more successful transition economies.

1. DATA SOURCES ON LIVING STANDARDS IN CENTRAL ASIA

The USSR had a relatively egalitarian income distribution, which was also true of the Central Asian republics even though they had the highest poverty rates in the USSR. The move to a more market-oriented economy has everywhere increased inequality (Cornia, 1996; Milanovic, 1998). If inequality has increased in these already poor countries, this has serious implications for living standards; we want to know not only what happened to average living standards but also how the changes in living standards varied across and within countries.

The major source on living standards data in the Soviet Union was the household budget surveys (HBS). These samples were biased, since they concentrated on households with earners in state factories or on collective farms and, to a lesser extent, on pensioners. Both tails of the income distribution were underrepresented, as households whose main employee worked in the private sector or was not working were absent and certain occupations were excluded (for example, party officials, high level bureaucrats, and military officers). Rural households were undersampled, which is especially important for the Central Asian republics, which were the most rural of the Soviet economies. Furthermore, the samples were not rotated; once the sample was established in the early 1950s, households were only removed by attrition. Falkingham et al. (1997, 48) characterize the HBS as 'a survey with a long history and a terrible reputation'. After independence the new national statistical authorities continued to follow the methodology of the HBS. The practices and standards diverged more than previously, but the HBS remains the main source for intertemporal comparisons.[1] The HBS can provide some guide to average (or, more precisely, median) household consumption levels, but the nature of the sample makes the HBS data a poor guide to changes in income distribution or in the number of people in poverty.

A potentially better data set for analysing living standards is the surveys supported by the World Bank as part of the Living Standards Measurement Study (LSMS).[2] The first such survey in Central Asia was the Kyrgyzstan Multipurpose Poverty Survey (KMPS) conducted in October and November 1993 with a sample of about 2000 households, that is, twice the size of the HBS sample and with much greater care taken to ensure a representative sample. The KMPS is distinguished from the standard LSMS surveys by its extensive additional questions, especially on nutrition. Surveys conducted in February and March 1996 in the Kyrgyz Republic used a similar questionnaire to that used in 1993, as did a 1996 LSMS in Kazakhstan and an LSMS begun but not completed in Uzbekistan in 1997. A series of annual LSMS surveys in the Kyrgyz Republic began in October/November 1996 with a new sampling frame and a longer questionnaire focusing on the changing environment brought about by transition to a market economy and omitting the nutrition questions of the KMPS. National LSMS surveys were conducted in Turkmenistan in spring 1998 and in Tajikistan in spring 1999, and a pilot survey was conducted in one region of Uzbekistan in 1999. The LSMS surveys are clearly superior to the HBS in sampling methodology and coverage, but so far have been little analysed. They are the basic sources for the analysis in this book, and they are described in greater detail in the Appendix.

There have also been a number of household surveys focussing on specific issues which cast some light on living standards, as well as studies of limited geographic areas or rapid appraisal methods. As the most open of the Central Asian countries, the Kyrgyz Republic has benefited most from external assistance, some of which has included finance for surveys, as well as being the country most willing to permit independent studies. Moreover, because this pattern dates back to 1993, the Kyrgyz Republic is the only Central Asian country with good quality data from the early stages of transition, permitting the closest thing we have to a before and after comparison. In sum, our best knowledge of the characteristics of gainers and losers comes from the Kyrgyz Republic, which has by far the best set of post-independence household survey data.

2. OUTLINE OF THE BOOK

The next two chapters review the background of the Central Asian economies before and after independence, and the evidence from the main economic performance indicators. The nature of our household survey data means that we cannot readily answer questions about performance over time and across countries. Rather we are examining, given the differing policy environments and post-independence economic performance, the characteristics of gainers and losers from the transition. These questions are addressed in Chapters 4 and 5.

Because the Kyrgyz Republic is the only Central Asian country with multiple LSMS-style surveys in the 1990s, our analysis starts with that country. The Kyrgyz Republic survey data are especially interesting because the 1993 survey can plausibly be considered to capture the situation before the establishment of a market economy. Although the USSR dissolved in December 1991, the Central Asian successor states' attention was focussed in 1992–93 on nation building and such elementary matters as establishing economic institutions and national currencies. By 1996 the Kyrgyz Republic had one of the most liberal economies in the Commonwealth of Independent States, so that the LSMS survey data present a before and after picture, followed by annual snapshots. In Chapter 4 we present analysis of the characteristics of poor households in 1993 and 1996 and more sophisticated analysis of the determinants of living standards across the entire distribution.[3]

Chapter 5 utilizes the publicly available LSMS data from the Kazakhstan and Tajikistan national surveys and the Uzbekistan pilot survey to compare the outcomes in these countries to the results from the Kyrgyz Republic. Although care has to be taken in making cross-country comparisons, especially when the surveys are from different years (1996 in Kazakhstan, and 1999 in Tajikistan and the Fergana province of Uzbekistan) at differing points in the transitional cycle, the uniform methodology of the LSMS surveys make the data a good source for comparative analysis. Indeed, the degree of data comparability is remarkably high for a group of non-OECD countries.[4]

The position of women in the Islamic former Soviet republics has been a controversial issue. Many observers saw improved social and economic status of women as one of the great benefits of the Soviet era and feared that these gains would be eroded after the dissolution of the Soviet Union. Much of the anecdotal evidence on the status of women in Central Asia since 1991 is disturbing, but it raises the question of how representative such evidence is. Chapter 6 contributes to our knowledge by analysing the Kyrgyz Republic LSMS data to draw conclusions about the position of women in the workforce. Given the high labour force participation rate of women, this is an important aspect of gender equity, although it is clearly an incomplete picture of the status of women which also depends upon intra-household resource allocation and on non-economic aspects.

A general finding from formerly centrally planned economies (and elsewhere) is that economic growth has been fuelled by new enterprises. Early debates about the transition from central planning focused on how to privatize state-owned enterprises, but by the early 2000s the emphasis had shifted from how to reform state enterprises to consideration of how to foster new enterprises. Chapter 7 uses the Kyrgyz Republic LSMS surveys to identify the characteristics of entrepreneurs. By their nature the surveys restrict this analysis to household businesses, that is, 'small' rather than small and medium-sized enterprises (SMEs). The survey data are, however, a rich source insofar as they allow comparison of the early and more mature phases of the transition and because they contain specific questions for households with non-farm businesses.

Chapter 8 draws conclusions and presents social policy implications obtained from our results.

NOTES

1. Before independence, completed questionnaires were sent to Moscow for processing, so that local analytical capacity was not developed (Falkingham et al., 1997, 43), and deliberate attempts were made to falsify published results (Dmitrieva, 1996, 100). Atkinson and Micklewright (1992, 265–269) review the methodology of the HBS. Marnie and Micklewright (1997) assess cross-tabulations from the 1989 HBS data for the Uzbek republic.
2. Deaton (1997) and Grosh and Glewwe (1998) describe the LSMS surveys. The core questions of the Central Asian surveys are based on Russian surveys initiated in 1992, which facilitates eventual comparability with other Soviet successor states. Klugman and Braithwaite (1998) review the Russian surveys.
3. The statistical analysis in chapters 4–7 was conducted with STATA. Details

and results referred to but not reported here are available from kathryn.anderson@vanderbilt.edu.

4. The small number of World Bank staff and outside consultants associated with the Central Asian LSMS surveys in the 1990s, with the same people often working on different countries, reinforced the uniformity and comparability of the survey data used in this book. Atkinson and Brandolini (2001) analyse pitfalls associated with cross-country analysis of household data when survey design, definitions, income and expenditure coverage, and so forth, vary.

2. The Central Asian economies before and after independence

The economies of Kazakhstan, the Kyrgyz Republic, Tajikistan, Turkmenistan and Uzbekistan were all centrally planned during the Soviet era and followed development strategies determined in Moscow. Since independence in late 1991, despite some similarity of economic structure, they have pursued differing development strategies. By the end of the twentieth century the transition to a market-oriented economy was essentially over, in the sense that Soviet-era central planning had ceased to exist and in all five countries market forces operate, although the countries have diverged to quite different economic systems with the five governments seeking to maintain economic control in different ways and to differing degrees. The aim of this chapter is to describe the initial conditions and national economic polices. The next chapter analyses the macroeconomic outcomes.

The five countries had no experience of nationhood before they were incorporated into the Russian empire during the eighteenth and nineteenth centuries, and they faced completely unexpected challenges of nation-building when the Soviet Union collapsed during the latter part of 1991. Their economic structures were similar in their emphasis on primary products, although the natural resource endowment varied from country to country (Pomfret, 1995). The region had been planned as a single unit, or perhaps more accurately as part of the single unit that had been the Soviet economy, and all five countries suffered severe disruption from the replacement of the USSR by fifteen independent countries. Attempts to maintain common economic links by retaining the ruble as a common currency in 1992–93 exacerbated the problem of hyperinflation and had been abandoned by the end of 1993. Within these common bounds, the five countries gradually became more differentiated as their governments introduced national strategies for transition to a market-based economy.

Surprisingly diverse economic strategies were adopted by the national leaders, despite the similarity of the inherited political structures. The Kyrgyz Republic embraced advice from western institutions advocating rapid change, and its president fostered the emergence of the most liberal regime in the region. Turkmenistan is at the opposite end of the spectrum; the president personalized absolute authority and limited economic change. Kazakhstan initially appeared to follow the Kyrgyz Republic on a liberal path, but as the 1990s progressed the economy became more like an economy of favours and influence than the market economy envisioned by reformers; dependence on hydrocarbon exports added to the atmosphere of rent-seeking, although it also helped to fuel a boom as oil prices rose rapidly in 1999 and 2000. Uzbekistan retained a tightly controlled political system and has been cautious in undertaking economic reforms, but its strategy of gradual economic change has, so far, been relatively successful. Tajikistan was the only one of the five countries not to evolve peacefully from Soviet republic to independent state under unchanged leadership, and the bloody civil war of 1992–93, which reignited in 1996–97, delayed implementation of a serious and consistent economic strategy; even during the relative peace of the last five years, the government has exerted uneven physical control over the country, but in the economic sphere it retains tight control where it can.

1. INITIAL CONDITIONS

The new independent countries of Central Asia started from fairly similar initial conditions. Before independence they were all republics of the Soviet Union, and had the same economic system. Although during the Gorbachev era some local economic experiments had taken place in the Baltic republics, parts of the Russian republic and elsewhere in the USSR, these had been absent from Central Asia, which was generally viewed as the most conservative area in the USSR. Together with Azerbaijan, the Central Asian republics had the largest proportion of households living below the poverty line (Table 2.1).

Per capita output in 1990 has been estimated at between $1130 and $1690 for the four southernmost republics and $2600 for the Kazakh republic. The relative values in Table 2.1 are a reasonable guide to the ranking of Soviet republics by living standards, but the absolute dollar values must be treated with caution due to the insoluble problems of the Soviet Union's artificial relative prices (Pomfret, 1995, 171–6). The estimates in Table 2.1 place the Kazakh republic's per capita GNP on a par with that of Hungary and somewhat lower than Iran's, while the other four republics had per capita GNP comparable to that of Turkey or Thailand; post-1991 experience suggests that they were behind all of these comparators.[1]

Consequences of creating a market economy

Table 2.1 Initial conditions: republics of the USSR 1989/91

	Popula. (mill.) mid- 1990	GNP per capita[a] 1990	Gini coeff 1989	Poverty (% of pop.)[b] 1989	Life Expect (years) 1991	Adult Literacy (%) 1991	Terms of trade[c]
Kazak	16.8	2600	0.289	15.5	69	97.5	+19
Kyrgyz	4.4	1570	0.287	32.9	68	97.0	+1
Tajik	5.3	1130	0.308	51.2	70	96.7	−7
Turkm	3.7	1690	0.307	35.0	66	97.7	+50
Uzbek	20.5	1340	0.304	43.6	69	97.2	−3
USSR	289.3	2870	0.289	11.1			

Notes:
[a] GNP per capita in US dollars computed by the World Bank's synthetic *Atlas* method.
[b] Poverty = individuals in households with gross per capita monthly income less than 75 rubles.
[c] Impact on terms of trade of moving to world prices, calculated at 105-sector level of aggregation using 1990 weights.

Sources: Columns 1–2, World Bank (1992, 3–4); columns 3–4, Atkinson and Micklewright (1992, Table U13) based on Goskomstat household survey data; columns 5–6, UNDP (1994); column 7, Tarr (1994).

The Central Asian republics' role in the Soviet division of labour was as producers of raw materials. The Kazakh republic's higher living standards reflect a more diversified economy with grain exports and a variety of mineral and energy resources. The Uzbek republic's economy was dominated by cotton, as were neighbouring parts of the other republics. Turkmenistan experienced a boom in natural gas production during the closing decade of the USSR, while the mainly mountainous Kyrgyz and Tajik republics had fewer exploitable resources.[2] Estimates of the impact of moving from Soviet to world prices show large gains for the Kazakh and Turkmen republics because energy resources were severely undervalued at Soviet prices (Table 2.1), but realization of the benefits from Turkmenistan's natural gas wealth or from Kazakhstan's minerals and oil was limited during the 1990s because existing pipeline routes left them dependent on Russia and other CIS countries for transit facilities and end-user payments. At least in the short term, Uzbekistan's resource endowment may have been more favourable because Uzbekistan was able to reduce its dependence on imported fuel and because world cotton prices boomed during the first half of the 1990s.

The Kyrgyz, Tajik, Turkmen and Uzbek republics had, together with Azerbaijan, the lowest per capita incomes in the USSR. The last four of these also had the most unequal income distribution, although the Gini coefficients, while high by Soviet standards, were still low relative to most lower and middle income countries.[3] The 1989 poverty rates for the Central Asian and Caucasus republics were substantially higher than in other Soviet republics (Table 2.1).

Within the USSR neither poverty nor unemployment officially existed. Until the mid 1960s, the official position was that with full employment poverty was impossible and only the wilfully idle could be poor (McAuley, 1994, 188–9). There was thus not only no unemployment insurance, but also no general means-tested programme of social assistance. The position was softened during the late 1960s and early 1970s, by raising the minimum wage and extending the child allowance system, but the general design of the welfare system was unchanged. A 1974 decree defined underprovisioned households as those with less than 50 rubles per person, and provided a monthly supplement to them.[4] During the 1980s hidden unemployment and the proportion of families receiving less than the minimum consumption basket increased. These trends were exacerbated by the abolition of central planning in 1987, the disintegration of the USSR in 1991, and the price reforms of January 1992.

The correlates of poverty in the USSR are debated, in large part due to the inadequate database with various researchers using differing sources to reach conflicting conclusions. McAuley (1979, 88) concluded that among non-agricultural state employees the minimum wage in the 1970s was sufficient to ensure that employed individuals lived above the poverty line, so that deprivation depended on having a non-working spouse and the number of dependents. Ofer and Vinokur (1992) challenged this conclusion, claiming that poverty existed among all kinds of Soviet households, including where both husband and wife worked. Household budget data for the Uzbek republic showed a significant relationship between household income and number of children (Marnie and Micklewright, 1997).

The status of women in the USSR is also a matter of interpretation, especially in Central Asia where the starting point was low. Positive views emphasise the emancipation of women, improved educational opportunities for girls and the incorporation of women into the labour force (Patnaik, 1989; Ubaidullaeva, 1982). In the USSR as a whole, women worked slightly fewer hours than men in paid employment, but at much lower wages than men, and spent twice as much time as men on household chores; the wage differentials cannot be fully explained by differences in human capital (Swafford, 1978; Ofer and Vinokur, 1992, 229–70). Independence was widely forecast to exacerbate gender discrimination in Central Asia, and reduce female participation in paid employment as traditional pre-Soviet gender roles were re-established.

The study by Lubin (1984), based on a year spent in Tashkent in 1978/9 and a brief return visit in 1981, mainly addresses the role of ethnicity, questioning the hypothesis that Central Asians were discriminated against in Soviet Central Asia.

Although their incomes were lower than the incomes of Slavs or other nationalities, the Central Asians accepted this by choice due to cultural preferences (for example unwillingness to leave the extended family) or preferring positions with potential for informal economic activity over higher-paying jobs which provided fewer opportunities to benefit from the shadow economy.[5]

The Soviet welfare system was strongly influenced by characteristics of the central planning system (McAuley, 1994). Because virtually all productive enterprises were owned by the state, the distinction between state and enterprise was blurred. Taxation and tax administration were poorly developed, because there was little need to distinguish between what belonged to enterprises and what belonged to the state. There was also a confusion of function as many enterprises provided an array of services ranging from pre-school child care to housing. With physical allocation of goods and services, the welfare system functioned reasonably well (although shortages engendered corruption and inefficient allocation by queuing), but it was a poor starting point for the provision of welfare services during the transition to a market economy.

Pension eligibility was generous in the USSR. After twenty years of employment, men were eligible for a state pension at 60 and women at 55, and in many circumstances earlier retirement was possible, for example military personnel, miners and, especially important for Central Asia, women who had borne many children. Pensions could frequently be drawn while continuing to work for wages. After independence these pension entitlements were difficult to change and ate up a large part of government budgets; even when the value of pensions was eroded, the sheer numbers made for a large aggregate bill. Universal pension rights were well-suited to economies with flat income distributions, but the absence of administrative capacity to target needy old people created a serious problem after independence.[6] With large numbers of eligible pensioners, fiscal constraints led to the pension budget being spread thinly, so that poor pensioners were insufficiently provided for or payments delayed.

In sum, although living standards in Soviet Central Asia were low by the standards of the USSR, income distribution was not perceived as a major problem either nationally or within individual republics. Although 'underprovisioned households' were assisted after 1974, poverty was neither explicitly recognized nor extensively analysed during the Soviet era. Correspondingly, the welfare system was designed for an egalitarian society in which universal entitlement to pensions, child support, health, education and other social services was the norm, and in the centrally planned economy it mattered little whether delivery was through the government or the enterprise.

2. INDEPENDENCE AND CHOICE OF NATIONAL ECONOMIC POLICIES

The Central Asian republics were almost totally unprepared for the rapid dissolution of the Soviet Union in 1991. As new independent states at the end of that year, they faced three major economic shocks: transition from central planning, dissolution of the Soviet Union, and hyperinflation. Dismantling the centrally planned economy created severe disorganization problems, which led to output decline everywhere in central and eastern Europe (Blanchard, 1997). The dissolution of the Soviet Union added to these problems as new national borders, and attempts to retain resources within these borders, disrupted supply links. In Central Asia the absence of any tradition of nationhood and the need to create new national institutions compounded these difficulties. The new governments faced a fiscal squeeze, with demands for public expenditure to meet entitlements and to shelter enterprises and individuals from income loss, but with little capacity to levy taxes. Attempts to maintain existing trade, commercial and political links by retaining a common currency fuelled hyperinflation.

Table 2.2 Inflation, 1991-2000*

	Kazakhstan	Kyrgyz Republic	Tajikistan	Turkmenistan	Uzbekistan
1991	79	85	112	103	82
1992	1381	855	1157	493	645
1993	1662	772	2195	3102	534
1994	1892	229	350	1748	1568
1995	176	41	609	1005	305
1996	39	31	418	992	54
1997	17	26	88	84	59
1998	8	36	28	24	29
1999	7	12	43	17	18
2000	13	19	34	8	50

Note: * Annual increase in consumer price index (end of year).

Source: EBRD (2001, 16).

Prices increased very rapidly in 1992, by more than 50 percent per month in all five countries (Table 2.2). The currency became the dominant economic issue in 1993, and four of the countries introduced national currencies: the Kyrgyz Republic in May, and Turkmenistan, Kazakhstan and Uzbekistan in November (Pomfret, 1996, 118–29). A national currency was a prerequisite for gaining control over inflation and hence establishing a functioning market economy in which *relative* price changes could be observed and perform their allocative function. Tajikistan was torn by civil war and did not introduce a national currency until May 1995.[7]

A national currency may have been a necessary condition for macroeconomic stability and effective economic reform but it was not a sufficient condition, and each of the countries moved along a different reform path. The various synthetic measures of the speed and extent of liberalization in transition economies typically divide the Central Asian transition economies into two groups. The Kyrgyz Republic and Kazakhstan are somewhere in the middle, and Uzbekistan, Turkmenistan and Tajikistan at the bottom of the list. Tajikistan is sometimes put in a separate category of those countries affected by regional tensions; it is viewed as making a delayed attempt at reform since 1997.[8] Turkmenistan has committed to minimizing economic change.

The Kyrgyz Republic is usually considered to be one of the most dynamic reformers among the former Soviet republics. In Central Asia, the Kyrgyz Republic was the first of the new independent countries to curb hyperinflation, bringing the annual inflation rate below 50 percent in 1995. Speed in addressing hyperinflation is closely correlated with the speed with which the transition to a more market-oriented economy has been pursued. In the Kyrgyz Republic, state orders were eliminated in 1993 and practically all prices liberalized by 1994. Enterprise reform has been less dramatic than in Central or Eastern Europe or the Russian Federation, but more extensive than elsewhere in Central Asia. The financial sector has also been transformed, so that both the exchange rate and interest rates are market-determined, although thin markets have limited allocative efficiency. In July 1998 the Kyrgyz Republic became the first successor state to the USSR to join the World Trade Organization, reflecting the country's liberal trade regime. Progress in creating the institutions needed to support a functioning market economy is, however, controversial. Important markets like the foreign exchange, domestic capital and national labour markets do not function effectively in allocating resources. This may reflect the initial backwardness of the economy, not just in income levels but also in human capital, which has been exacerbated by substantial emigration.[9]

Kazakhstan had a better base for creating a market economy, given its higher living standards and human capital endowments, and it too was initially viewed as one of the more reformist Soviet successor states. Although macroeconomic control was attained more slowly than in the

Kyrgyz Republic, with an annual inflation rate of 50 percent achieved in 1996, Kazakhstan did move fairly quickly with price liberalization and enterprise reform. The privatization process, or more specifically the policies towards energy and minerals rights, has, however, been associated with widespread corruption similar to that which emerged in Russia in 1995–96. In the second half of the 1990s concerns increased over the government's failure to establish a suitable framework for a well-functioning market economy.[10] Agents of the government are frequently seen to be benefiting from their position rather than enforcing law and order or maintaining public services, and privatization largely benefited insiders without obvious efficiency gains. Nevertheless, since 1996 Kazakhstan has, like the Kyrgyz Republic and unlike Uzbekistan or Turkmenistan, accepted currency convertibility on current account, and prices in Kazakhstan are essentially market-determined and subject to world market forces.

Uzbekistan is often viewed as one of the least liberalized among economies in transition from central planning.[11] Although the political regime is authoritarian and illiberal, the economy has been gradually reformed since independence. Price and enterprise reform proceeded slowly, but practically all prices had been liberalized by 1996 and housing and small enterprises have been privatized. Trade policy is liberal as export taxes imposed in the early 1990s have been removed, but its impact is negated by stringent foreign exchange controls which were reintroduced in the second half of 1996. Macroeconomic control was achieved more slowly than in the Kyrgyz Republic or Kazakhstan, with inflation only dropping below 50 percent in 1998; prices have been less free than in those countries, and privatization has proceeded at a glacial speed. Nevertheless, the government has moved albeit cautiously to establish a market economy and has provided good governance in moderating corruption, providing infrastructure and maintaining social expenditures (Pomfret and Anderson, 1997). By 1998 the European Bank for Reconstruction and Development ranked Uzbekistan ahead of Kazakhstan in its annual index of cumulative progress towards establishing a market economy.[12] The government, however, took a major step backwards in October 1996 when, in response to balance of payments problems following a decline in world cotton prices, draconian exchange controls were re-introduced; the consequence in the remainder of the 1990s was a steadily widening gap between the official and the black market exchange rates, leading to substantial resource misallocation (Rosenberg and de Zeeuw, 2000). A hallmark of the Uzbekistan government's economic strategy has, however, been a willingness to reassess and change policies when faced with evidence that they are not working well, and in 2000 and 2001 there were signs of increased support for private sector activities and liberalization of the exchange controls (Pomfret, 2000c).[13]

Turkmenistan is also classified as a slow reformer, and in this case indisputably so. The president has adopted populist policies aimed at minimizing fundamental change. Initially, he promised the people a range of free utilities and other services, to be paid for by natural gas export revenues, but the pipeline system channelled gas exports to other former Soviet republics and allowed little opportunity for market diversification; problems receiving payment for such exports undermined the presidential promises (Ochs, 1997; Lubin, 1999). Eventually in the first half of 1997 Turkmenistan cut off supplies, which were only resumed after a solution to the payments problems was negotiated in early 1999. The decline in GDP in 1997 was exacerbated by a poor 1996 cotton harvest.[14]   In this context, Turkmenistan moved to a more serious economic reform. Prices of important consumer goods such as meat, vegetable oil, tea and sugar were gradually freed during 1997, and price subsidies on these goods were largely removed in January 1998, leaving subsidies only on bread and flour, utilities and communal services, petrol, transportation and building materials. Despite promises of reforms after 1997, however, there is still little evidence of change, either economically or politically. National resources have been frittered away on prestige projects such as a magnificent presidential palace and a new national airport, and a large debt has been accumulated to fund import-substitution projects which are unlikely to ever generate (or save) foreign currency with which to repay the loans (Pastor and van Rooden, 2000; Pomfret, 2001). After the president declared himself president for life in 1999, the European Bank for Reconstruction and Development took the unprecedented step of banning all public sector loans to Turkmenistan, which underlined the increasing isolation of the country.[15]

Tajikistan is sometimes viewed as having made progress towards establishing a market-based economy, but implementation of consistent economic policies has been frustrated by the intermittent civil war throughout the 1990s. The economic disruption is captured in the huge decline in per capita output during the first half of the 1990s, and even after peace was negotiated in 1997 the political situation remained fragile and economic progress difficult. The poor security situation discouraged investment, and lack of unified control also deterred economic activity because separate agencies seek to raise revenue by taxes and fees.[16] The government was kept afloat in the early and mid 1990s by military loans from Russia and after 1997 by aid from the multilateral international financial institutions and other donors.

A summary of commonly used indicators of progress in transition from central planning or the degree of economic liberalization is presented in Table 2.3. The division between Kazakhstan and the Kyrgyz Republic on the one hand and the remaining countries on the other hand is clear.

Although Kazakhstan had the most cumulative liberalization by 1997, the Kyrgyz Republic had the most liberalized economy in 1999 by the EBRD index and had the best institutional quality. The IMF institutional quality index is, however, low for all five countries, and Tajikistan, Turkmenistan and Uzbekistan rank (together with Yugoslavia and Laos) among the five worst of all transition economies. The openness indicators, WTO status and current account convertibility, suggest that Tajikistan should perhaps be grouped with Kazakhstan and the Kyrgyz Republic in terms of intention to liberalize the economy, although the three indices show that Tajikistan still has substantial ground to make up.

Economic performance is related to initial conditions and other exogenous forces, as well as to policies. Given the pre-existing specialization in primary products, the national development strategies have been outward-oriented. Although there have been measures to encourage greater food and energy self-sufficiency, to protect domestic industries and to tax exports, trade policies have generally been liberal with low formal trade barriers. Trade performance has, however, been disappointing, especially the ability to find new export markets (Pomfret, 1999b). Turkmenistan and Kazakhstan, which had been expected to benefit substantially from the shift to world prices for their exports (Tarr, 1994), found themselves tied to old Soviet pipelines for their oil and gas exports, and Turkmenistan had great difficulty in collecting payment for its gas exports to Ukraine and Georgia. Uzbekistan turned out to have more favourable initial conditions insofar as its cotton and gold exports could be transported and sold for hard currency (Taube and Zettelmeyer, 1998).

Capital flows and external assistance have differed from country to country, and are not independent of economic policies. Direct foreign investment to Central Asia has gone overwhelmingly to Kazakhstan and to the energy sector. In the early post-independence era, the main source of external funds was the Bretton Woods institutions, which had a strong predilection for rapid reform and especially for macroeconomic stabilization and open trade and exchange policies. The Kyrgyz Republic benefited most from World Bank and IMF assistance, while Turkmenistan's and Uzbekistan's relations with these institutions have been frosty.[17] After 1997 Tajikistan became a major beneficiary of multilateral assistance, and by 2001 both the Kyrgyz Republic and Tajikistan had built up large debts, $1.7 billion (130 percent of GDP) and $1.2 billion respectively at the end of 2001, albeit at concessional rates.[18] Turkmenistan is believed to have accumulated a substantial external debt at commercial (or higher) rates, but the capital account of its balance of payments is not transparent. The severity of the debt problems is unclear, although it may be eased by a more supportive attitude towards the region's rulers by western creditors after the September 2001 terrorist acts in the USA.

Table 2.3 Summary indicators of transition

	EBRD Transition Index 1999	World Bank Liber. Index 1989–97	IMF Index of Inst.Quality 1997–98	WTO Status[a]	Currency Convertibility
Kazakhstan	2.7	4.35	–7.9	WP 1996	Yes
Kyrgyz Republic	2.8	3.39	–6.5	Joined 1998	Yes
Tajikistan	2.0	2.21	–17.3	WP 2001	Yes
Turkmenistan	1.4	1.53	–16.1	None	No
Uzbekistan	2.1	2.83	–13.8	WP 1994	No

Note: The WTO dates are for establishment of the Working Party; this does not necessarily reflect the current stage of negotiations.

Sources: The first three columns, taken from the summary table in IMF (2000b, 180–83), report the EBRD average of eight indicators, the similar index used by the World Bank summed over the years 1989–97, and the IMF index ranging from +25 to –25 (low institutional quality).

NOTES

1. Figures for the other countries are Iran $3200, Hungary $2590, Turkey $1370 and Thailand $1220 (World Bank, *1991 World Development Report*, 204–5).
2. The Tajik economy, however, benefited from a huge investment programme during the 1980s. The South Tajik Territorial Production Complex utilized hydroelectricity resources to develop an aluminium smelter, an electrochemical plant and other activities. Until the collapse of the USSR, investment in this project was expected to continue on a large scale in the 1990s.
3. In the USSR the elite benefited from important non-pecuniary privileges. On the other hand, public services reinforced the egalitarian outcome; Buckley and Gurenko (1997) show that imputed income from subsidized housing (including maintenance and utilities) played a major role in reducing economic inequality in the USSR. Atkinson and Micklewright (1992) compare income distributions in the USSR and eastern Europe. Milanovic (1998) reviews the distributional evidence from the 1990s.
4. This followed calculations by Soviet economists Sarkisyan and Kuznetsova who established a minimum material satisfaction budget for a family of four in the

mid 1960s of 205.60 rubles per month. Among western scholars, McAuley (1979) used the 50 ruble level as his primary criterion of poverty, while Matthews (1986) used 70 rubles per month as his poverty line and consequently produced a much gloomier picture of poverty in the USSR. Matthews' study identifies the USSR with the non-Islamic republics, apart from appending a brief unofficial report on 'Poverty in Central Asia' which is impressionistic and not very helpful. Although McAuley has three chapters on inequality among Soviet republics (and personal experience of Central Asia), he says nothing about intra-republic inequality.

5. In dealing with ethnicity there are serious multicollinearity problems because Turkic and Tajik groups have bigger families and other characteristics which may separately affect household living standards.

6. In Uzbekistan, maintenance of the entitlements after independence imposed a severe budgetary burden, which was exacerbated by an unsustainable indexation policy in 1993 when pension payments amounted to 11.4 percent of GDP (Griffin, 1996, 155–7).   After a change of indexation rules, however, expenditures halved in 1994.

7. The Tajik ruble was replaced by the somoni in October 2000. Despite concerns about yet another currency reform undermining confidence in financial assets (after the confiscatory reforms of 1993 and 1995), this primarily involved a rescaling as one somoni replaced 1000 Tajik rubles.

8. Attempts to accelerate reforms and establish macroeconomic stability after the introduction of the Tajik ruble in May 1995 were disrupted by renewed civil war in late 1996, and only revived after the June 1997 peace agreement. Despite a rhetoric of reform since 1997, there are few concrete achievements and critics see a pathology of aid dependence, in which the government mollifies donors by promising reforms but lacks the will or ability to implement serious reforms.

9. During the first half of the 1990s, both the Kyrgyz Republic and Kazakhstan experienced large net emigration, predominantly of ethnic Germans and Slavs, many of whom had above-average education and skill levels. Emigration from Tajikistan has also been substantial and, especially in recent years, included hundreds of thousands of ethnic Tajiks, reflecting the dearth of economic opportunities; many of these emigrants view their move as temporary, and they send remittances to their families, at least for a while.

10. Two books on Kazakhstan which appeared in 1998 (Kalyuzhnova, 1998; Olcott, 1998) were both sceptical about the country's economic and political liberalization, in contrast to more up-beat assessments in earlier reports by international institutions and independent commentators (for example World Bank, 1996).

11. To some extent, this reflects jaundiced views by the international financial institutions, with which Uzbekistan was on frosty terms throughout the 1990s, and a conflation of political and economic considerations. Gürgen et al. (1999, especially 3–4 and 73) is typical in its asserted rather than substantiated

contrast between the favourable record of the faster reformers, Kazakhstan and the Kyrgyz Republic, and the less successful other Central Asian economies. The IMF has, however, continued to be an impartial collector of data and empirical studies by some IMF staff, such as those by Taube and Zettelmeyer (1998), are admirably objective.   Relations between Uzbekistan and the Washington institutions appear to have improved since the change of government in Afghanistan in late 2001.

12. In EBRD (1998, Table 2.2.1) the unweighted average of the EBRD's eight indicators (on an ascending scale of 1–4) for the Central Asian countries was for Kazakhstan 2.1, the Kyrgyz Republic 2.9, Tajikistan 1.9, Turkmenistan 1.5 and Uzbekistan 2.3, although the following year Kazakhstan was ranked above Uzbekistan (see Table 2.3 in the text).

13. The black market premium peaked at 470 percent in January 2000. Signs of a policy reversal appeared in the first half of 2000 when the black market premium dropped to 160 percent in June 2000, where it remained for the next twelve months.   This reflected a substantial depreciation of the official exchange rate from around 140 to 325 sum/$ over the year 2000, including a devaluation from 148 to 231 on 1 May 2000.   Moreover, access to foreign exchange at better than the official rate was widened, especially after the 62 percent devaluation of the 'commercial exchange rate' on 1 July 2000 (*Uzbekistan Economic Trends, January–March 2001*, p.35).

14. In 1993 natural gas and cotton accounted for three fifths of Turkmenistan's GDP (IMF, 1998b, 8).

15. As with many judgments in this chapter, the situation remains fluid. In 2000 Turkmenistan became the last of the Central Asian countries to join the Asian Development Bank, which could signal a renewed interest in international links. On the other hand, Turkmenistan is the only Soviet successor state not to have applied for WTO membership.

16. A recurring number quoted in interviews in July 2001 is that small and medium-sized enterprises pay 17 separate taxes, with the consequence that few new private enterprises have emerged in Tajikistan.

17. Cumulative World Bank loan commitments up until the end of the 1996 fiscal year amounted to $70 per head for the Kyrgyz Republic, $49 for Kazakhstan, $11 for Uzbekistan, $6 for Turkmenistan and $1 for Tajikistan – calculated from data reported in the World Bank newsletter, *Transition*, **8**, February 1997. The Kyrgyz Republic also received concessional financing from the IMF, and by 1996 had the second-highest debt/GDP ratio (43 percent) of any former Soviet republic; the debt/GDP ratio for Tajikistan was 84 percent (mainly war-related concessional loans from Russia), Turkmenistan 32 percent, Kazakhstan 19 percent and Uzbekistan 17 percent, with the last three having acquired most of their debt on commercial terms (Kapur and van der Mensbrugghe, 1997).

18. The majority of Tajikistan's debt is bilateral debt and this has been rescheduled. As of July 2001, Tajikistan had suspended servicing of its debts to Russia, Kazakhstan and India and was negotiating payments on debts to Uzbekistan on an annual basis, but was servicing other external debts fully (IMF, 2001, 10). In March 2002 the Kyrgyz Republic had initiated Paris Club

negotiations with its major bilateral creditors, but the majority of its debt is with multilateral institutions (led by the World Bank and Asian Development Bank). In light of its low per capita GNP, the Kyrgyz Republic may qualify for leniency under the Highly Indebted Poor Countries (HIPC) Initiative.

3. Economic performance since independence: output, distribution, and poverty

This chapter reports measures of the output performance and of changes in inequality and poverty in the Central Asian countries since 1991. All suffered a severe recession in the early and mid 1990s and, although they all enjoyed positive economic growth by the end of the 1990s, reported levels of real GDP were still less than at the start of the decade. For the least well endowed with exploitable natural resources, the Kyrgyz Republic and Tajikistan, the outcome has been very low per capita incomes.[1] The move to market-based economies led to greater income inequality and increased poverty, especially in the countries with the lowest average incomes.

A decade after independence should be a long enough time for the effects of differing economic policies and strategies to be apparent, but patterns are not clear-cut. Countries have changed strategies, and especially in Uzbekistan there have been several policy changes within the generally gradualist framework. Exogenous factors, such as the world prices of crucial primary product exports, also complicate assessment of longer-term relationships between policies and performance, especially for Kazakhstan and Turkmenistan. Finally, for the Kyrgyz Republic and Tajikistan, and possibly also Turkmenistan, a growing external debt has raised questions about the sustainability of recent performance. Here, we will provide proximate explanations for economic performance, but eschew attempting to prove definitive links between policies and performance.[2]

1. OUTPUT

All of the Central Asian countries suffered a sharp drop in real output during the first half of the 1990s, whose impact on living standards was exacerbated by the cessation of intra-USSR transfers and by increased economic inequality. The initial decline in output is difficult to measure because of the problems of valuing Soviet-era output for which there was no demand after the end of central planning and because of quality changes and new products.[3] Revaluation of energy products provided a boost to estimated GDP in Kazakhstan and Turkmenistan, which partly offset the decline in quantities. In Tajikistan the disruption of civil war led to an exceptionally sharp fall in output in 1992, which continued until 1995–6. With these caveats in mind, we can attempt to relate changes in real GDP to the initial conditions and policies described in the previous chapter.

Table 3.1 reveals very different time paths of real GDP in the five countries up to 1997. Tajikistan is the easiest to explain, with the civil war destroying economic activity until the 1996 ceasefire, when real output had fallen to just over two-fifths of its level at independence. Turkmenistan, which had more abundant natural resources and has enjoyed a decade of peace, had the same outcome by 1997, albeit with a different time path. Turkmenistan's decline in real GDP was comparatively slow in 1992–93, accelerated in 1994–96, and went into collapse in 1997. There are some questions about the reliability of Turkmen economic data after the mid 1990s, but no doubt that the economy has been in serious trouble and that this is due to poor and unsustainable economic policies.[4] The other three countries' experience is more complex and more interesting.

Table 3.1 Real GDP, 1991–97 (index 1991 = 100)

	1991	1992	1993	1994	1995	1996	1997
Kazakh	100	94.7	86.0	75.2	69.0	69.3	70.7
Kyrgyz Republic	100	86.1	72.8	58.2	55.0	58.9	62.8
Tajik	100	71.0	63.2	51.3	44.9	42.9	43.8
Turkmen	100	94.7	85.0	68.9	63.2	58.4	43.8
Uzbek	100	89.0	86.9	83.3	82.5	83.8	85.6
CIS average	100	78.8	69.8	59.1	55.6	55.4	56.1

Source: National authorities and IMF staff estimates as reported in Mercer-Blackman and Unigovskaya (2000, 4).

Table 3.2 Growth in real GDP, 1992–2000 (per cent)

	92	93	94	95	96	97	98	99	00
Kazakh	–3	–9	–13	–8	1	2	–2	2	10
Kyrgyz Republic	–19	–16	–20	–5	7	10	2	4	5
Tajik	–29	–11	–19	–13	–4	2	5	4	8
Turkm	–5	–10	–17	–7	–7	–11	5	16	18
Uzbek	–11	–2	–4	–1	2	3	4	4	2
CIS average	–14	–9	–14	–5	–4	1	–4	3	7

Source: EBRD (2001, Table A.1). Data for 2000 are preliminary actuals.

The Kyrgyz Republic saw real GDP decline by 45 percent between 1991 and 1995. This was due to the three shocks described in the previous chapter, whose impact was not softened by possession of readily tradeable natural resources. The decision to adopt the most radical economic reforms in the region and the most rapid macroeconomic stabilization also exacerbated the severity of the post-independence recession. The theory of rapid reform, which has been to some extent vindicated by Polish experience but is still a matter of debate, implies that after the pain the Kyrgyz Republic should have been best placed to grow once it had the institutions of a market economy in place. The Kyrgyz economy did indeed grow by 15 percent between 1995 and 1997, but it is unclear to what extent that is sustainable. Much of the economic growth originated in one project, the Kumtor goldmine, which boosted real GDP during the investment stage in 1996–97 and has added to real GDP since then.[5] In 1998 economic growth was slower, in part due to temporary shocks such as the Russian economic crisis and poor agricultural performance, compared to the bumper harvests of 1996 and 1997. Growth in 1999, 2000 and 2001 was in the 4–5 percent per annum range (Table 3.2).

Kazakhstan's decline in real GDP in the first half of the 1990s was less than that of the Kyrgyz Republic, which may reflect the former's more abundant resources and perhaps its less radical reforms, but Kazakhstan did not enjoy the growth that the Kyrgyz Republic had in 1996–97. The Kazakhstan economy was then buffeted by the Russian crisis in 1998 and real GDP was probably little different by the end of the century than it had been in 1995. The proximate causes of the disappointing 1990s growth performance by the potentially best-placed new independent state in Central Asia were exogenous developments such as commodity price trends, interminable delays in establishing new oil pipeline routes from the Caspian Basin to non-CIS markets, and the August 1998 Russian economic crisis. More fundamentally, the poor performance reflected a failure to truly reform the economy so that it could better weather such shocks. Central planning appears to have been replaced by a rentier economy in which insiders live off the resource rents rather than generating new non-resource-related output. Output growth did return in 2000, driven by booming oil prices and positive real developments in the hydrocarbon sector, but it is highly dependent on that single sector.[6]

Uzbekistan's economic performance has been the greatest puzzle among all former Soviet republics. The initial decline in real GDP was fairly moderate – at least by the awful standards of the former Soviet Union in 1992–93. This could be ascribed to the avoidance of reform, but such stability has proven short-lived in other non-reformers such as Belarus or Turkmenistan whose unreformed economies continued to stagnate or decline in the second half of the 1990s. Uzbekistan in contrast halted the decline in real GDP in the mid 1990s and enjoyed modest economic growth during the second half of the decade. The relatively good performance between 1991 and 1996 was helped by buoyant world prices for Uzbekistan's two main exports, cotton and gold, although this appears to be only a partial explanation.[7] Although both commodities' prices fell substantially in the second half of the decade, Uzbekistan's GDP grew fairly steadily after 1995, albeit with a worrying slowdown in 2000. Measures of cumulative decline in real GDP over the 1990s (as in Table 3.3) show Uzbekistan to have had the smallest decline of any Soviet successor state.

Table 3.3 Real GDP in 1996 and 1999 (as percent of 1989)

	1996	1997
Kazakhstan	45	59
Kyrgyz Republic	52	62
Tajikistan	37	43
Turkmenistan	57	53
Uzbekistan	84	89

Sources: EBRD (1997b, 7 and 9; 1999, Table 1.1).

In all five countries aggregate output was increasing by the late 1990s (Table 3.2). The timing of the onset of growth varied, however, and

Kazakhstan suffered a setback in 1998. These variations in the timepath of output represent a potential pitfall for our study, insofar as we compare the situation in different countries at times determined by when the surveys were conducted, which may have been at differing points in the transformational recession or recovery. Our time-series analysis of the Kyrgyz Republic must also bear in mind that the 1993 LSMS survey was done in the midst of the output decline, while the 1996 and *a fortiori* 1997 and subsequent surveys were carried out after the recovery had begun.

2. DISTRIBUTION

In all countries in transition from central planning, income inequality has increased. In the most thorough attempt to assemble comparative data, Milanovic (1998) collected estimates of Gini coefficients in 1987/8 and in 1993/5 for most of the eastern European and former Soviet economies, and he reports estimates for all Central Asian countries except Tajikistan (Table 3.4). According to Milanovic, the Kyrgyz Republic suffered the largest changes in inequality. The ranking is plausible given the initial conditions and rapid reform in the Kyrgyz Republic, but the absolute numbers in Table 3.4 are of dubious comparative value, given that the Kyrgyz 1993 data are from the fall 1993 LSMS survey and all other data are from the HBS. The three non-Kyrgyz observations for 1993/5 are remarkably similar, which is surprising in view of the diverging policies of Kazakhstan, Turkmenistan and Uzbekistan. Milanovic has done heroic work in bringing together household survey data from most transition economies on a roughly comparable basis, but comparisons based on flawed data sets must be treated with caution.[8]

Table 3.4 Inequality in Central Asia (Milanovic)*

	Gini coefficient (income)	
	1987/8	1993/5
Kazakhstan	·0.26	0.33
Kyrgyz Republic	0.26	0.55
Turkmenistan	0.26	0.36
Uzbekistan	0.28	0.33

Note: *Data are household income taken from HBS, apart from Kyrgyz 1993 (LSMS); Turkmenistan's Gini coefficient is from 1989 not 1987/8.

Source: Milanovic (1998, 41).

Table 3.5 reports summary statistics on inequality derived from the LSMS data sets. The Gini coefficients in Table 3.5 provide a more nuanced picture of the situation during the 1990s than that provided by Milanovic's summary in Table 3.4. Although inequality was very high in the Kyrgyz Republic in fall 1993, this is likely to have been at a peak, when hyperinflation was still rampant, delayed payment of incomes was widespread and the initial economic disruption was likely at its worst. The Gini coefficients for 1996, although still high, show that inequality had begun to moderate after mid-decade.[9] In the second half of the decade inequality was most severe in Tajikistan and more pronounced in Turkmenistan than in Kazakhstan. The relatively low inequality in Kazakhstan according to the LSMS survey data is an antidote to anecdotal literature of large variations in wealth; some people may have gained disproportionately from the new opportunities, but it is important to keep the individual excesses in perspective.[10]

Table 3.5 Gini coefficients from LSMS data

	Gini coefficient (expenditure)
Kyrgyz Republic (1993)	0.54
Kyrgyz Republic (spring 1996)	0.46
Kyrgyz Republic (fall 1996)	0.41
Azerbaijan (1995)	0.35
Kazakhstan (1996)	0.35
Turkmenistan (1998)	0.41
Tajikistan (1999)	0.47

Source: World Bank (2000, 19).

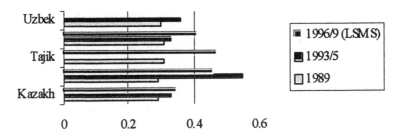

Source: Tables 3.4 and 3.5

Figure 3.1 Gini coefficients

Unemployment has increased, although this is difficult to measure in partially reformed economies without incentives to sign on as unemployed. Hidden unemployment certainly increased in Central Asia, and the phenomenon of unpaid work became commonplace as wage payments were delayed and erratic, but unemployment figures are inconsistent and difficult to interpret. In the Kyrgyz Republic reported unemployment was low in the 1993 household survey (the KMPS), although by the spring 1996 LSMS survey it had risen to 17 percent in rural areas and 21 percent in urban areas.[11] More clear-cut has been the decline in employment during the 1990s, especially in Kazakhstan.[12] In Tajikistan the labour force participation rate declined from 74 percent in 1991 to 64 percent in 1996.[13] Uzbekistan is the odd one out with total employment, according to official figures, increasing by about 4 percent between 1990 and 1995, although these data are problematic due to the widespread hidden unemployment (Klugman, 1998, 99–109).[14]

These distributional considerations raise the important question of who have been the gainers and losers from the transition from Soviet central planning to the more market-oriented national economies. Here we will briefly mention some spatial aspects. The next two chapters will address household and individual living standards in depth.

The regional shifts are clearest and have been best documented in Kazakhstan. The coalmining oblasts (provinces) of Karaganda and Pavlodar had 16.6 percent of the national population and 29.3 percent of GDP in 1993 with per capita product about double the national level, but by 1998 they were producing only 19.1 percent of GDP, their population share had fallen to 14.8 percent, and per capita product was only 25–30 percent above the national level.[15] Meanwhile, the population share of Almaty, the Soviet-era capital city, and its surrounding oblast increased from 16.7 percent to 18.0 percent and share of GDP from 14.2 percent to 21.4 percent. Per capita income in Almaty jumped from 40 percent above the national average in 1994 to more than double the national average in 1998. These are large changes over such a brief period. The petroleum producing regions of Atyrau and Mangistau only increased their combined share of GDP from 9.0 percent to 9.5 percent, implying that although Kazakhstan's growth was fuelled by the hydrocarbon sector the real beneficiaries were in the commercial capital rather than near the oilfields. There is also a widely reported phenomenon of 50–60 'sick towns' which depended on a single large enterprise in the Soviet era (Bauer et al., 1998, 40–41). The regional picture is less pronounced in the other countries, but everywhere the position of the capital city's residents has strengthened since independence.

3. POVERTY

For the Central Asian countries, with their initial relatively high incidence of poverty, the consequence of lower average income and increased inequality has been high poverty rates. The most quoted comparative figures on poverty are those assembled by Milanovic (1998) for all Central Asian countries except Tajikistan. For the four countries the poverty headcount, using a common measuring rod of $120 per month, increased from 15 percent of the population in 1987/8 to 66 percent in 1993/5, representing an increase from 6.5 million to 30.7 million people.[16] According to Milanovic, the Kyrgyz Republic suffered the largest changes in both poverty and inequality, and he found that in 1993–95 the Kyrgyz Republic had the highest poverty rate of any eastern European or former Soviet economy (Table 3.6 and Figure 3.2).[17] Anecdotal evidence supports the conclusion that poverty increased markedly in the Kyrgyz Republic during the early years after independence (for example Howell, 1996a, 1996b), but the poverty rates given by Milanovic are difficult to compare across countries with vastly different survey data.[18]

*Table 3.6: Poverty in Central Asia**

| | Poverty headcount (percent) | |
	1987/8	1993/5
Kazakhstan	5	65 (62)
Kyrgyz Republic	12	88 (86)
Turkmenistan	12	61 (57)
Uzbekistan	24	63 (39)

Note: *Based on HBS income. Numbers in parentheses are based on an across-the-board upward adjustment in income to capture the difference between incomes reported in the HBS and incomes in the national accounts.

Source: Milanovic (1998, 68–9 and 75).

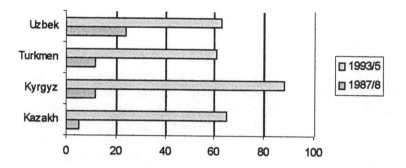

Source: Table 3.6 (unadjusted poverty rates).

Figure 3.2 Poverty headcount rates

The poverty rates are, of course, lower when lower cut-off lines are used. World Bank estimates for three of the Central Asian countries in 1993 show that, with a dollar-a-day standard, severe poverty was less than 5 percent in Kazakhstan and Turkmenistan, although almost a fifth of the Kyrgyz Republic's population was living in severe poverty (Table 3.7).[19]

Table 3.7. Share of population living on less than $1 per day, 1993*

	Poverty share (percent)
Kazakhstan	<2.0
Kyrgyz Republic	18.9
Turkmenistan	4.9

Notes: *The poverty line is $1 per day at purchasing power parity prices in 1985 US dollars; figures for Tajikistan and Uzbekistan are not reported.

Source: World Bank (1998, 65–6).

Poverty headcount measures based on the LSMS survey data indicate poverty increasing more or less in line with increased inequality in Central Asia. Using the yardstick of $2.15 per person per day for the poverty line, the headcount varies widely from 6–7 percent in Kazakhstan and Turkmenistan to 65 percent in Tajikistan (Table 3.8). Although *any* increase in open poverty has been difficult to bear in countries unused to the concept, the former two countries appear to have done substantially better than Russia by this measure. This likely also applies to Uzbekistan, although strictly comparable national data are unavailable.

Table 3.8 Poverty headcount from LSMS data ($2.15 PPP per day)

	Headcount (percent)
Tajikistan (1999)	65.4
Turkmenistan (1998	7.0
Kyrgyz Republic (spring 1996)	49.1
Kazakhstan (1996)	5.7
Azerbaijan (1995)	23.5
Russia	18.9

Table 3.9 illustrates the pitfalls of relying too heavily on headcount measures of poverty, that is, the proportion of the population living in households with per capita expenditure below the poverty line. In Tajikistan, headcount measures for 1999 vary from 17 percent to 96 percent depending upon which of three, all plausible, poverty lines are used; the minimum consumption basket is as defined by the government in 1998 and valued at 1999 prices, while the two PPP poverty lines are ones in common use in World Bank cross-country comparisons. The poverty gap measure (P1) is an indicator of the redistribution needed to bring everybody above the poverty line, and it too varies considerably with the choice of poverty line. Finally, P2 is the Foster–Greer–Thorbecke measure of the depth of poverty and it too can show either a chillingly depressing picture with the minimum consumption basket or a more cheerful picture of little deep poverty if the $1 per day yardstick is used.

Other measures are, however, also problematic. The IMF reported dollar values of the average monthly wage in the Central Asian countries (Table 3.10). This measure underlines the relative prosperity of Kazakhstan and the dire situation in Tajikistan, but whether it is a better indicator than the poverty rates in Tables 3.6–3.8 of the true position with regards to living standards in Turkmenistan and the Kyrgyz Republic is unclear.

Table 3.9 Sensitivity to choice of poverty line (Tajikistan, 1999)

	Measure
(a) Minimum consumption basket	
(TR32 083)	
Headcount (percent poor)	95.7
P1	56.4
P2	36.8
(b) $2.15 PPP per day (TR15 111)	
Headcount (percent poor)	65.4
P1	22.9
P2	10.9
(c) $1.075 PPP per day (TR7 557)	
Headcount (percent poor)	16.9
P1	4.4
P2	1.7

Source: World Bank (2000, 18).

Table 3.10 Average monthly wage in US dollars, 1997

	Average wage ($)
Kazakhstan	120
Kyrgyz Republic	40
Tajikistan	6
Turkmenistan	35
Uzbekistan	53

Source: IMF (1998a, 21; 1998b, 19).

4. CONCLUSIONS

The five new independent states of Central Asia emerged from the Soviet Union with similar economic systems and some similarity of economic structure. A decade later their economic experiences are becoming differentiated. The energy abundant economies of Kazakhstan and Turkmenistan found it more difficult than expected to benefit from the windfall gain of earning world prices rather than Soviet prices for their oil and gas exports. Tied into pre-existing pipeline infrastructure, their choice of export destinations has been constrained and their bargaining power weak.[20] Political developments in both countries have not been positive;

Kazakhstan appeared to be a potentially liberal country but turned towards authoritarian politics and crony capitalism, while Turkmenistan's president established an extreme personality cult from the start. Nevertheless, there is a big difference between the relative openness of Kazakhstan, which has potential for evolutionary change, and the individual despotism of Turkmenistan.

The two poorest-placed countries have done less well economically. The Kyrgyz Republic adopted rapid and basic reforms but, due to its backwardness, had difficulty establishing a well-functioning market economy. The severe decline in living standards may have been exacerbated by the rapid reform strategy, but this is unclear, as is the relationship between the degree of liberalization and the growth of the late 1990s and prospects for the 2000s. Tajikistan has had a grim economic experience since independence, but this was largely shaped by the civil war which raged on and off for most of the 1990s. Since 1997 the government has adopted a more coherent economic strategy, but has had difficulty in implementing it. Neither country has abundant exploitable natural resources, and by the early 2000s both countries were heavily indebted.

Uzbekistan, although often characterized as a slow reformer, had the best economic performance of all Soviet successor states during the 1990s. Critics point to the failure to establish a well-functioning market economy as a fatal flaw which will prevent future growth, but that argument becomes more jejune with time. Perhaps Uzbekistan could be performing even better with a different economic system, but clearly the government has done well enough on the policy front to limit the economic decline and even generate modest economic growth during the second half of the 1990s. This mainly seems to be due to good governance, at least by the low standards of the region.[21]

The common features of the Central Asian countries' post-independence economic experience have been a severe transformational recession during the first half of the 1990s followed by positive but generally sluggish growth since the late 1990s. In all five countries, the new governments had difficulty in mobilizing resources, and competing expenditure demands often crowded out social expenditures, although the degree to which this occurred varied, with Uzbekistan notable for maintaining public sector revenue and delivering social services. As in all eastern European and former Soviet economies in transition from central planning, inequality increased and, combined with the larger than expected transformational recession, this was associated with increased poverty throughout Central Asia during the 1990s. There is, however, ample evidence that there were gainers as well as losers.[22] Stories of profiteering and corruption are backed up by the presence of

Mercedes and BMW cars. Everywhere members of the old elite in the capital cities were the people best able to protect themselves against economic hardship and to benefit from new opportunities, while most employees of the state enterprises in heavy industries and of state farms have lost their economic advantages. In the following chapters we investigate who were the gainers and the losers from the establishment of market-based economies.

NOTES

1. World Bank estimates of per capita GNP at market prices and exchange rates placed Tajikistan ($158) and the Kyrgyz Republic ($263) among the world's poorest countries in 2000. These estimates overstate real deprivation because purchasing power parity incomes are much higher and because Central Asian households still have stocks of durable goods from the Soviet era, but the numbers do highlight the magnitude of the decline experienced by people who in 1990 were living in a superpower which a few decades earlier aimed to catch up with the most economically advanced western countries.

2. In Pomfret and Anderson (2001) we do make some judgments about such links. Pomfret (2002b) attempts a broader review of policies and performance across all transition economies.

3. There are also measurement difficulties due to reporting biases, the growth of the informal economy and index number problems (Pomfret, 1995, 171–6; Fischer et al., 1996; Falkingham et al., 1997, 21–41; Bloem et al., 1998).

4. Turkmenistan's economy has recovered since 1997 with high growth rates from that low base. The balance of payments problems have been addressed by draconian exchange controls since December 1998, and the resumption of natural gas exports to CIS markets in 1999 provided a major boost (Table 3.2).

5. Kumtor accounts for over two-fifths of industrial output, and its share in GDP increased from 8 percent in the first quarter of 2000 to 16 percent in the first quarter of 2001; Center for Social and Economic Research in Kyrgyzstan (2001, 9).

6. Growth was also stimulated by a currency depreciation from 85 tenge/$ in the first quarter of 1999 to 140 tenge/$ in the fourth quarter of 1999, but the incremental output in 2000 was dominated by oil and oil products exports, which increased by 63 percent; see *Kazakhstan Economic Trends January– March 2001*, 62.

7. Taube and Zettelmeyer (1998) and Zettelmeyer (1998) analyse the Uzbek puzzle and conclude that data deficiencies and favourable initial conditions and exogenous events only explain part of Uzbekistan's relatively good 1992–96 output performance, and policy must be given some of the credit. Spechler (1999) and Pomfret (2000c) also analyse Uzbekistan's policies and performance. Tashkent, the capital of Uzbekistan, was the principal

administrative centre for Soviet Central Asia and one advantage Uzbekistan had upon independence was the relatively large stock of experienced administrators.

8. Before making cross-country comparisons care must be taken that Gini coefficients are calculated in a similar way, for example for households or for individuals and over the same intervals. For the late 1980s there are implausible variations between Milanovic's 1987/8 Ginis and those calculated, also from the HBS, by Atkinson and Micklewright for 1989 cited in Table 2.1.

9. According to Falkingham (1999b, 11), the income Gini rose to 0.63 in the 1993 LSMS survey and fell to a still high 0.51 in 1996. It is unclear why these figures differ from Milanovic's calculations for 1993, but such differences among Ginis calculated from similar sources reflect the sensitivity of Gini coefficients to the method of calculation from household data.

10. The expenditure Gini of 0.35 from the 1996 Kazakhstan LSMS survey is less than the comparable 0.46 or 0.41 from the Kyrgyz Republic's 1996 LSMS surveys. Income-based Kyrgyz Ginis are substantially higher than expenditure Ginis, so that the 0.35 figure suggests that the HBS-based income Gini of 0.33 in Table 3.4 is too low for Kazakhstan. Wealth inequality has widened more than income or expenditure inequality after privatization; in the rural areas this has been especially apparent as entrepreneurs who gained control over key resources such as pastures or hay fields have been accumulating an ever-increasing share of the livestock.

11. Falkingham (1999b, 6; 2000b, 9) reports open unemployment rates of 30 percent in Tajikistan, 20 percent in the Kyrgyz Republic, 11 percent for men and 6 percent for women in Uzbekistan, and around 6 percent for Kazakhstan. These numbers come from differing 1998 sources and, although they all presumably refer to 1996 or 1997, it is not clear whether they are seasonally adjusted or based on comparable concepts of unemployment; the low rate for Kazakhstan, in particular, is at odds with casual observation.

12. The number employed in Kazakhstan fell from 6.5 million in 1990 to 4.3 million at the end of 1995, when registered unemployment was reported at 4 percent (Bauer, Boschmann and Green, 1997, 3). The number employed at large and medium-sized enterprises, which still appears to cover over four-fifths of the employed workforce declined from over 3 million in 1997 to 2 015 000 in 1999 before recovering slightly to 2 229 000 in 2000 (*Kazakhstan Economic Trends, January–March 2001*, 104).

13. IMF (1998a).

14. On the basis of the 1995 European University Institute and University of Essex Survey of Uzbekistan (EESU), Klugman estimates that as many as a quarter of the labour force might be included in 'hidden unemployment', in the sense of not having been paid over the previous month. Before and after transition comparisons are, however, fraught, because before 1991 many people were on enterprises' or farms' books as employed, but were not working. Allowing for all the measurement problems, Klugman (1998, 115) concludes that Uzbekistan's employment record during transition has been less adverse than in other former Soviet republics.

15. Figures in this paragraph are taken from Table 1 in Esentugelov (2000, 23). A similar picture is drawn in IMF (2000a). De Broeck and Koen (2000, 12) report that the regional variation in the decline in industrial output during the 1990s was greater in Kazakhstan than in other large former Soviet republics.

16. International dollar (I$) values are calculated by valuing quantities at purchasing power parity prices, using 1985 US dollars.

17. The IMF's *World Economic Outlook* (IMF, 1998c, 110) provides a comparative list.

18. The adjustments in brackets suggest that changes in assumptions can make big differences in the calculated incidence of poverty. The expenditure-based headcount measure of poverty in the Kyrgyz Republic increased from 45 percent in 1993 to 69 percent of individuals in 1996; these figures calculated from the 1993 and spring 1996 surveys are comparable to the figure in Table 2.1. Using households rather than individuals as the unit, the headcount, poverty gap and FGT P2 measures of poverty (Foster et al., 1984) increased between 1993 and 1996 from 40 percent to 49 percent, 20 percent to 24 percent and 13 percent to 15 percent respectively, indicating that the depth of poverty increased as well as the number of poor.

19. The World Bank (1997) estimates that 19 percent of the Kyrgyz Republic's population was below the international poverty line of US$1 per day at 1985 prices, with a poverty gap of 5.0 percent, that is, lower figures than most but not all African, Latin American or South Asian countries (Tanzania and Mexico, for example, have fewer poor and a smaller poverty gap than the Kyrgyz Republic).

20. The two countries may, however, not be equally affected. In 2000–2001 Kazakhstan experienced a boom due to high world oil prices. Kazakhstan also appears set to benefit during the first decade of the twenty-first century from new pipeline options, as well as from potentially large new oilfields.

21. Corruption is pervasive in Uzbekistan, but appears to be on a smaller scale than in other Central Asian countries – petty larceny rather than grand theft – and the government seems to have succeeded in creating a stable economic policy environment and providing physical infrastructure and law and order. EBRD (1999), reporting the results of a survey of 3000 firms in 20 transition economies, found that almost half of the Uzbek firms bribed frequently (the third highest among the twenty countries), but, when asked about the quality of governance under various headings, Uzbekistan came out positively, ranking fourth behind Hungary, Slovenia and Estonia, ahead of reform leaders like Poland and far ahead of Kazakhstan (fourteenth) and the Kyrgyz Republic (nineteenth); Tajikistan and Turkmenistan were not included in the survey, but would surely have ranked poorly on governance.

22. Jovanovic (2001) and Rutkowski (2001) have identified considerable mobility within the income distribution in other eastern European and former Soviet economies.

4. Living standards in the Kyrgyz Republic

In this chapter we use data from the LSMS survey conducted in the Kyrgyz Republic between 1993 and 1997 to analyse the characteristics of households which fell below the poverty line and the determinants of household consumption levels. The Kyrgyz survey data are especially rich because they cover a number of years, and they start at a very early stage in the country's transition from central planning. The Kyrgyz Republic is also an interesting starting point because its relatively liberal policies during the early and mid 1990s should be associated with relatively rapid establishment of market-based relationships. Finally, the poverty picture is likely to be put into sharp perspective because during the 1990s the Kyrgyz Republic suffered a deep decline in income levels with real per capita income falling by almost half and a large increase in inequality.

The Kyrgyz Republic clearly suffered a substantial drop in consumption levels during the first half of the 1990s. Roberts (1997) analysed the Kyrgyz HBS data, and estimates that private household consumption fell by 33 percent during 1990–93 and rose by 7 percent in 1995. This is substantially smaller than the fall in consumption implied by GDP estimates (Table 3.1) or official estimates of a 44 percent decline in 1990–93 followed by a further 5 percent drop in 1995. The main reason for the discrepancy is the rapid growth of the private sector, especially in 1991, to the extent that by 1995 the shadow economy was supplying between a quarter and a half of household consumption. Although Roberts presents a less gloomy picture than official figures, his estimates still represent a large drop in consumption during the first half of the 1990s.

The aggregate picture is supported by anecdotal evidence. In June 1995 the World Bank surveyed 150 households in Bishkek to appraise capacity and willingness to pay for heating and hot water. The responses to the income and expenditure questions revealed that households spent on average 70 percent of their income on food and 10 percent on energy, but the lowest quartile spent 78 percent of income on food and 22 percent on energy (Finkel and Garcia, 1997, 194). Such figures paint a grim picture of a substantial part of the population of the capital city having inadequate incomes to cover basic needs and being vulnerable to even minor policy shifts with respect to provision of subsidized services such as district heating.[1]

Even more vivid pictures of people living on the brink emerge from the report on interviews of adults in 154 poor households in the southern oblasts of Osh and Djalalabad in September and October 1994 (Howell, 1996a, 1996b).   Howell highlights the variety of coping strategies, but the overwhelming impression is of choices having to satisfy basic needs, often at the expense of future income. Should an animal be sold to buy supplies for schoolchildren or should the children be kept at home on the farm? Should a fruit tree be chopped down to save expenditure on coal? Non-essential items such as furniture or sheets or towels were being sold by urban dwellers who had no plot of land to fall back on for food.

1. POVERTY IN THE KYRGYZ REPUBLIC IN 1993

The 1993 KMPS has been used to make more firmly based generalizations about the evolution of poverty during transition in the Kyrgyz Republic. The World Bank (1995) provided the initial poverty assessment.   Simple cross-tabulations show that the poor in the Kyrgyz Republic in 1993 tended to be rural, with the poverty rate lowest in the capital city, Bishkek, and highest in the south of the country. Poverty was associated with large families, and with ethnicity; Slav households were less likely to be poor than Turkic households. Education, gender or pensioner effects were not strong. This accords with common perceptions about poverty in the southern republics of the Soviet Union (see Chapter 2.1) and suggests that, although there had been a sharp increase in the level of poverty after the dissolution of the USSR, the determinants of poverty had not changed by autumn 1993.

In 1993 poverty was greater in rural areas. By the expenditure measure 56 percent of the rural population lived in households with an average expenditure below the poverty line, and 31 percent were very poor (that is, per capita household expenditure was less than half of the poverty line); the comparable figures for urban areas were 34 percent and 13 percent (Pomfret and Anderson, 1998). Green and Vokes (1997, 265–66), referring to Asian Development Bank field studies, argue that rural–urban wage differentials in the Kyrgyz Republic widened markedly during the first half of the 1990s. Farmers suffered from the near collapse of input supplies (no fertiliser, pesticides or herbicides, inferior seeds, disrupted supply of fuel and spare parts), large adverse relative price changes and mushrooming rural debt. Ackland and Falkingham (1997) also claim that non-payment of farm wages and lack of rural credit widened the rural–urban gap after 1993, although net increases in livestock during 1993 suggest that people were not yet running down productive assets to maintain current consumption.[2] The rural–urban comparison is sensitive to assumptions about consumption of non-marketed produce, which was large but likely to have been misreported even in the KMPS.[3]

Multivariate analyses of the 1993 survey data have aimed to identify more clearly the underlying determinants of poverty. In the KMPS the primary unit is the household. Individual questionnaires were also completed, but there is little or no information on intra-household economic relations. The household income data are polluted by the disrupted economic conditions of 1993. The income distribution is discontinuous, and there is no relationship between income and expenditure. A primary reason for this was the common practice in 1993 of enterprises not paying the monthly wages on time, so that many workers recorded zero income during the reporting period while others who happened to receive a backlog of several months' wages reported high incomes; employees were still continuing to work on the assumption that they would eventually be paid or at least remain on their employer's books, so that open unemployment was still low (6 percent, in contrast to 20 percent by the time of the 1996 LSMS).

The dependent variable in the following analysis is based on expenditure per head. Expenditure is calculated at the household level, and then divided by the number of people in the household. This simplistic approach ignores economies of scale in households, but at least as a first pass it is unclear what specific equivalence scale would be superior. Even with expenditure data rather than income, there is a large range across households in 1993. In this section we focus on the lower part of the distribution, that is, on the probability of an individual living in a household whose per capita expenditure is below a poverty line.

The poverty line used is a nutrition-based measure compiled by the World Bank (1995).[4] The concept of a poverty line has come under some criticism, and Peter Lanjouw (1997) has castigated the World Bank's line for the Kyrgyz Republic. Lanjouw challenges use of a nutrition-based line for a country where obesity is widespread; the problem is not lack of food, but poor diets. He also criticizes the lack of transparency in the published descriptions of the poverty line's construction. There is, however, little alternative to using the World Bank's poverty line. Some rough sensitivity analysis was done by also considering the very poor, that is, people living in households with expenditure less than half the poverty line. The line dividing the very poor from the rest of the population is obviously open to Lanjouw's criticisms too, but presumably includes the truly destitute households as a larger proportion among its subset of the poor.

The analysis in this and the next section is based on a binary response model where the dependent variable is equal to 0 if the household is not poor (by the standard above) and 1 if the household is poor. We estimate the probability of a household's per capita expenditure (y) being below the poverty line, conditional on a number of explanatory variables ($\mathbf{x}$):

$$E[y|\mathbf{x}] = 0[1 - F(\beta'\mathbf{x})] + 1[F(\beta'\mathbf{x})] = F(\beta'\mathbf{x}) \tag{4.1}$$

The conditional probability is constrained to lie between zero and one by assuming that the cumulative distribution function is s-shaped with these lower and upper bounds. Specifically, we use probit models, which assume the cumulative distribution function $F(\cdot)$ is a normal distribution, and estimate the parameters by maximum likelihood.[5] The probit coefficients are given in Table 4.1.

From the probit coefficients in Table 4.1, we estimate the marginal effects of variables on the probability of being poor. If the independent variable (X_1, for example) is continuous, the marginal effect is computed as in (4.2a) below:

$$\frac{\partial E[y \mid x]}{\partial Y_1} = (\beta' x)\beta_1 \tag{4.2a}$$

where $\varphi(\cdot)$ is the standard normal density function evaluated at the mean values of x and β_1 is the probit coefficient on X_1. If X_1 is a dummy variable, then the effect of moving from $X_1 = 0$ to $X_1 = 1$ is given in (4.2b) below:

$$\Phi(\beta'x|X_1{=}1) - \Phi(\beta'x|X_1{=}0) \tag{4.2b}$$

where $\Phi(\cdot)$ is the standard normal cumulative distribution function evaluated at the mean values of all x when X_1 is equal to 1 and when X_1 is equal to zero. For the Kyrgyz 1993 sample, the marginal effects of the explanatory variables other than location in Bishkek and higher education are small.

For the total sample, at the mean values of the explanatory variables and using the probit coefficients in Table 4.1, the marginal effect of residence in Bishkek is –0.25 and of higher education is –0.14, while no other marginal effect has an absolute magnitude above 0.1. Education has a larger negative impact on poverty in the urban areas than in the rural regions. Residence in Chyi oblast (the Northern rural region) is the only other region in the Kyrgyz Republic where poverty is lower than in Osh. Having an additional child increases the probability of a household being poor by 0.04 and an extra adult raises the probability by

0.01, but dependent children have a larger impact on poverty in the urban than in the rural areas.

Table 4.1 Regional, ethnic, demographic and educational effects, 1993*

	Total	Urban	Rural
Constant	−0.105	−0.305	0.022
Region (oblast)			
Narun	0.166	0.134	0.186
Talas	−0.158	−0.125	−0.132
Djalalabad	0.028	−0.306	**0.476**
Issuk-Kul	−0.100	−0.380	0.106
Chyi	**−0.255**	−0.029	**−0.350**
Bishkek	**−0.677**	**−0.556**	−
Ethnicity of household head			
Russian	−0.167	0.084	−0.179
Other Slavic	**−0.388**	0.040	**−0.518**
Uzbek	−0.251	−0.108	−0.186
Demographic characteristics			
Female head	**0.221**	**0.360**	0.046
Number of adults	0.030	−0.018	0.026
Number of children	**0.094**	**0.141**	**0.063**
Education level of head			
Less than complete secondary	0.052	−0.134	0.137
Higher	**−0.300**	**−0.393**	**−0.249**
Sample size	1929	828	1101
Chi-square (14 df)	**189.480**	**66.880**	**98.710**
Log Likelihood	−1227.75	−4820.58	−7110.64

Note: ***Boldface** = significant at the 5 percent level..

The differences in coefficients between the rural and urban results suggest that poverty is not only more widespread in the countryside, but also that there are differences in the nature of rural and urban poverty. The regional coefficients confirm a well-known divide between poorer southern oblasts (Djalalabad, Narun and Osh – the base category) and richer northern oblasts. The strongest finding is of the likelihood of rural households in Djalalabad being poor. Urban poverty appears to be most likely in the omitted region, Osh. On the other hand, households in the capital, Bishkek, are less likely to be poor. The negative coefficient for Chyi oblast may reflect proximity to the capital or the successful response of farmers switching to previously illegal crops.[6]

Simple cross-tabulations from the KMPS show Turkic-headed households to be more likely than Slav-headed households to be below the poverty line (Ackland and Falkingham., 1997, 90), but this ethnic relationship is only weakly supported in Table 4.1. In rural areas, all ethnic groups are less likely to be poor than Kyrgyz-headed households, but the negative coefficient is only significant for the miscellaneous 'Other Slav' households.[7] In urban areas, none of the ethnicity coefficients is significant. Although the crosstabs reflect widespread perceptions of the ethnic dimension of poverty in Central Asia, the probit results are consistent with the conclusions of Lubin (1984), who found that Slavs in Uzbekistan had higher-wage jobs because they were better educated; Central Asians often chose not to pursue educational opportunities and gravitated to occupations offering opportunities for unofficial income.

Having more children is associated with being poor, whether in an urban or a rural location. For urban households, having more adults in the household is associated with a lower probability of being poor, but in rural households the relationship between number of adults and poverty is positive, but in neither case is the coefficient statistically significant. Female-headed households are more likely to be poor than male-headed households, the relationship is statistically significant for urban households, but not for rural households.

The negative relationship between the household head's education level and the probability of being poor is as expected. Whether in urban or rural locations, if the household head has a college education, then the household is significantly less likely to be below the poverty line. The relationship between completion of secondary education and poverty is, however, inconclusive.

The relationship between ethnicity and poverty is examined further in Table 4.2. The poverty model is estimated over all households and separately over households in the three major ethnic groups: Kyrgyz, Russians and Uzbeks.

The most striking feature of Table 4.2 is in the results for the demographic variables. In Kyrgyz households the number of children is positively related to the probability of being poor, but the gender of the household head is not significant. For Russian households family size is not significant, but having a female head is significant as a positive determinant of poverty. The results for Uzbek households are weaker due to the small number in the sample, but they are similar to the Kyrgyz pattern of the number of children being marginally significant at the 10 percent level and the head's gender not significant. Thus, although ethnicity is not identified

Table 4.2 Poverty and ethnicity, 1993

	Total	Kyrgyz	Russian	Uzbek
Constant	**−0.251**	0.042	−0.291	−0.547
Region (oblast)				
Narun	**0.315**	0.116	Dropped	dropped
Talas	−0.052	−0.181	−0.566	−0.085
Djalalabad	0.058	−0.026	**−1.113**	−1.441
Issuk-Kul	0.016	−0.136	0.073	0.283
Chyi	**−0.235**	**−0.328**	−0.066	−0.609
Bishkek	**−0.664**	**−0.945**	**−0.480**	−0.939
Demographic characteristics				
Female head	**0.221**	0.036	**0.378**	0.560
Number of adults	0.026	0.042	−0.002	0.092
Number of children	**0.099**	**0.089**	0.010	0.319
Education of household head				
Less than complete secondary	0.006	−0.111	0.007	0.465
Higher education	**−0.297**	**−0.423**	−0.256	−0.209
Sample size	1929	983	463	93
Chi-square (11 df)	**166.19**	**89.69**	**29.44**	**18.60**
Log Likelihood	−1239.389	−635.195	−276.149	−48.411

Note: ***Boldface** = significant at the 5 percent level. Narun oblast was dropped in the Russian and Uzbek runs due to collinearity.

as a determinant of poverty, there is a difference in the pattern of poverty within the main ethnic groups. In Kyrgyz and Uzbek households large numbers of children are associated with poverty, but having a female head is not. In Russian households family size is not a problem, but not having a working age male is.

2. EVOLUTION OF THE DETERMINANTS OF POVERTY, 1993–96

By 1996 the Kyrgyz Republic had passed through the initial stages of the transition from central planning. Price reform was largely complete and inflation subdued, although the emergence of a flourishing private sector remained in the future. This section compares the determinants of poverty in 1993 and 1996.

Between the 1993 and 1996 surveys poverty levels stabilized, but it is to be expected that the determinants of poverty changed. Education was undervalued in the steady state of Soviet planning where rules of thumb held good and initiative was not desired, but the shocks associated with the dissolution of the USSR created disequilibria and, to deal with disequilibrium, education would become more valuable. Pressures on the social security system after independence increase the likelihood of pensioners and large families being poor in 1996.[8] The social and economic status of women was widely expected to deteriorate in the Islamic successor states of the former Soviet South, although casual observation suggests that the Kyrgyz Republic, especially in the Northern region, has remained a predominantly secular society. The regional incidence of poverty during transition could change in any direction. Liberalization of labour markets and increased labour mobility should reduce regional income variations, but despite large-scale international migration since independence internal migration has been limited.[9] There may also be virtuous or vicious circles as better-off regions more vigorously pursue economic change that will stimulate growth, while poorer regions engage in short-term behaviour detrimental to long-term economic growth.[10]

Two LSMS-style household surveys were completed in 1996. The first was done in the spring using the 1993 questionnaire and the second in the autumn. Although the questions and procedures differed slightly, the autumn 1996 survey appears to have been better conducted and its use avoids seasonality problems when comparisons with 1993 are made. The sample size in autumn 1996 was 1951 and the composition of the sample was similar to that of the 1993 KMPS in the dimensions used in the probit analysis of poverty.

Aggregate analysis of the 1996 data yielded results similar to those in the first column of Table 4.1. The regional effects are strong with households in Bishkek less likely to be poor and households in the mountain and southern oblasts more likely to be poor. Households with college-educated heads are less likely to be poor. The head's gender is no longer significant, but the number of household members seems to be more strongly related to poverty than in 1993.

In order to examine the impact of ethnicity, household size, education and other head characteristics more carefully, the 1996 analysis was done with separate regional samples. The results for common categories in 1993 and 1996 are given in Table 4.3. The smaller sample sizes mean that fewer coefficients are significant than in Tables 4.1 and 4.2, but some interesting patterns emerge. The higher education variable is always negatively related to poverty, but the impact is more often statistically significant in 1996. The ethnicity variables, however, which showed poverty in 1993 to be more likely amongst Kyrgyz households in the south, are universally insignificant in 1996. There is also fairly consistent evidence of the costs of larger families, with such families more likely to fall below the poverty line in 1996 than in 1993.

Table 4.3 Regional poverty analysis, 1993 and 1996[*]

(a) 1993

	Bishkek	Chyi	Mountain	South
Constant	−0.393	−0.098	−0.024	0.106
Russian ethnicity	0.137	−0.182	−0.369	**−0.502**
Uzbek ethnicity	0.470	−0.358	−1.049	**−0.425**
Other non-Kyrgyz ethnicity	−0.103	**−0.394**	−0.386	−0.294
Number of pensioners in household	**0.341**	−0.061	0.214	−0.039
Number of children	0.117	0.043	0.079	**0.114**
Number of other adults	−0.026	0.032	0.009	0.033
Head has primary education only	−0.258	−0.028	0.034	−0.072
Head has other training (sec.equivalent)	−0.209	−0.110	−0.233	−0.123
Head has higher education	−0.470	−0.334	−0.319	**−0.401**
Male head	**−0.558**	−0.101	0.030	−0.120
Pensioner head	−0.212	0.355	−0.309	0.174
Sample size	320	473	383	753
Chi-square (11 df)	**22.95**	14.11	19.64	**57.66**
Log Likelihood	−155.347	−308.596	−255.361	−492.201

(b) 1996

	Bishkek	Chyi	Mountain	South
Constant	**−0.754**	−0.043	−0.345	−0.337
Russian ethnicity	−0.089	0.249	-0.202	−0.141
Uzbek ethnicity	0.257	−0.164	–	−0.216
Other non-Kyrgyz ethnicity	−0.259	−0.037	0.024	−0.230
Number of pensioners in household	**0.486**	0.002	0.166	0.060
Number of children	0.152	**0.165**	**0.116**	**0.233**
Number of adults	0.109	**0.146**	**0.203**	**0.151**
Head has primary education only	−0.021	0.009	0.115	−0.078
Head has other training (sec.equivalent)	0.015	-0.158	0.002	0.047
Head has higher education	**−0.625**	−0.329	**−0.484**	**−0.470**
Male head	−0.269	**−0.457**	0.162	**0.511**
Pensioner head	−0.547	−0.124	0.084	−0.100
Sample size	390	366	380	809
Chi-square (11 df)	**43.06**	**26.34**	**36.69**	**127.12**
Log Likelihood	−201.542	−239.974	−213.785	−344.294

Note: ***Boldface** = significant at the 5 percent level. The Mountain observations for 1996 included only one Uzbek headed household, which was dropped from the analysis.

These results are consistent with expectations about the process of transition. Better educated people are better able to deal with rapidly changing circumstances, while ethnic discrimination is likely to be eroded by market forces. The improvement in the position of Kyrgyz households may also reflect discrimination in favour of the titular nationality in the independent Kyrgyz Republic. The higher cost of dependents is an expected consequence of the decline in social support since the dissolution of the Soviet Union, although pensioners appear to have maintained their position better than other dependents.

On the other hand, the education results are weaker than might be expected from human capital models. The generally low number of significant coefficients in Table 4.3(b) may reflect incomplete transition, but may also be due to the limited ability of probit analysis to distinguish among households when most households are below the poverty line. The analysis focuses on position above or below the poverty line, while ignoring any other changes in the distribution.

In the probit analysis the strongest associations are that residence in the capital and having a college-educated household head reduce the probability of a household being poor, while nothing else had much of an effect. Given the very high poverty rate, this implies that a small group, presumably the old elite, had weathered the storm of the early 1990s better than anybody else. Households in Bishkek are least likely to be poor, and urban poverty appears to be most likely in Osh, the second largest city, located in the south. The regional dimension supports Howell's decision to focus on Djalalabad and Osh when studying coping strategies.

Probit analysis of household survey data can help to identify the correlates of poverty and thus provide some guidance to poverty alleviation strategies. Poverty is highest in rural areas, especially those far from the capital. Female-headed households are more likely to be poor than male-headed households, but this relationship is only significant in urban locations and appears to apply particularly to Russian households. Households with a large number of children are more likely to be poor, although this applies particularly to Kyrgyz and Uzbek households. Variations in the education level of the household head are generally not significant below the tertiary level, but having a household head with higher education is negatively related to the probability of being poor. The marginal effects of the explanatory variables (for example, in Pomfret and Anderson 1998, Table 3) are small, apart from location in Bishkek and higher education; at mean values the marginal effect of residence in Bishkek is −0.25 (that is, reduces by 25 percent the probability of a household being poor) and of a household head having higher education is −0.14, while no other marginal effect has an absolute value above 0.1.

3. LIVING STANDARDS ACROSS THE ENTIRE DISTRIBUTION

Poverty studies have relied on simple cross-tabulations or on probit analysis of the determinants of the probability of a household being above or below a poverty line. By focusing on the binary response (above or below the line) these studies fail to utilize most of the information in the expenditure distribution, as well as being sensitive to the construction of the poverty line. In this section we analyse the entire expenditure distribution, avoiding the need to draw a poverty line. These are important advantages in analysing

Kyrgyz Republic data given the criticisms of the World Bank's poverty line and the high headcount measures of poverty.

The distribution of consumption expenditures is skewed to the right. To take this nonlinearity into account, we estimate a semi-logarithmic expenditure function where the logarithm of total expenditure (y) is regressed on the explanatory variables (x) described in the previous section; the regression coefficient on x is β. We use two different approaches to estimate this model: ordinary least squares and quantile regression.

We first estimate the model with ordinary least squares (OLS). This is primarily for comparability with Grootaert and Braithwaite (1998) who applied OLS to a reduced form equation with real household expenditure per equivalent adult in 1993 as the dependent variable and various household and environmental characteristics as the independent variables. The explanatory power of their OLS equation is low (adjusted $R^2 = 0.10$), and as with the probit analysis the sharpest change in household welfare is implied by moving to the capital.

We prefer quantile regression, which utilizes the entire expenditure distribution, without imposing the condition from OLS regression that all income groups have the same underlying structural equation.[11] In quantile regression analysis the same explanatory variables are tested for all income groups, but the magnitude of the relationship between each variable and household expenditure is allowed to differ between rich and poor households. The quantile regressions can differ from each other for two reasons.

1. The expectation of the disturbance differs at the various quantiles if X_j is not independent of ε_j;
2. The quantile regressions also differ if the effect of the explanatory variables differs at different quantiles of the distribution of the dependent variable.

To obtain an estimate for quantile q, the values of $y_j - X_j\beta$ at the estimated value of β are weighted; if a residual is negative, it is weighted $-(1-q)$, and if a residual is positive, it is weighted q. To illustrate, suppose the quantile regression for the seventy-fifth percentile is estimated. The weight for negative residuals is -0.25, while the weight for positive residuals is 0.75. Minimizing the sum of the residuals using these weights is equivalent to using the absolute values of residuals with weights of 0.25 and 0.75 or a ratio of one to three. Note that this weighting scheme with weights of -0.5 and $+0.5$ minimizes one half of the sum of the absolute values of the residuals, which provides a conditional estimate at the median. The general interpretation of the estimated coefficients is that they provide the best linear approximation of the effect of explanatory variables at various quantiles of the dependent variable.

We estimate the model at the median or fiftieth percentile, and at the tenth, twenty-fifth, seventy-fifth and ninetieth percentiles. We can then determine whether position in the expenditure distribution differentially affects how household characteristics are related to consumption. We use the Wald test to test whether the regressions differ significantly across quantiles.[12] In both 1993 and 1996 Wald tests reject the hypothesis that the separate quantile regressions are equivalent; $F(55,1904) = 8.07$ in 1993 and $F(60,1938) = 22.56$ in 1996.

3.1 Full Sample Results

The quantile regression results for 1993 and 1996 are presented in Tables 4.4 and 4.5.[13] For comparison, we also present the results from an OLS version of the model in the first column of the two tables. The standard error on β is bootstrapped; we draw 1000 samples with replacement.[14]

Family size is negatively related to household living standards. In both 1993 and 1996, additional children and working age adults decrease per capita expenditure in the household, but children have a much larger effect on consumption than adults. At the median, an additional child lowers per capita expenditure by 11 percent in 1993 and by 17 percent in 1996 while an additional adult lowers consumption by an insignificant 3 percent in 1993 and 7 percent in 1996. Wald tests indicate that the differences across quantiles are significant for children in both years and for adults in 1996, but these interquantile differences are small.[15] The effects at the median or the mean increase over time and suggest that children during transition became more costly in terms of foregone household consumption.

The presence and number of elderly persons in the household has no significant effect on per capita consumption in 1993. Income contributed by pensioners compensates the household for the increase in consumption, both on average and in all income groups other than the top decile. However, by 1996, expenditure falls with the addition of a pensioner to the household and the negative coefficient is insignificant at all but the lowest quantiles in the expenditure distribution; the interquantile differences are significant $(F(5,1938) = 2.47)$. In general, the reduction in consumption from the addition of an elderly adult is much smaller than the reduction from the addition of a child.

Consequences of creating a market economy

Table 4.4 Quantile regressions of per capita expenditure, fall 1993[*]

Variables	Mean	Percentile 10th	Percentile 25th	Percentile 50th	Percentile 75th	Percentile 90th
Constant	**4.798**	**3.724**	**4.11**	**4.985**	**5.685**	**6.153**
	[0.102]	[0.273]	[0.154]	[0.108]	[0.104]	[0.120]
Region						
Bishkek	**0.340**	**0.413**	**0.444**	**0.278**	**0.184**	**0.264**
	[0.079]	[0.151]	[0.105]	[0.078]	[0.073]	[0.092]
South	**−0.205**	**−0.455**	**−0.175**	**−0.200**	**−0.213**	**−0.267**
	[0.067]	[0.171]	[0.089]	[0.078]	[0.066]	[0.071]
Mountain	**−0.331**	**−0.635**	**−0.311**	**−0.268**	**−0.255**	**−0.225**
	[0.075]	[0.190]	[0.119]	[0.085]	[0.075]	[0.083]
Education of head						
Primary	**0.244**	0.258	**0.287**	**0.234**	0.107	0.033
	[0.078]	[0.181]	[0.140]	[0.100]	[0.078]	[0.110]
Some	**0.306**	**0.371**	**0.386**	**0.265**	**0.168**	0.087
training	[0.078]	[0.168]	[0.131]	[0.111]	[0.081]	[0.103]
College	**0.439**	**0.509**	**0.541**	**0.419**	**0.247**	0.09
	[0.078]	[0.172]	[0.129]	[0.094]	[0.076]	[0.099]
Male head	0.099	0.099	0.197	0.04	0.071	0.112
	[0.069]	[0.199]	[0.106]	[0.070]	[0.074]	[0.076]
Pensioner	**−0.25**	**−0.784**	**−0.405**	−0.141	−0.086	0.188
head	[0.107]	[0.315]	[0.183]	[0.112]	[0.112]	[0.136]
Household members						
Children	**−0.112**	**−0.112**	**−0.114**	**−0.112**	**−0.110**	**−0.071**
	[0.017]	[0.040]	[0.024]	[0.019]	[0.018]	[0.018]
Adults	**−0.037**	−0.053	−0.059	−0.033	**−0.038**	**−0.045**
	[0.017]	[0.036]	[0.030]	[0.019]	[0.015]	[0.021]
Pensioners	0.001	0.023	0.071	−0.022	−0.032	**−0.101**
	[0.043]	[0.088]	[0.065]	[0.045]	[0.039]	0[.053]
Sample size	1916	1916	1916	1916	1916	1916
R-square	0.114	0.077	0.066	0.064	0.071	0.066

Note: *Coefficient [standard error]. **Boldface** = significant at the 5 percent level.

Table 4.5 Quantile regressions of per capita expenditure, fall 1996

Variables	Mean	10th	25th	50th	75th	90th
			Percentile			
Constant	**6.781**	**5.741**	**6.075**	**6.837**	**7.432**	**7.88**
	[0.077]	[0.133]	[0.086]	[0.104]	[0.111]	[0.130]
Region						
Bishkek	**0.423**	**0.481**	**0.484**	**0.355**	**0.413**	**0.302**
	[0.061]	[0.129]	[0.075]	[0.076]	[0.065]	[0.114]
South	**−0.463**	**−0.647**	**−0.604**	**−0.503**	**−0.433**	**−0.333**
	[0.054]	[0.093]	[0.079]	[0.074]	[0.065]	[0.104]
Mountain	**−0.143**	−0.060	**−0.174**	**−0.230**	**−0.212**	−0.084
	[0.060]	[0.094]	[0.070]	[0.079]	[0.068]	[0.116]
Education of head						
Primary	0.069	−0.084	0.044	0.056	**0.183**	0.119
	[0.061]	[0.090]	[0.076]	[0.081]	[0.089]	[0.097]
Some	**0.091**	**0.249**	**0.216**	0.072	0.005	−0.013
training	[0.045]	[0.080]	[0.058]	[0.059]	[0.055]	[0.084]
College	**0.366**	**0.442**	**0.467**	**0.302**	**0.284**	**0.293**
	[0.057]	[0.112]	[0.060]	[0.073]	[0.069]	[0.109]
Male head	−0.021	0.042	0.026	0.047	−0.105	−0.079
	[0.057]	[0.098]	[0.064]	[0.077]	[0.093]	[0.093]
Pensioner head	0.089	0.059	0.178	0.099	−0.004	0.083
	[0.084]	[0.138]	[0.101]	[0.116]	[0.113]	[0.174]
Household members						
Children	**−0.174**	**−0.157**	**−0.144**	**−0.184**	**−0.171**	**−0.197**
	[0.015]	[0.029]	[0.022]	[0.019]	[0.019]	[0.028]
Adults	**−0.067**	**−0.054**	−0.025	**−0.071**	**−0.076**	**−0.086**
	[0.013]	[0.026]	[0.017]	[0.016]	[0.016]	[0.021]
Pensioners	**−0.083**	−0.061	**−0.094**	**−0.095**	**−0.107**	**−0.111**
	[0.028]	[0.056]	[0.037]	[0.038]	[0.043]	[0.054]
Sample size	1822	1822	1822	1822	1822	1822
R-squared (pseudo)	0.347	0.199	0.213	0.206	0.200	0.201

Note: * Coefficient [standard error]. **Boldface** = significant at the 5 percent level.

Second, gender of the household head has no effect on per capita expenditure in either 1993 or 1996, and these results are stable across quantiles. In 1993, household expenditure was on average 25 percent lower in households headed by an elderly adult than in other households; this mean effect was the result of the large reduction in expenditures (40–78 percent) experienced by pensioner-headed households below the twenty-fifth percentile.[16] By 1996, households in the lower quantiles are less likely to be headed by an elderly adult, and the head's age has no effect on household consumption at any point in the distribution.

Third, region has large and significant effects on consumption in both 1993 and 1996; these regional differences increase over time and the differences across quantiles are significant.[17] Households in Bishkek are less poor and have higher per capita expenditure than households in other regions, while the poorest households are in the mountain and the southern, primarily rural, oblasts.   In 1993, households in the mountain oblasts are the poorest on average and in all quantiles except the ninetieth; at this point in the distribution, there is no difference in the consumption of mountain and southern households.   By 1996, the South is clearly the poorest region in the Kyrgyz Republic, and the regional differences are much larger than in 1993.   At the median, per capita expenditure is 28 percent higher in Bishkek, 20 percent lower in Osh and Djalalabad, and 27 percent lower in the mountain region than in Chyi in 1993. By 1996, expenditure is 35 percent higher in Bishkek, 48 percent lower in Osh and Djalalabad, and 21 percent lower in the mountain region than in Chyi. This same pattern is evident at every point in the distribution. The regional changes have clear and important implications, suggesting that poor people in pastoral regions did relatively well during the Kyrgyz Republic's transition, but poor people in sedentary agriculture in the southern regions did not progress.

Finally, education is an important determinant of household consumption, and the returns to high-skill training change over time. In 1993 and 1996, at the mean and the median, expenditure is highest in households with a college-educated head, but the return to college education is lower in 1996 than in 1993. At the median, households with college-educated heads consume 42 percent more in 1993, but 30 percent more in 1996, than households in which the head has only secondary education. In both 1993 and 1996 in the lower quantiles, households with college-educated heads have the highest returns, in terms of per capita expenditure, to the head's education; in these quantiles, non-college training beyond secondary school also pays off at a higher rate than at other points in the distribution. The differences across quantiles are not significant for primary education in 1993 and 1996, but interquantile differences are significant for higher education in both years.[18]

A plausible interpretation of these results is that college education became more important in 1996 than in 1993 to upward mobility, while more narrow vocational further education still helped raise incomes in poorer households but did not assist the household head in moving the household upward in the income distribution. In 1993, 15–20 percent of all households in the lower half of the distribution have college-educated heads and 20–27 percent have heads with post-secondary training below college level. (See Table 4A.1 at the end of this chapter.) By 1996, heads with post-secondary training are concentrated in the top half of the expenditure distribution; 15–29 percent of heads in households above the median have college education in comparison to 4–10 percent of poorer households.[19] The 1996 college returns in the lower quantiles are driven by the behaviour of a small sample of agricultural households in Osh that perform relatively better than other low income households but are unable to significantly move up the income distribution over time.

In summary, from our analysis of the full sample of households, we find three important changes in the expenditure distribution over time. Returns to education fall over time, but education, college education in particular, is important in the movement of households to higher quantiles. In both years, returns to higher education are higher among the poorest households. Second, we find increases in the costs of children and pensioners between 1993 and 1996, and these cost increases are similar across quantiles. Third, we find large regional changes. In 1993, the mountain region is the poorest region, and Bishkek is the wealthiest; by 1996, the southern region is clearly the poorest, and the return to residence in Bishkek is even higher. The poorest households receive the largest benefit from living in the capital and bear the highest cost from residence in the South in both years. In view of the strong regional effects, we next consider whether the region rather than the nation would provide a more appropriate unit of analysis.

3.2 Regional Models

We estimate the expenditure models separately for four regions, Bishkek, Chyi, the South (Osh and Djalalabad) and the Mountain region (Narun, Talas and Issyk-kul), with the same variables as in Tables 4.4 and 4.5 apart from replacing the regional variables with three ethnic variables (Russian, Uzbek and other non-Kyrgyz groups). The sample sizes are much smaller in these regional models, and the standard errors are higher. Overall, we find few statistically significant effects of gender or age of the head on expenditure at any point in the distribution in the region.[20] However, there are some interesting regional differences in returns to college and post-

Consequences of creating a market economy

Table 4.6 Returns to education, by region and quantile[*]

	Mean	Percentile				
		10th	25th	50th	75th	90th
Fall 1993						
Bishkek						
Primary	0.271	−0.162	0.182	−0.018	0.228	0.297
Other training	0.312	−0.226	0.208	0.152	0.261	0.524
College	**0.414**	0.176	0.366	0.136	0.271	**0.632**
Chyi						
Primary	−0.117	−0.368	−0.173	0.097	0.114	−0.180
Other training	−0.054	−0.167	−0.027	0.177	0.110	−0.304
College	0.227	0.317	0.198	0.274	0.321	−0.100
South						
Primary	**0.243**	0.336	0.320	0.218	0.129	−0.109
Other training	**0.288**	0.197	0.320	0.145	0.190	0.061
College	**0.458**	0.408	**0.532**	**0.465**	**0.273**	0.118
Mountain						
Primary	0.166	−0.241	0.120	0.041	−0.088	−0.279
Other training	**0.545**	0.629	**0.732**	0.171	0.353	0.097
College	**0.419**	−0.034	0.566	0.411	0.183	−0.063
Fall 1996						
Bishkek						
Primary	−0.001	0.314	0.163	0.192	0.223	0.555
Other training	0.084	0.205	0.028	−0.018	−0.044	−0.023
College	0.300	0.386	**0.320**	**0.289**	**0.244**	**0.407**
Chyi						
Primary	0.265	**−0.486**	**−0.410**	0.054	**0.352**	**0.511**
Other training	−0.009	−0.052	0.030	0.150	0.103	**0.344**
College	**0.335**	0.477	**0.372**	**0.453**	0.345	0.460
South						
Primary	0.169	0.214	0.204	**0.317**	0.170	0.040
Other training	0.104	**0.260**	**0.252**	**0.211**	0.048	-0.072
College	**0.405**	**0.277**	**0.543**	**0.486**	**0.336**	0.250
Mountain						
Primary	−0.106	−0.156	−0.050	−0.321	−0.015	0.082
Other training	0.131	**0.316**	**0.226**	0.038	−0.043	0.049
College	**0.366**	**0.434**	**0.461**	0.185	0.162	0.486

Note: *****Boldface** = significant at the 5 percent level.

secondary training presented in Table 4.6, the costs of children and adults presented in Table 4.7, and ethnicity presented in Table 4.8.

Table 4.6 shows that college education for the household head has a strong effect, but one which varies by region and over time. In 1993, expenditure at the mean is 41–45 percent higher if the head has a college education in comparison to households in which the head has only completed secondary education. This result holds in every region except Chyi, where there are no differences in household expenditures by education of the head. In the South, the high returns to college education are concentrated in the middle of the expenditure distribution. In the mountain region non-college vocational education is important on average, and quantile differences are minimal. In Bishkek the position differs from elsewhere in the country, with the return to college education being only significant in the top decile, but being substantial for that group. In Bishkek college returns are three times as high among high income households than among other households, and within the top decile having a college-educated head added over 60 percent to household per capita expenditure over secondary education alone. The phenomenon of high-income college-educated people being concentrated in the capital city is not surprising.

Between 1993 and 1996 the return to college education declined nationally, but there are large regional variations. In Bishkek in 1996, the return is still highest in the top decile, but this is less of an extreme outlier than in 1993. By 1996 the positive impact of college education on household expenditure is significant for all groups other than the lowest decile; the return to college is over 30 percent in all quantiles. In the neighbouring Chyi oblast the return to college education is higher in 1996 than in 1993 at every point in the expenditure distribution, although the positive coefficient is only statistically significant at the median. The South and the Mountain region show the strongest evidence of the sorting effect as the returns to college and vocational education increase for the poorest households, and yet decline at the mean.

Overall, Table 4.6 provides support for the hypothesis that education became a more important determinant of material living standards between 1993 and 1996. In 1993, the data are dominated by the high-income college educated group in Bishkek, and are spotted with anomalies such as the higher expenditure levels of households whose heads had only primary education than of households whose heads had completed secondary school. By 1996, although the return to college education declined in aggregate, the regional quantile regressions show a more generalized positive impact of higher education (11 of 20 positive coefficients for college education in Table 4.6 are significant in 1996, up from 4 out of 20 in 1993).

Table 4.7 compares the expenditure costs of children and adults in 1993 and 1996. First, a child lowers per capita expenditure in both years, but the costs are higher in 1996 in all regions except the Mountain region when evaluated at the mean. At the mean, the regional differences are small; costs increase between 1993 and 1996 from 12 percent to 17 percent in Bishkek, 9 percent to 17 percent in the South, and 3 (insignificant) percent to 16 percent in Chyi, and fall from 15 percent to 13 percent in the Mountain region. These costs are borne at every point in the expenditure distribution, but the wealthiest households in general experience the highest costs.

Elderly and non-elderly adults also become more expensive over time. The elderly cause no reduction in expenditure in 1993, but by 1996 significant regional effects are found in Bishkek and in the Mountain region. An elderly householder reduces consumption on average 42 percent in Bishkek and 12 percent in the Mountain region. In Bishkek, these effects on expenditure are measured at every quantile; in the Mountain region, we only measure significant reductions among the poorest households although the point estimates are similar across all quantiles.

Non-elderly adults do not affect per capita consumption in 1993; by 1996, however, expenditure falls in every region with the addition of non-elderly adults to the household. The regional effects are similar at the mean, ranging from a 5 percent reduction in the South to a 10 percent reduction in the Mountain region. No pattern is found across the quantiles.

Table 4.8 examines ethnic changes over time and region. Ethnic effects compare Russian, Uzbek, and other ethnic groups to Kyrgyz. In Bishkek, there are no ethnic effects on consumption in 1993 or 1996 at the mean or at any point in the distribution. In the Mountain region, ethnic effects are also weak in both years. Mean effects are never significant, but we detect some Uzbek–Kyrgyz differences at some of the quantiles; in general, Uzbek households are better off relative to Kyrgyz households in 1993 and worse off relative to Kyrgyz households in 1996 in this region. In Chyi, we observe a significant reduction in ethnic differences in consumption over time. At the mean in 1993, Russians consume 31 percent more and other ethnic groups consume 42 percent more than Kyrgyz; these differences vanish in 1996 at the mean and at every point in the distribution. In the South, ethnic differences remain in 1996 but are much smaller. At the mean, Russians earn 41 percent more than Kyrgyz in 1993, but there is no difference in expenditures between Kyrgyz and Russian households in 1996; this change is concentrated among the poorest households. Differences between Uzbek and Kyrgyz households fall from 40 percent in 1993 to 23 percent in 1996, and the difference between other ethnic groups and Kyrgyz

Table 4.7 Costs of children, the elderly, and other adults by region and quantile[*]

	Mean	10th	Percentile 25th	50th	75th	90th
Children						
Fall 1993						
Bishkek	**−0.117**	−0.074	−0.119	**−0.181**	**−0.163**	−.199
Chyi	−0.029	−0.010	−0.024	−0.043	−0.036	0.004
South	**−0.091**	−0.064	−0.070	**−0.097**	**−0.121**	**−0.113**
Mountain	**−0.154**	−0.328	**−0.131**	**−0.100**	0.105	−0.018
Fall 1996						
Bishkek	**−0.174**	−0.091	**−0.113**	**−0.158**	**−0.230**	**−0.202**
Chyi	**−0.157**	**−0.245**	**−0.217**	**−0.172**	**−0.149**	**−0.164**
South	**−0.166**	**−0.106**	**−0.139**	**−0.174**	**−0.180**	**−0.208**
Mountain	**−0.130**	**−0.115**	**−0.082**	**−0.116**	**−0.133**	**−0.195**
Elderly						
Fall 1993						
Bishkek	−0.134	−0.217	−0.107	**−0.250**	−0.180	−0.210
Chyi	−0.017	−0.078	0.023	−0.033	0.040	0.031
South	0.033	0.198	0.134	0.008	0.023	− 00003
Mountain	−0.088	−0.075	0.105	−0.062	**−0.208**	**−0.286**
Fall 1996						
Bishkek	**−0.416**	**−0.379**	**−0.274**	**−0.317**	**−0.433**	**−0.451**
Chyi	−0.006	0.008	−0.089	−0.089	0.002	−0.119
South	0.027	0.065	0.120	0.082	0.006	−0.017
Mountain	**−0.122**	**−0.159**	**−0.148**	−0.147	−0.100	−0.141
Other Adults						
Fall 1993						
Bishkek	−0.050	0.034	0.001	−0.086	−0.140	**−0.123**
Chyi	−0.021	−0.022	−0.056	−0.014	−0.025	−0.025
South	**−0.042**	−0.048	−0.050	−0.031	−0.035	−0.037
Mountain	−0.010	0.007	−0.020	−0.018	−0.048	−0.026
Fall 1996						
Bishkek	**−0.078**	−0.035	−0.075	**−0.101**	**−0.099**	**−0.104**
Chyi	**−0.086**	**−0.135**	**−0.135**	−0.096	−0.071	−0.039
South	**−0.052**	−0.003	0.005	−0.033	**−0.069**	**−0.086**
Mountain	**−0.101**	**−0.135**	**−0.082**	**−0.089**	−0.078	−0.072

Note: ***Boldface** = significant at the 5 percent level. Sample sizes, in 1993 are: Bishkek = 320, Chyi = 473, South = 753, Mountain region = 383, and in 1996: Bishkek = 391, Chyi = 370, South = 809, Mountain region = 381.

*Table 4.8 Ethnic effects on expenditures by region and quantile**

		Percentile				
	Mean	10th	25th	50th	75th	90th
Russian						
Fall 1993						
Bishkek	0.008	0.149	–0.104	0.119	0.056	0.151
Chyi	**0.312**	**0.813**	0.198	0.119	0.040	0.136
South	**0.411**	**0.941**	**0.622**	**0.413**	0.229	0.093
Mountain	0.163	0.406	0.397	0.187	–0.060	–0.083
Fall 1996						
Bishkek	0.008	0.0001	–0.066	0.037	–0.061	0.039
Chyi	–0.034	0.095	–0.138	–0.129	–0.106	–0.170
South	0.261	**0.704**	0.294	0.145	0.170	–0.150
Mountain	0.080	–0.018	0.147	0.135	0.140	–0.143
Uzbek						
Fall 1993						
Bishkek	–0.378	–0.246	–0.386	–0.064	–0.266	–0.401
Chyi	0.706	0.883	0.200	0.612	0.577	0.658
South	**0.404**	**0.577**	**0.511**	**0.409**	**0.202**	0.111
Mountain	0.801	**1.939**	**1.287**	0.719	0.536	0.861
Fall 1996						
Bishkek	–0.059	0.414	–0.217	–0.000	0.0009	0.111
Chyi	0.511	0.766	0.374	0.524	0.063	1.527
South	**0.226**	**0.429**	0.210	**0.225**	0.078	0.103
Mountain	–0.774	0.131	–0.234	–0.687	**–1.240**	**–1.937**
Other ethnicity						
Fall 1993						
Bishkek	–0.085	0.318	0.036	0.118	0.251	0.365
Chyi	**0.421**	**0.737**	0.331	0.281	**0.297**	0.274
South	**0.366**	**0.834**	**0.506**	**0.343**	0.101	0.092
Mountain	0.474	0.617	0.485	0.515	0.157	0.166
Fall 1996						
Bishkek	0.211	0.249	0.048	0.177	0.244	0.285
Chyi	0.083	0.209	0.112	–0.003	–0.079	–0.053
South	**0.219**	0.138	0.129	0.126	0.083	0.210
Mountain	0.193	–0.013	0.143	0.109	0.122	0.106

Note: ***Boldface** = significant at the 5 percent level of significance. Sample sizes in 1993: Bishkek = 320, Chyi = 473, South = 753, Mountain region = 383; in 1996: Bishkek = 391, Chyi = 370, South = 809, Mountain region = 381.

falls from 37 percent in 1993 to 22 percent in 1996; these changes are also concentrated among the poorest households. Overall, transition resulted in less expenditure discrimination based on ethnicity.

In summary, from the regional analyses, the most interesting results are the increases in the costs of large families over time, and the decline in ethnic differences in consumption across regions and over time. The regional analysis reinforces the conclusion that children generally impose a higher burden on household consumption than pensioners, but highlight the special (and highly adverse) impact of pensioners on household welfare in Bishkek. The education effects are more complex with the regional analysis indicating lower returns to education over time, but also providing support for the existence of sorting effects. The education and family size effects are strongest in Bishkek, while the ethnic changes are strongest in the agricultural regions of Chyi, Osh, and Djalalabad and are particularly noticeable among the poorest households.

3.3 Conclusions from Quantile Regressions

The determinants of household expenditure have been analysed by quantile regression using a human capital model with demographic and location control variables. The overall fit of the model to Kyrgyz Republic data improves substantially between 1993 at the start of transition and 1996 when reforms were well under way. The pseudo R^2 at the mean is 0.114 in 1993 and 0.347 in 1996; the 1993 value is similar to the R^2 of the OLS regression reported by Grootaert and Braithwaite (1998). Some of the results are specific to the Kyrgyz Republic or similar economies, while others appear more general, such as the increased cost of large families during transition. Particularly interesting are the results with respect to education, suggesting its enhanced role during a period of disequilibrium in determining a household's place in the income distribution.

The results from the quantile regressions of household expenditures reveal differences in consumption across groups and by quantile that are potentially of importance when policies are developed that may affect a household's standard of living. The results also differ from findings based on a simple division between poor and non-poor households, where the only strong results show negative relationships between poverty and residence in Bishkek and between poverty and the head having a tertiary education. The quantile regressions highlight the special nature of college-educated household heads in Bishkek in the top decile of the distribution. In a country with a very high poverty headcount, poverty analysis is perverted into wealth analysis, and potentially important correlates of poverty are swamped by the attributes of the rich.

The gender and age of the household head are generally not important determinants of household expenditure. Among the poorest 25 percent of households in 1993, having a pensioner head was significantly negatively related to expenditure, but by 1996 this effect was no longer significant, probably because of the decline in the share of poor households headed by pensioners. An exception to these generalizations may be a group of female pensioners living alone in Bishkek. These women tended to be Russian. In contrast, many non-Russian pensioners were taken into the household of their extended family as the real value of pensions fell.

Region, ethnicity, family size and education are important determinants of household consumption following transition. We also find changes in the relative impact of the variables over time, across regions, and among households.   Over time regional disparities increased in the Kyrgyz Republic; residence in the large urban centre of Bishkek yielded higher returns in 1996 than in 1993, the South replaced the mountain region as the most depressed region of the country, the North–South gap widened, and ethnic differences narrowed within regions.[21]   The poorest households display more regional disparity than wealthier households but, within regions, the poorest households experience larger reductions in ethnic differences in consumption. This could be interpreted as evidence of the increased play of market forces as inter-regional differences are reduced, but cultural or institutional barriers to internal migration remain strong especially for the poorest families.

Additional children lower per capita expenditure and significantly increase the probability that a household is poor; these negative effects were larger in the later stages of transition than in the beginning. By 1996, the number of adults and the elderly are also significant predictors of lower household per capita expenditure, although the quantile regressions indicate that pensioners reduce per capita expenditure across the entire income spectrum with smaller effects at the bottom end of the distribution. These results suggest that the cost of children, measured as foregone household consumption, increases with transition and that the income contributed by elderly and non-elderly adults is less likely to cover their additional consumption in the market-based economy. The payoff to smaller families is higher as transition progresses.

Finally, high skill training, particularly at the college level, is an important factor in household well-being. While the marginal return to college education falls over time, college education seems to be more important to household consumption in 1996 than in 1993 as returns to lower levels of education fall and educated households sort into wealthier quantiles of the distribution. We observe a sharp decline in the percentage of heads with a college education between 1993 and 1996 particularly in the lower quantiles. The aggregate decline is related to the large-scale net emigration from the Kyrgyz Republic; emigrants consisted disproportionately of college-educated Slavs and Germans. However, education does appear to have a larger impact on expenditures in the lower half of the distribution. Our results suggest that households, particularly the poorest, have significantly benefited from having a head with post-secondary training. This result sheds little direct light on current education debates centred on the erosion of educational provision at all levels since 1991. This means that in the next generation the norm will no longer be completed secondary school, and, with varying quality of educational institutions, it will matter to a greater extent where kindergarten, primary, secondary and tertiary education are attained.

The overall conclusion from our quantile regression analysis of the Kyrgyz Republic is that transition to a market economy has had large effects on the standard of living of many households. Transition reduced economic disparities based on ethnicity and, to a lesser extent, location. Dismantlement of the extensive social protection system inherited from central planning increased the private cost of large families. The relatively privileged position of pensioners in the Soviet Union was no longer apparent by 1996, although at the bottom of the income distribution having a pensioner in the household did not lower household consumption. On the positive side, location in the capital city became even more important as a determinant of household expenditure, education appears to have also increased in importance as a determinant of a household's place in the expenditure distribution. Replacement of the administered labour markets of the centrally planned economy by market forces has increased inequality and has also changed the reward pattern; although still moderated by location and to a diminishing extent ethnicity, the costs of dependents are clearly increasing, as are the returns to human capital.

4. CONCLUSIONS

The various approaches to poverty and living standards in the Kyrgyz Republic during the transition to a market-oriented economy shed considerable light on the transition process. Most of all, it is a slow process. In the early 1990s the Kyrgyz economy suffered from a huge negative shock and those best able to shelter their households from the shock were residents of the capital city and household heads with tertiary education, that is, a small part of the population incorporating many of the old elite. The strong regional effects in analyses based on 1993 data indicate low levels of internal labour mobility. Applying standard human capital models to the determination of household living standards works much better with 1996 data than with 1993 data, but still less well than in developed market economies, suggesting that the shift to a functioning market economy has been slow and, almost a decade after the abolition of central planning, remains incomplete.

The results provide strong evidence of the decline in social protection offered by the state, and of the increased cost of raising children as benefits (such as kindergarten or school meals) previously provided by the state or the enterprise have disappeared. Households with many adults or pensioners were also more poorly placed in 1996 than in 1993, indicating that the value of the generous Soviet era pensions was being eroded but they still helped to protect pensioners in poor households.[22] Although age and gender effects are believed to be related to poverty, the quantitative studies provide little supporting evidence of such effects in the Kyrgyz Republic in 1993.

Changes in the wealth distribution are likely to have been even more pronounced than changes in the expenditure or income distribution, although it is difficult to find data on wealth. Especially in Kazakhstan privatization transferred valuable public assets to a small group, but everywhere there is a feeling that those in power could use their position to obtain rents that were transformed into cars and other consumer durables or invested abroad. Privatization of the housing stock with priority to current occupiers favoured the old elite which had the best housing and, especially in the capital cities, could benefit from a tiny market in good quality apartments to earn substantial rents from expatriates. For poor people privatization of housing created new burdens on the household, which was now responsible for maintenance, and as provision of heating, hot water and other utilities was gradually shifted to a user-pay system.[23]

The distributional effects of the economic strategies adopted during the transition from central planning can be modified by individual responses and by social policy. The increased cost of children has been associated with a declining birth rate; in the Kyrgyz Republic the crude birth rate was 32.0 per thousand population in 1985, 29.3 in 1990 and 27.5 in 1996. This will eventually lead to smaller families but will take decades to work its way through, and meanwhile the current generation of children will grow up with poorer education than their parents, and with a significant number of children outside family care.[24] Although private health and education provision is emerging and is in some respects more efficient than the old state monopoly, many people are excluded from these services by poverty. Reduced human capital will harm future growth prospects and emergence of an alienated under-class will challenge social stability, so there are strong reasons for active public policies.

NOTES

1. District heating is a central system of providing heating to a community. About a quarter of households in the Kyrgyz Republic have access to the district heating network; 80 percent of these are in Bishkek.

2. The net increases are at the national level and hide regional variations. The two poor pastoral areas included in Howell's 1994 survey recorded high rates of selling livestock (55 percent of households in one and 79 percent in the other) in order to buy food, coal, medicine, bus tickets and clothes, especially to enable children to continue attending school.

3. In the KMPS 43 percent of urban and 71 percent of rural households reported having had access to a private plot of land during the preceding twelve months.

4. The poverty line was constructed for each of seven demographic groups (1–6, 7–10, 11–13, 14–17, male 18–59, female 18–54 and pensioner) based on minimum nutrition needs valued at market prices and adjusted for non-food needs valued at one fifth of total expenditure. Each household has a poverty line reflecting the age/sex composition of its members, so that scale economies enter indirectly and in a non-transparent manner. Because number and gender effects are built into the poverty line, it is difficult to separate out analytically the impact of family size and composition when using the definition of poor households in World Bank (1995).

5. Greene (2000) provides a textbook treatment, and Horowitz and Savin (2001) discuss recent developments in the use of binary response models.

6. In the mid 1990s the UN Drug Control Programme estimated that four- fifths of the heroin consumed in Europe came from Central Asia (Kaser and Mehrotra, 1996, 248). The best growing areas are in the Kyrgyz Republic, especially in the Chyi oblast. Before 1917 what is now the Kyrgyz Republic accounted for a fifth of world opium output.

7. German and Jewish household heads were included in the other Slav category while Korean and Farsi were in the other category, which is sometimes referred to as 'other Turkic'.

8. Pensioners also suffered from the high inflation of 1992–5 and from housing privatization. Imputed income from subsidized housing, including maintenance and utilities, played a major role in reducing inequality in the USSR (Buckley and Gurenko, 1997). Privatization of housing shifted the burden of maintenance on to householders, and the gradual shift towards user-pay systems for heating, hot water and other utilities impinged heavily on poor households (Finkel and Garcia, 1997). After any financial savings had been wiped out by

hyperinflation, pensioners were poorly placed to deal with the shift to payment for maintenance and services.

9. Net emigration between 1989 and 1996 was, by World Bank estimates, 370 000 (8.6 percent of the 1989 population, and the largest proportion of any former Soviet republic), of which 200 000 were Russian (Heleniak, 1997). The Kyrgyz Republic's German population dropped from 102 000 in 1989 to 38 000 by early 1995 (Olcott, 1996, 550). The 1997 *Human Development Report* (UNDP, 1997a) for the Kyrgyz Republic reports the ethnic composition having changed from 52 percent Kyrgyz, 22 percent Russian and 13 percent Uzbek in 1989 to 60 percent Kyrgyz, 16 percent Russian and 14 percent Uzbek in 1996. The limited internal migration in the Kyrgyz Republic, as in the rest of Central Asia, is usually explained by strong extended kinship networks and culturally prescribed preferences for kin proximity (Buckley, 1998, 72).

10. Howell (1996a; 1996b) reports cases of poverty forcing poor families in rural areas of the south to slaughter or sell livestock which they need for breeding or to cut down fruit trees for firewood. Klugman (1997) cites Asian Development Bank field reports that almost two-thirds of children in the Bel-Adei district of Djalalabad oblast did not attend school in winter 1994 for lack of winter clothing and shoes. Poor parents are under financial pressure to skimp on providing basic school supplies which are no longer free; Klugman reports a decline in real educational expenditure of over 60 percent between 1990 and 1996 while the number of teachers remained constant, implying a huge squeeze on material supplies. The serious decline in kindergarten places has been more pronounced in rural areas (Klugman et al., 1997). In Chyi oblast, the better-off farmers have pushed agrarian reform fastest; by the end of 1996 three-fifths of farms in Chyi were individually owned, while in Osh and Djalalabad oblasts restructuring had mainly created agricultural cooperatives (Mudahar, 1998). The cooperatives, often conservatively run by former state farm managers, could inhibit progress in the south, while the northern farmers pursue more dynamic strategies. The mountain regions have a distinctive economic base with emphasis on pastoral activities.

11. In ordinary least squares regression, $y_j = x_j\,\beta + \varepsilon_j$ and $E(y_j|\ x_j) = x_j\beta$. By imposing constant parameters over the entire distribution, OLS assumes that the underlying structural equations do not differ across income groups. Quantile regression assumes that a linear function or approximation describes not $E(y_j|$ $X_j)$, but $f(y_j|X_j)$, for a quantile q of the distribution where $0 < q < 1$. The technique was developed by Koenker and Bassett (1978), and is discussed in Deaton (1997, 80–85), and in greater detail in Buchinsky (1998) and Koenker and Hallock (2001).

12. The test statistic is: $W = (Rb-r)'(RVR')^{-1}(Rb-r)$ where W is distributed as a chi-squared with q degrees of freedom, and b is the estimate of β, $Rb-r$ is the set of hypotheses being tested, and q is the number of restrictions. W/q is distributed as an F-statistic with q and d degrees of freedom; $d = n-k-1$, where k is the number of coefficients estimated in each quantile regression.

13. Summary statistics for the variables included in the quantile regressions are given in Tables 4A.1 and 4A.2 in Appendix 4A.

14. Brownstone and Valletta (2001) provide an introduction to the bootstrap as a means of improving the accuracy of standard error estimates and hence improving the efficiency of hypothesis tests. Efron and Tibshirani (1993) describe bootstrap methods. For more recent syntheses, see the contributions of Horowitz (2001) and Brownstone and Kazimi (2001) to the *Handbook of Econometrics* vol. 5.

15. For children, $F(5,1904) = 10.41$ in 1993 and $F(5,1938) = 24.45$ in 1996. For working age adults, $F(5,1904) = 1.86$ in 1993 and $F(5,1938) = 7.68$ in 1996.

16. This effect in the lower quantiles is not caused by disproportionate representation of elderly heads in these two quantiles. In 1993, 10–15 percent of households in every quantile were headed by persons eligible for (and likely to receive) a pension. (See Table 4A.1 in Appendix 4A.)

17. In 1993, $F(5,1904) = 4.86$ for Bishkek, 4.16 for the Mountain region, and 4.39 for the South. In 1996, $F(5,1938) = 12.92$ for Bishkek, 3.23 for the Mountain region, and 16.17 for the South.

18. In 1993, $F(5,1904) = 1.47$ for primary education, 2.51 for post-secondary vocational training and 5.17 for college education. In 1996, $F(5,1938) = 1.57$ for primary education, 3.47 for post-secondary vocational training and 14.62 for college education.

19. A similar pattern of college-educated household heads becoming more concentrated in the upper quantiles occurred in other transition economies (see, for example, Keane and Prasad, 1999, 6, on Poland).

20. A striking exception is that in Bishkek male headship is associated with 63 percent higher per capita household expenditure among the lowest decile in 1993. This is likely to pick up the effect of elderly females living alone (Grootaert and Braithwaite, 1998, 27). A large and negative link between female headship in households where the head is retired and consumption among the poorest households is consistent with considerable research on poverty among the elderly in the United States and Europe (Smeeding, 1990), perhaps implying a more 'modern' economic and social structure in the capital.

21. The greater resilience of pastoral to crop agriculture during transition is also evident in Mongolia and Kazakhstan (Pomfret, 2000a). Moreover, the largest foreign investment project in the Kyrgyz Republic, the Kumtor goldmine, located in Issyk-kul oblast in the Mountain region, had begun to play a significant role in the national economy by 1996 due to construction work, although output only began to flow in 1997.

22. The fiscal costs of defined-benefit pay-as-you-go pension schemes have, however, been a large burden, which will increase further due to the future liability to post-1945 baby boomers. Kazakhstan instituted a personal-account system on the Chilean model in 1998 (see the papers in *Kazakstan Economic Trends*, October–December 1999), and the Kyrgyz Republic is seriously considering pension reform (Anderson and Becker, 1999).

23. Finkel and Garcia (1997) analyse options for pricing heating in the Kyrgyz Republic and find that many users in the capital city could not afford user fees

set at any level. Outside the capital the under-funded heating system often failed, and this was associated with deteriorating health (Bauer et al., 1998, 48).

24. The increasing number of children outside the household system is a new phenomenon in post-independence Central Asia. Although orphanages existed in the USSR, they rarely catered to Central Asian children, who were taken care of within the extended family. The phenomenon of street children is still not fully accepted, let alone accurately measured; one symptom is the increased number of children being held in detention centres on vagrancy charges (Bauer et al., 1998, 108).

APPENDIX 4A

Table 4A.1 Summary statistics: full sample and by quantile, fall 1993[a]

Variables	All households	Percentile					
		<=10th[b]	10–25th[c]	25–50th[d]	50–75th[e]	75–90th[f]	>90th[g]
Per capita expenditure	176.721 [168.398]	24.140	62.814	127.512	127.512	237.936	382.593
Region							
Bishkek	0.166	0.036	0.072	0.119	0.119	0.280	0.313
Chyi	0.245	0.172	0.216	0.234	0.324	0.277	0.328
South	0.390	0.495	0.478	0.443	0.377	0.273	0.234
Mountain	0.199	0.297	0.234	0.204	0.180	0.170	0.125
Ethnicity							
Kyrgyz	0.510	0.746	0.626	0.501	0.462	0.428	0.349
Russian	0.240	0.099	0.175	0.214	0.267	0.322	0.354
Uzbek	0.114	0.078	0.117	0.135	0.132	0.087	0.083
Other	0.136	0.077	0.082	0.150	0.139	0.163	0.214
Education of head							
Primary	0.334	0.349	0.323	0.335	0.335	0.301	0.385
Secondary	0.170	0.292	0.214	0.168	0.148	0.128	0.104
Some training	0.245	0.203	0.271	0.270	0.213	0.273	0.219
College	0.251	0.156	0.192	0.227	0.304	0.298	0.292
Male head	0.818	0.839,	0.808	0.83	0.824	0.824	0.760
Pensioner head	0.119	0.135	0.110	0.104	0.112	0.131	0.151
Household members							
Children	1.821 [1.690]	2.271 [1.873]	2.309 [1.821]	2.029 [1.732]	1.675 [1.509]	1.374 [1.559]	1.161 [1.365]
Adults	3.112 [1.792]	3.406 [1.920]	3.419 [2.053]	3.198 [1.826]	3.176 [1.757]	2.768 [1.485]	2.505 [1.425]
Pensioners	0.513 [0.740]	0.500 [0.686]	0.515 [0.758]	0.561 [0.759]	0.534 [0.746]	0.471 [0.745]	0.417 [0.689]
Sample size	1929	192	291	481	483	289	192

Notes :
[a]Mean [standard deviation].
[b]Expenditure at 10th percentile; other statistics for persons with expenditure <=10th percentile.
[c]Expenditure at 25th percentile; other statistics for persons with expenditure >10th and <=25th percentile.
[d]Expenditure at 50th percentile; other statistics for persons with expenditure >25th and <=50th percentile.
[e]Expenditure at 50th percentile; other statistics for persons with expenditure >50th and <=75th percentile.
[f]Expenditure at 75th percentile; other statistics for persons with expenditure >75th and <=90th percentile.
[g]Expenditure at 90th percentile; other statistics for persons with expenditure >90th percentile.

Table 4A.2 Summary statistics: full sample and by quantile, fall 1996[a]

Variables	All households	Percentile <=10th[b]	10–25th[c]	25–50th[d]	50–75th[e]	75–90th[f]	>90th[g]
Per capita expenditure	803.526 [940.038]	147.382	272.495	517.851	517.851	989.405	1698.313
Region							
Bishkek	0.200	0.020	0.034	0.074	0.260	0.377	0.533
Chyi	0.190	0.097	0.108	0.202	0.230	0.249	0.185
South	0.415	0.786	0.659	0.446	0.295	0.240	0.159
Mountain	0.195	0.097	0.199	0.278	0.215	0.134	0.123
Ethnicity							
Kyrgyz	0.572	0.821	0.704	0.642	0.545	0.445	0.431
Russian	0.233	0.036	0.110	0.176	0.289	0.384	0.395
Uzbek	0.081	0.087	0.134	0.092	0.066	0.051	0.056
Other	0.113	0.056	0.052	0.090	0.100	0.120	0.118
Education of head							
Primary	0.143	0.077	0.150	0.137	0.138	0.151	0.210
Secondary	0.461	0.693	0.544	0.521	0.425	0.373	0.288
Some training	0.253	0.194	0.237	0.284	0.285	0.229	0.210
College	0.143	0.036	0.069	0.100	0.152	0.247	0.292
Male head	0.847	0.954	0.887	0.881	0.805	0.825	0.728
Pensioner Head	0.125	0.026	0.069	0.084	0.154	0.188	0.241
Household members							
Children	1.524 [1.426]	2.500 [1.311]	2.127 [1.446]	1.748 [1.434]	1.318 [1.313]	0.935 [1.151]	0.482 [0.864]
Adults	2.533 [1.691]	2.985 [1.744]	3.055 [1.778]	2.765 [1.685]	2.371 [1.626]	2.154 [1.52]	1.692 [1.402]
Pensioners	0.528 [0.743]	0.383 [0.731]	0.467 [0.706]	0.562 [0.766]	0.590 [0.761]	0.538 [0.714]	0.508 [0.728]
Sample size	1951	196	291	489	488	292	195

Notes:

[a]Mean [standard deviation].

[b]Expenditure at 10th percentile; other statistics for persons with expenditure <=10th percentile.

[c]Expenditure at 25th percentile; other statistics for persons with expenditure >10th and <=25th percentile.

[d]Expenditure at 50th percentile; other statistics for persons with expenditure >25th and <=50th percentile.

[e]Expenditure at 50th percentile; other statistics for persons with expenditure >50th and <=75th percentile.

[f]Expenditure at 75th percentile; other statistics for persons with expenditure >75th and <=90th percentile.

[g]Expenditure at 90th percentile; other statistics for persons with expenditure >90th percentile.

5. Cross-country comparisons of the determinants of living standards

In this chapter we examine household data from four of the five Central Asian states to analyse how household expenditure levels are determined in newly established market economies.[1] Our focus is on identifying patterns which are robust across countries, rather than nation-specific explanations of living standards as in the previous chapter. Three sets of variables prove to be robust explanators: location, household composition and education level.

1. PREVIOUS STUDIES OF KAZAKHSTAN, UZBEKISTAN, TURKMENISTAN AND TAJIKISTAN

Living standards in other Central Asian countries are more difficult to assess due to the poorer raw data than in the Kyrgyz Republic. Kazakhstan and Uzbekistan have been relatively extensively studied, although the basic data are much poorer than in the Kyrgyz Republic, with continuing reliance on the HBS apart from the 1996 LSMS in Kazakhstan and a 1995 household survey of three oblasts in Uzbekistan conducted under the auspices of the European University Institute and the University of Essex.[2] For Turkmenistan household data are significantly poorer, despite the existence of a 1998 LSMS survey (which is not in the public domain), and for Tajikistan due to the civil unrest they are virtually non-existent before the 1999 LSMS survey; in both countries, however, the limited evidence points to increasingly severe poverty (Falkingham, 1999b, 19).

Kazakhstan was less vulnerable than the other four new independent Central Asian countries to increased poverty because of its higher initial living standards. The National Statistics Committee paints a much less negative picture from HBS data than that provided by Milanovic's data in Table 3.6. Using a poverty line intended to match in real terms the 75 rubles per month in 1989 used in Table 2.1, the poverty rate increased from 15.5 percent in 1989 to 22.6 percent in 1995, although the rate was higher in rural areas (35 percent in 1995) and other quality of life indicators had also declined during the first half of the 1990s (Akanov and Suzhikova, 1998, 235–36). Since independence birth rates have declined, although this continues a trend from the 1980s, and death rates have risen.[3] Deteriorating health standards are also evidenced in anthropometric data, anaemia levels and so forth, but many of these indicators reflect pre-existing social and cultural values or arise from environmental consequences of Soviet policies.[4]   Without wishing to downplay the severe health problems in many parts of Kazakhstan, the mortality situation is less severe than in, say, Russia, and direct links between transition and increased morbidity are uncertain.

The Kazakhstan government is, however, widely believed to have failed to provide the framework of good governance necessary for a successful market economy.   Moreover, widening inequality and severe reductions in public spending on education and health undermine future growth prospects.[5]   A special problem in Kazakhstan is the phenomenon of 'company town', usually related to minerals and processing activities, whose economic collapse after the dissolution of the USSR led to severe localized deprivation (see Chapter 3.2).

Uzbekistan has pursued a more gradual transition strategy, which can be directly linked to the smaller fall in GDP and less severe inequality than in the Kyrgyz Republic (Falkingham et al., 1997, 114).   Milanovic's Gini coefficient of 0.28 in 1987–88 was the highest among the eighteen countries in his study, while the 0.33 in 1993–95 is lower than for any former Soviet republic except Latvia.   Table 3.4 suggests that the increase in inequality in Uzbekistan during the first half of the 1990s was much lower than in neighbouring countries. Milanovic's poverty measures indicate an increase in the headcount measure from 24 percent in 1987–88 to 63 percent in 1993–95, which is severe, but smaller than the increase in the other Central Asian countries – from 5 percent to 65 percent in Kazakhstan, from 12 percent to 88 percent in the Kyrgyz Republic and from 12 percent to 61 percent in Turkmenistan.

Alternative poverty measures for Uzbekistan have been estimated by the Centre on Economic Research in Tashkent using HBS data. With a nutrition-based poverty line, CER (1997) reports a crude headcount measure of 58 percent in December 1996.   Home production is, however, negatively correlated with money income and inclusion of home production in household resources, reduces the poverty rate to 46 percent. Adjustment for household size and composition, because larger families have lower per capita consumption but benefit from scale economies and because children consume less than adults, reduces the poverty count to 22 percent. The CER numbers are lower than those of Milanovic, which reflects primarily a lower poverty line, but the adjustments are difficult to assess.   Marnie and Micklewright (1997) discounted the importance of scale economies before transition, but since housing privatization their argument holds to a lesser degree and it also seems plausible that home production has become relatively more important since independence, but how much to allow for these two factors is unclear.[6]

Despite these reservations about the quantitative results, it seems incontrovertible that there have been shifts in the income distribution and increases in poverty during Uzbekistan's transition. Although economic change has been limited by gradual policies and a small decline in output, the forces for increased income disparities inherent in a market economy are present in Uzbekistan, as in all transition economies. In sum, the direction if not the extent of distributional changes is predictable. The relatively stable output-mix and heavy government hand on the economy suggest that the emergence of *nouveaux riches* in the private sector may be a lesser phenomenon in Uzbekistan than in other transition economies. The new poor may also be less numerous and less suddenly impoverished than elsewhere. Pomfret and Anderson (1997) review the mechanisms by which the government has restricted the extent of welfare changes and in particular how prudent government policies have softened the decline in key social services and provided an effective social safety net.

Who have been the winners and losers? Coudouel's analysis of data from the EESU 1995 survey of three oblasts reveals patterns common to many transition economies (Coudouel, 1998; summarized in CER, 1997, 21–25). Large families have lower per capita incomes and expenditures; households with seven members or more account for 30 percent of poor households and half of the individuals in poverty. As elsewhere in the former USSR, gender and age are not strong determinants of poverty in the early transition years. There is an ethnic dimension to poverty, at least based on simple cross-tabulations; Central Asians make up 79 percent of the population and 92 percent of those in poverty, while Slavs make up 16 percent of the population and only 4 percent of the poor. Regional differences between the three oblasts are large, ranging from a 10 percent poverty rate in Tashkent to 60 percent in Karakalpakstan. Rural–urban differences are large, but not robust when output measures are used; other measures suggest large rural–urban differences in living standards, for example washing machine ownership is highest in Tashkent and higher in other urban locations than in rural households.[7] Poverty among the elderly remains limited in Uzbekistan; old people still receive some protection through the pension system and, especially when they are living in an extended family household, old people are not a major group in poverty, although single pensioners in urban areas are emerging as a group in poverty.

Education has played a role in Uzbekistan as in other transition economies, with tertiary education being a significant determinant of individual economic performance. While the returns to education have declined during the 1990s, individuals with tertiary qualifications have moved up the income distribution; Klugman (1998) describes this as a cohort effect, and it is similar to the sorting effect identified from more extensive data in the Kyrgyz Republic

(Anderson and Pomfret, 2000). Klugman (1998, 298 and 203–33) estimates that the returns to education are higher for women than for men, although women's subsequent returns to experience in the labour force are significantly reduced by breaks in employment.

Ethnic effects continue to exist. Smith (1995), on the basis of a small survey in Tashkent, reported that Uzbeks had lower educational qualifications than Russians, and had lower average incomes. Holding sex, age, education and occupation constant, Smith found that being Russian had a significant positive effect on income. This is consistent with the results of Lubin's work conducted fifteen years earlier. Klugman (1998, 281) found similar results on the basis of her larger sample covering three oblasts in 1995. Klugman explains the persistence of ethnic effects in the face of independence and large Slavic emigration by self-selection as less well-paid Slavs would leave first, by the earnings premium capturing skills not measured in the formal modelling, and by the emigration being based on expectations rather than on current discrimination or falling relative incomes for Slavs.

In part, the relative success in protecting those most threatened by transition may be due to policy innovations such as decentralization of social assistance through the mahallah system (analysed in greater depth by Coudouel and Marnie, 1999) or to private transfers (Coudouel et al., 1997), but quantitative assessments of these relationships is difficult. What can be more readily documented is that Uzbekistan has been the most successful of the new independent states in Central Asia in protecting the level of government spending and minimizing cuts in health and education spending, which could augur well for the future. In Uzbekistan, however, the government still keeps a heavy hand on the allocative mechanism, which discourages entrepreneurship and, especially, the creation of new private enterprises.

The impact of Turkmenistan's economic policies on living standards is difficult to assess with any accuracy because reliable data are hard to find.[8] Until 1996 the absence of reform possibly helped to reduce the negative impact on living standards by moderating both the decline in GDP and the increase in inequality, but this strategy stored up future problems which became apparent in 1997. Thus, Turkmenistan's GDP had fallen by less than that of Kazakhstan and the Kyrgyz Republic between 1989 and 1996, but whereas the latter two countries were enjoying some economic recovery by 1996–99 Turkmenistan's GDP continued to decline (Table 3.3).[9] The conservative economic policy with generous provisions for basic needs helped to avoid the rapid increase in poverty seen in the Kyrgyz Republic in the early 1990s (Table 3.6), but average wages were low (Table 3.10) and living standards have further deteriorated, possibly rapidly, in the second half of the

1990s. The LSMS survey conducted in 1998 has remained confidential, although World Bank references suggest relatively low poverty rates.

Living standards in Tajikistan during the 1990s are also difficult to assess, mainly due to the ongoing civil strife. The government has tried to implement economic reforms, especially in 1996 and since June 1997, but its success has been mixed, in part because the central government has not controlled all of the national territory. The output performance since independence has been the worst in Central Asia, and the demands of war finance have constantly disrupted attempts at macroeconomic stabilization. A 1995–96 survey by CARE International of 1848 households at risk (reported in UNDP, 1997b, 51–2) painted a grim picture of almost universal poverty and malnutrition. The 1999 LSMS survey reaffirmed this picture, with 96 percent of people having below the minimum consumption basket, although the picture is less grim with higher poverty lines (Table 3.4) (Falkingham, 2000c). The civil war has created 20 000 widows and over 55 000 orphans; female-headed households appear to be more likely to be poor, and there is an obvious problem of increased child labour (visible, for example, in the car windscreen washers on the streets of the capital city, Dushanbe) whose absence from school has repercussions for human capital formation and future living standards.

A few generalizations about the region can be made. Everywhere, transition was accompanied by an initial decline in living standards, as GDP fell and inequality increased, but by the late 1990s the trough had been passed and positive real GDP growth was ubiquitous in 1999 and 2000. The differing national timepaths of transformational recession and subsequent growth are related to the speed and intensity of reform. As the transition process progresses the determinants of living standards evolve, in line with expectations from established market economies. Human capital becomes a more important determinant of living standards, although the quantitative evidence for Central Asia is so far only strong with respect to tertiary education.[10] There is evidence that the distribution of human capital is becoming less egalitarian with changes in the delivery of education and healthcare. Particularly worrying for long-term growth is the drop in kindergarten enrolments (in the Kyrgyz Republic from about a third of the age group in 1990 to below 10 percent in 1994, and in Kazakhstan from half to less than 30 percent in the same period), as state enterprises and collective farms came under pressure to impose charges or reduce quality or divest themselves of kindergartens (Klugman et al., 1997). Such asset inequality reinforces the likelihood that underprivileged children will grow up to be poor and reduces the prospects for long-term growth.

2. DATA AND SUMMARY STATISTICS

The data for our analysis are obtained from five household surveys. Four of these are nationwide Living Standards Measurement Study (LSMS) surveys: the 1993 and 1997 Kyrgyz Republic surveys, the 1996 Kazakhstan LSMS, and the 1999 Tajikistan LSMS. For Uzbekistan, we use data on households collected in the Fergana oblast in 1999 as a pilot study for redesign of the national Household Budget Survey.[11] The sample sizes are for the Kyrgyz Republic 1926 households in 1993 and 2618 in 1997, Kazakhstan 1890 households, Tajikistan 1983 households, and Uzbekistan 542 households.

Summary statistics for each survey are given in Appendix Table A2. Despite the four countries' historical, cultural and geographical similarities, there are differences in the samples. The differences largely reflect the higher incomes and more 'European' culture of Kazakhstan, and the more traditionally Central Asian society in Tajikistan and the Fergana oblast of Uzbekistan. The Kazakhstan sample is the most urban, with 44 percent of households living in rural communities, which is fewer than in the Kyrgyz Republic (57 percent in 1993 and 62 percent in 1997), the Fergana oblast of Uzbekistan (72 percent) or Tajikistan (73 percent). Households in Kazakhstan are less likely to be headed by a man and the head is less likely to be married than households in the Kyrgyz Republic, Tajikistan or the Fergana oblast of Uzbekistan. Finally, household heads in Kazakhstan are older (46 years), on average, than heads in the Kyrgyz Republic (40–41), Tajikistan (40), and Uzbekistan (39).

Households are smaller in Kazakhstan than in Tajikistan, Uzbekistan or the Kyrgyz Republic. In 1996 the average household in Kazakhstan contains 3.6 members, which is less than in the Kyrgyz Republic (4.9 in 1993 and 5.5 in 1997), Uzbekistan (6) and Tajikistan (7). The average number of children in a household in Kazakhstan is 1.3, which is less than in the Kyrgyz Republic (1.8 in 1993 and 2.2 in 1997), Uzbekistan (3.0) or Tajikistan (3.5), while the number of elderly household members is similar in each country (0.4–0.5). The number of children is substantially higher than in European transition economies or elsewhere in the CIS.

The education variables indicate the high education level, relative to income levels, of these countries. Over two-fifths of household heads in each country have post-secondary education. In Kazakhstan the proportion with university education is slightly higher than in Tajikistan or the Fergana oblast of Uzbekistan. The Kyrgyz surveys, especially that of 1997, report substantially higher proportions of college-educated heads, and fewer heads having other post-secondary education than in the other countries, and there is also a sharp increase in the proportion of household heads completing secondary education and drop in those with incomplete secondary education from 1993 to 1997.[12] The other human capital variable, reported health of the household head, also has implausible variations with much worse reported health in Kazakhstan and much better in the Kyrgyz Republic.

Comparison of the samples' characteristics suggests that, in many respects, households in the Kyrgyz Republic and Kazakhstan are more similar to each other than to households in Tajikistan and the Fergana oblast of Uzbekistan. In the Kyrgyz Republic and Kazakhstan, compared to the other two countries, households are more likely to be headed by women or by an unmarried head, heads are younger and better educated, and households are less likely to be in rural areas. In addition, households are smaller and contain fewer dependents in Kazakhstan and the Kyrgyz Republic than in Tajikistan or the Fergana oblast of Uzbekistan.

The LSMS data have provided the basis for poverty analyses by the World Bank and other researchers. The picture of poverty presented by descriptive analysis is that poverty is higher in rural areas, varies across regions, and is related to ethnicity, education and dependency. However, many of the characteristics are inter-related. Multivariate analysis of household poverty isolates the impact of the different household characteristics on poverty, holding other things constant, and probit models have identified the overwhelming role of location in the capital city, the household head's education, and the number of dependents as key determinants of the probability of a household being above or below the poverty line.[13] Poverty is one measure of the well-being of households, but by focusing on poverty a great deal of information about households is lost because poverty analysis depends on arbitrary poverty lines to classify households as poor or non-poor. And it is also difficult to compare poverty across countries where poverty lines may represent different consumption standards. A preferable approach to the analysis of material well-being is to examine the distribution of household income or expenditures.

3. MODEL AND VARIABLES

We estimate a human capital model in which the per capita expenditure of households is affected by the level of human capital, the number of household members and other demographic characteristics of the household, and the location of the household (Anderson and Pomfret, 2002a). The dependent variable is household expenditures per capita, based on a headcount of household members and reported expenditures on goods (excluding vehicles), food, health, education and other services, housing, utilities, communication and transportation.[14] Because the log of expenditure more closely follows a normal distribution, we estimate semi-logarithmic regressions of the log of per capita expenditure on the household characteristics.

To capture household human capital, we include measures of the education and health of the household head. For all countries we use dummy variables for college education, other post-secondary training, and completed secondary education, with incomplete secondary schooling as the omitted education category. For Kazakhstan, we include two non-college post-secondary training variables, differentiating between PTU training and Tecnikum education.[15] Health is measured by a subjective assessment of the head's health status; the dummy variable is equal to one if the head reports good or very good health and equal to zero if health is average, poor, or very poor.

Household composition is measured by three variables describing the number of children under the age of 18, the number of elderly, and the number of non-elderly adults in the household. An adult is defined as elderly if he or she is eligible for a state pension, normally at age 60 for a man and age 55 for a woman. The other demographic characteristics include the age, measured in years, gender and marital status of the head of the household. Gender and marital status are captured by dummy variables, respectively equal to one if the head is a man and zero if the head is a woman, and equal to one if the head is married or cohabiting with a partner and equal to zero otherwise.

Location of the household is measured by a rural-urban dummy variable (one if rural, and zero if urban) and with region-specific variables. In the Kyrgyz Republic, we classify households into four groups: resident of Bishkek, resident of Chyi but not living in Bishkek, resident in the southern oblasts of Osh or Djalalabad, and resident in the mountain oblasts of Issuk-kul, Narun, or Talas. We divide Kazakhstan into six regions: Almaty, southern oblasts other than Almaty, northern oblasts, central oblasts, western oblasts and eastern oblasts.[16] We divide Tajikistan into five regions: Gorna-Badakhshan in the east, Leninabad in the northwest, Khatlon in the southwest and Dushanbe and the Rayons of Republican Subordination (RRS) in the central western area.[17] In each of these three countries, the omitted category for regional location is the largest city (Bishkek, Almaty and Dushanbe). In Uzbekistan, we only include the rural–urban variable because a single oblast was sampled.

In addition to the national level analysis, we make two attempts to compare similar locations in different countries. We compare the Fergana oblast of Uzbekistan in 1999 to the parts of the Kyrgyz Republic in 1997 and Tajikistan in 1999 also located in the Ferghana Valley.[18] The Ferghana region of the Kyrgyz Republic is defined as the Osh and Djalalabad oblasts, while the Ferghana region of Tajikistan is the Leninabad oblast. We also compare the experience of households in three capital cities: Almaty,

Bishkek, and Dushanbe. We have no data on Tashkent, the capital of Uzbekistan.

4. RESULTS

The results of the ordinary least squares regressions are presented in Tables 5.1a (Kazakhstan), 5.1b and 5.1c (the Kyrgyz Republic, 1993–97) and 5.1d (Tajikistan). The first and second columns in the tables for Kazakhstan and Tajikistan include the results from estimation of the model including regional variables and a rural–urban variable, while the third and fourth columns contain results from estimation of the model with region interacted with rural–urban residence. Table 5.1b contains results for the Kyrgyz Republic in 1993 and 1997 with the regional variables, and Table 5.1c contains the rural-region interactions for 1993 and 1997. The pooled model for the Kyrgyz Republic regresses the log of real per capita expenditures on the explanatory variables, with 1993 as the base year (price index = 100) and a 1997 price index equal to 369.

In Table 5.2, we present results from expenditure models for the Fergana oblast of Uzbekistan and for the Ferghana Valley regions of the Kyrgyz Republic and Tajikistan. In Table 5.3 we present the estimation for Almaty, Bishkek and Dushanbe. We use ordinary least squares regression in this chapter in order to have comparable cross-country estimates.[19]

4.1 Household Location

Location is an important factor in determining per capita household expenditure. Urban–rural differences in per capita expenditure are significant in Kazakhstan, the Kyrgyz Republic and the Fergana oblast of Uzbekistan, although not in Tajikistan. Within each country for which we have a national survey, households living in some regions are significantly wealthier than equivalent households living in other regions and the estimated coefficients are large.

In the Kyrgyz Republic, rural households' per capita expenditures are, other things equal, on average 28 percent lower than those of urban households, although the gap did narrow between 1993 and 1997. Households in the northern oblast of Chyi and the capital city of Bishkek are significantly wealthier than similar households in the other regions of the country. Living standards are lowest in the rural Mountain region and the rural Southern oblasts, followed by the urban Mountain and urban South areas. The regional differences widen over the transition period. In 1997, a Mountain region household is estimated to have 93 percent lower per capita expenditure than an identical household in Bishkek. The gap is smaller for the other regions, but still 74 percent for the South and 27 percent for Chyi, even though the latter is contiguous with Bishkek.[20]

*Table 5.1a Expenditure model: Kazakhstan, 1996**

Variables	Coefficient	t-statistic	Coefficient	t-statistic
Intercept	**8.590**	93.39	**8.570**	93.19
Head is male	0.046	1.34	0.040	1.15
Age of head	−0.002	−1.21	−0.001	−1.04
Head is married	0.045	1.11	0.043	1.07
Head is college graduate	**0.219**	5.11	**0.213**	4.99
Head has Tecnikum	**0.115**	2.85	**0.112**	2.78
Head has PTU	0.081	1.60	0.076	1.49
Head completed sec.	−0.010	−0.25	−0.009	−0.23
Head in good health	−0.030	−0.99	−0.026	−0.86
Rural community	**0.113**	3.98		
Central region	−0.028	−0.54		
Southern region	**−0.446**	−8.35		
Western region	0.092	1.47		
Northern region	**0.305**	5.86		
Eastern (not Almaty)	0.047	0.91		
Rural central region			0.100	1.64
Urban central region			−0.037	−0.67
Rural south region			**−0.357**	−5.72
Urban south region			**−0.431**	−7.29
Rural west region			0.024	0.30
Urban west region			**0.222**	3.10
Rural north region			**0.437**	7.62
Urban north region			**0.289**	5.06
Rural east region			**0.200**	3.47
Urban east region			0.002	0.03
Children in household	**−0.173**	−13.930	**−0.169**	−13.470
Elderly in household	**−0.122**	−4.010	**−0.114**	−3.740
Other adults in house.	**−0.058**	−4.170	**−0.055**	−3.910
R-square	0.297		0.303	
F-statistic	**46.59**		**38.69**	
Sample size	1890		1890	

Note: ***Boldface** if significant at the 5 percent level.

Table 5.1b Expenditure model: Kyrgyz Republic, 1993-1997[*]

Variables	1993-1997 Coefficient	t-stat	1993 Coefficient	t-stat	1997 Coefficient	t-stat
Intercept	**5.300**	61.56	**4.958**	30.62	**7.655**	94.03
Head is male	−0.015	−0.34	0.113	1.42	**−0.180**	−4.22
Age of head	−0.000	−0.02	−0.001	−0.31	0.001	0.69
Married head	0.041	1.06	0.089	1.19	**0.070**	1.99
Education/health of head						
College graduate	**0.174**	4.59	**0.211**	3.14	**0.118**	3.09
Postsecondary	0.059	1.39	0.102	1.43	−0.081	−1.73
Completed sec.	**−0.093**	−2.34	**−0.169**	−2.11	**−0.085**	−2.25
Good health	0.023	0.50	0.105	1.16	−0.017	−0.42
Household location						
Rural community	**−0.283**	−9.29	**−0.396**	−6.74	**−0.181**	−6.55
Chyi	**−0.164**	−3.51	−0.067	−0.79	**−0.270**	−6.00
South	**−0.528**	−12.56	**−0.367**	−4.65	**−0.735**	−18.84
Mountain	**−0.709**	−16.32	**−0.460**	−5.31	**−0.931**	−24.01
Household composition						
Children	**−0.128**	−14.97	**−0.121**	−6.94	**−0.122**	−16.67
Elderly	**−0.054**	−3.05	**−0.085**	−2.37	0.019	1.10
Other adults	**−0.030**	−3.57	0.001	0.05	**−0.088**	−10.01
Year						
1997	**0.663**	24.55				
R-square	0.320		0.147		0.537	
F-statistic	**141.37**		**23.30**		**214.33**	
Sample size	4531		1913		2618	

Note: *****Boldface** if significant at the 5 percent level.

Consequences of creating a market economy

Table 5.1c Expenditure model: Kyrgyz Republic, 1993–1997,
         rural–region interactions*

Variables	1993-1997		1993		1997	
	Coefficient	t-stat	Coefficient	t-stat	Coefficient	t-stat
Intercept	**5.195**	61.21	**4.863**	30.48	**7.547**	93.82
Head is male	−0.017	−0.39	0.104	1.31	**−0.179**	−4.16
Age of head	0.000	0.07	−0.001	−0.28	0.001	0.76
Married head	0.036	0.93	0.083	1.12	0.062	1.74
Education/health of head						
College grad.	**0.187**	4.96	**0.221**	3.29	**0.135**	3.51
Postsecondary	0.067	1.58	0.110	1.54	−0.073	−1.55
Complete sec.	−0.077	−1.93	−0.149	−1.88	−0.071	−1.87
Good health	0.032	0.71	0.111	1.22	−0.002	−0.06
Household location						
Rural Chyi	**−0.288**	−6.63	**−0.272**	−3.49	**−0.317**	−7.44
Rural South	**−0.744**	−18.28	**−0.694**	−8.72	**−0.839**	−22.91
Urban South	**−0.417**	−9.11	**−0.237**	−2.79	**−0.648**	−15.07
Rural mountain	**−0.940**	−23.10	**−0.853**	−9.80	**−1.048**	−29.99
Urban mountain	**−0.553**	−10.61	−0.185	−1.69	**−0.804**	−18.08
Household composition						
Children	**−0.128**	−15.01	**−0.123**	−7.03	**−0.125**	−16.61
Elderly	**−0.052**	−2.96	**−0.085**	−2.37	0.020	1.16
Nonelderly	**−0.028**	−3.35	0.002	0.10	**−0.085**	−9.69
Year						
1997	**0.666**	24.62				
R-square	0.319		0.150		0.537	
F-statistic	**131.57**		**22.34**		**201.45**	
Sample size	4515		1913		2618	

Note: ***Boldface** if significant at the 5 percent level.

Table 5.1d Expenditure model: Tajikistan, 1999[*]

Variables	Coefficient	t-statistic	Coefficient	t-statistic
Intercept	**9.917**	113.93	**9.911**	113.64
Head is male	0.016	0.29	0.017	0.30
Age of head	−0.001	−0.86	−0.001	−0.87
Head is married	0.068	1.46	0.069	1.49
Education/health of head				
College graduate	**0.337**	7.11	**0.339**	7.15
Postsecondary	**0.165**	4.06	**0.166**	4.08
Completed secondary	0.040	0.99	0.043	1.06
Good health	−0.010	−0.34	−0.009	−0.32
Household location				
Rural community	0.011	0.33		
Gorna-Badakhshan	**−0.593**	−7.50	**−0.585**	−7.82
RRS	**−0.061**	−1.06		
Leninabad	**−0.325**	−6.16		
Khatlon	**−0.339**	−6.26		
Rural RRS			−0.066	−1.25
Urban RRS			0.048	0.54
Rural Leninabad			**−0.315**	−6.21
Urban Leninabad			**−0.327**	−5.55
Rural Khatlon			**−0.324**	−6.51
Urban Khatlon			**−0.366**	−5.65
Household composition				
Children	**−0.088**	−12.76	**−0.087**	−12.73
Elderly	**−0.049**	−2.75	**−0.048**	−2.74
Other adults	−0.005	−0.71	−0.005	−0.59
R-square	0.176		0.177	
F-statistic	**28.09**		**24.93**	
Sample size	1983		1983	

Note: ***Boldface** if significant at the 5 percent level.

Table 5.2   Expenditure model: Ferghana region of Uzbekistan, Kyrgyz
*   Republic and Tajikistan**

	Uzbekistan		Kyrgyz Republic		Tajikistan	
Variables	Coeff.	t-stat	Coeff.	t-stat	Coeff.	t-stat
Intercept	**8.067**	32.56	**6.890**	53.95	**9.732**	67.90
Head male	0.0005	0.00	−0.012	−0.172	−0.108	−0.98
Age of head	**0.010**	2.60	0.0005	0.33	0.001	0.65
Married head	0.049	0.33	−0.060	−1.03	−0.011	−0.12
Education of head						
College grad.	**0.439**	3.12	0.110	1.73	**0.237**	2.63
Postsecondary	0.169	1.31	**−0.175**	−2.33	**0.180**	2.44
Completed sec.	0.127	1.01	−0.075	−1.19	0.044	0.60
Good health			−0.076	−1.11	0.064	1.28
Household location						
Rural	**−0.530**	−6.63	**−0.234**	−6.26	0.047	0.89
Household composition						
Children	**−0.105**	−4.27	**−0.114**	11.43	**−0.106**	−7.31
Elderly	**0.106**	2.24	**0.057**	2.08	−0.056	−1.85
Other adults	−0.026	−0.91	**−0.071**	−5.63	**−0.030**	−1.96
R-square	0.187		0.342		0.14	
F-statistic	**12.16**		**42.73**		**8.760**	
Sample size	541		915		603	

Note: ***Boldface** if significant at the 5 percent level.

*Table 5.3 Expenditure model: capital cities of Kazakhstan, Kyrgyz Republic and Tajikistan**

Variables	Almaty (Kaz)		Bishkek (Kyrg.)		Dushanbe (Taj)	
	Coeff.	t-stat	Coeff.	t-stat	Coeff.	t-stat
Intercept	**8.782**	34.01	**7.867**	40.35	**10.169**	41.91
Male head	0.133	1.46	**-0.312**	-3.46	-0.119	-0.63
Head age	-0.002	-0.48	-0.0006	-0.22	-0.005	-1.24
Married head	0.015	0.15	**0.185**	2.15	**0.330**	2.06
Head college grad.	**0.266**	2.44	0.049	0.48	0.242	1.67
Head postsecondary	0.077[a]	0.66	0.029	0.23	0.009	0.07
Head PTU	0.074	0.42				
Head completed sec.	0.083	0.69	0.093	0.82	-0.240	-1.59
Head good health	0.043	0.46	0.154	1.67	0.138	1.40
Household composition						
Children	**-0.214**	-4.42	**-0.158**	-6.26	**-0.144**	-4.88
Elderly	**-0.286**	-3.17	0.004	0.08	-0.130	-1.61
Other adults	**-0.133**	-3.32	**-0.191**	-7.18	0.003	0.09
R-square	0.248		0.300		0.220	
F-statistic	**4.970**		**16.57**		**4.600**	
Sample size	178		397		174	

Note: * **Boldface** if significant at the 5 percent level.

In Kazakhstan, rural households are significantly better off than equivalent urban households. Living standards are highest in the North and lowest in the South, and within both the North and the South rural households are better off than those in the cities. Per capita expenditure is also relatively high in the rural Eastern region and the urban West. The estimated coefficients are again large, although the size of the regional gaps is masked by the fact that the omitted location (Almaty) is not an outlier. A household in the South has 45 percent lower and a household in the North 31 percent higher per capita expenditures than a similar household in Almaty, which implies a more than a 100 percent gap between the best and the worst location.

In Tajikistan rural–urban differences are insignificant, but as in the other two countries regional differences are substantial. Households in Dushanbe and the surrounding Rayons of Republican Subordination (RRS) are significantly wealthier than identical households in the other areas of the country. Per capita household expenditure in Gorna-Badakhshan is 59 percent lower than in Dushanbe *ceteris paribus*, and in Leninabad 33 percent and in Khatlon 34 percent lower than in Dushanbe.

In the Fergana oblast of Uzbekistan, per capita expenditure is 53 percent lower in rural areas than in urban locations.[21] This is much larger than the effect of rural residence on expenditures in the Ferghana regions of the Kyrgyz Republic (23 percent) or Tajikistan (5 percent). In the Ferghana area of Tajikistan, as in the national sample, per capita household expenditures do not differ significantly between urban and rural areas.

4.2 Household Composition

In all four countries, household composition is an important determinant of per capita household expenditures. The costs of large households are substantial. A recurring result is that additional children lower per capita household expenditure by a larger amount than additional elderly or non-elderly adults.[22] Unsurprisingly, the costs of additional children, in terms of the negative impact on per capita household expenditure, are larger in the cities.

In Kazakhstan, an additional child reduces per capita household expenditure by 17 percent, an elderly adult reduces per capita expenditure by 11–12 percent, and a non-elderly adult reduces per capita expenditure by 6 percent. In the Kyrgyz Republic, an additional child reduces consumption by 12–13 percent in 1993 and 1997. An extra adult also reduces per capita household expenditure, but the pattern differs in 1993 and 1997; while elderly adults reduce it by 9 percent in 1993 and non-elderly adults have no significant impact, it is non-elderly adults that reduce per capita household expenditure in 1997, also by 9 percent, while the elderly have no effect. In Tajikistan, each additional child reduces per capita expenditure by 9 percent. The elderly have a smaller, negative effect, with each additional elderly adult reducing per capita household expenditure by 5 percent. The presence of additional working-age adults does not affect per capita household expenditure in Tajikistan.

When we compare the Ferghana regions of Uzbekistan, Tajikistan and the Kyrgyz Republic, we find similarities and differences. In all three countries, an additional child lowers per capita household expenditure by about 11 percent. The presence of a pensioner has no effect on per capita household expenditure in the Ferghana region of Tajikistan, but in the Ferghana region of the Kyrgyz Republic and in the Fergana oblast of Uzbekistan the presence of a pensioner increases per capita household expenditure – by 6 percent in the former and by 11 percent in the latter.[23] In contrast, non-elderly adults have no impact on per capita household expenditures in the Fergana oblast of Uzbekistan, but reduce expenditures in the Ferghana regions of Tajikistan and the Kyrgyz Republic in 1997; an additional non-elderly adult in the household lowers per capita expenditure by 3 percent in Tajikistan and by 7 percent in the Kyrgyz Republic. This suggests that in the Ferghana Valley, the labour market provides enough income to cover the average expenditures of adults in Uzbekistan, but cannot cover expenditure needs of adults in the poorer countries of Tajikistan and the Kyrgyz Republic.

We next compare the effects of household composition on expenditures in the capital cities: Almaty, Bishkek and Dushanbe. In all three cities, an additional child substantially lowers per capita household expenditure *ceteris paribus* – by 21 percent in Almaty, by 16 percent in Bishkek, and by 14 percent in Dushanbe. The negative impact of children on material well-being is stronger in the cities than in the poorer and rural Ferghana Valley. Additional elderly adults have no effect on per capita household expenditure in Bishkek or Dushanbe (a similar result to that for the Ferghana Valley), but the presence of a pensioner lowers per capita household expenditure significantly in Almaty. In Almaty, the effect of an additional elderly adult on expenditures is 29 percent and, uniquely, it is larger than the effect of an additional child.   An additional working-age adult lowers per capita household expenditure in Bishkek (by 19 percent) and in Almaty (by 13 percent), but has no effect in Dushanbe.

4.3 Education and Health of the Household's Head

In all four countries, having a college-educated head positively affects household living standards. In Kazakhstan and in the Kyrgyz Republic in 1993, per capita expenditure is 21–22 percent higher in households with a college-educated head than in households whose heads failed to complete secondary school.[24] In the Kyrgyz Republic, the effect of college education drops significantly during the transition period, to 12–14 percent in 1997. The effect of a college-educated head is larger in Tajikistan (34 percent higher per capita household expenditure than in households whose head failed to complete secondary education), and larger still in the Fergana oblast of Uzbekistan (44 percent).[25]   Overall, general high-skilled training has substantially helped household heads improve their families' standard of living.

In Kazakhstan having a head with Tecnikum training is associated with higher expenditures, but the impact is about half that of a university education, while PTU training has no significant impact. In Tajikistan having a head with non-college post-secondary training raises per capita household expenditure *ceteris paribus* by 17 percent – about half the impact of having a college-educated head.   Having a head with non-college, post-secondary training has no effect on per capita household expenditure in the Kyrgyz Republic.   The evidence from the Ferghana Valley on non-college post-secondary education is all over the place: it has no effect on household living standards in Uzbekistan, increases expenditures by 18 percent in Tajikistan, and lowers expenditures by 16 percent in the Kyrgyz Republic. Non-college post-secondary education has no impact on household expenditures in any of the capital cities. In general, the impact of less general, more vocational post-secondary training is mixed, and the Kazakhstan results suggest our empirical analysis could probably be improved by further disaggregation.

Completion of secondary education appears to have no benefits in terms of a head's ability to increase household expenditures relative to those of a household headed by somebody with only primary or incomplete secondary education. The second measure of human capital, self-reported health of the head, also has no impact on expenditures.

4.4 Demographic Traits

The demographic traits in our model – age, gender, and marital status of the head – are generally not significant determinants of household expenditures. The age coefficient is positive and significant for the Fergana oblast of Uzbekistan, but elsewhere it does not differ significantly from zero. In the Kyrgyz Republic in 1997, expenditures are 18 percent lower if the head is male, and the negative effect is even more pronounced in Bishkek, but this variable is never significant in any other country (nor with the 1993 Kyrgyz data). Having a married head is positive and significant in Bishkek and Dushanbe, but not in Almaty; nor is marital status significant in any of the national or Ferghana Valley samples.

4.5 Year

Tables 5.1b and 5.1c present estimation of the pooled expenditure regression for the Kyrgyz Republic, 1993–97. We find that real per capita expenditure is 66 percent higher in 1997 than in 1993, holding other determinants of household expenditure constant. Households are better off in the later transition period than in the early period after independence once we control for changes in education, region, household composition and the demographic characteristics of the household. It is also noteworthy that the fit of the human capital model is substantially better in 1997 than in 1993; the R-square increases from 0.15 to 0.54. Our interpretation of this is that the Kyrgyz economy is becoming more similar to established market economies where the human capital model provides an accepted explanation of differences in living standards.

4.6 Summary

In summary, the most important explanations for the variation in expenditures per capita in the region are household location, household composition, and education. We find large variation in per capita expenditure by location within each country, and the differences go beyond the simple rural–urban distinction. In the previous chapter's analysis of the Kyrgyz Republic over the transition period, we found that the costs of large families increased during transition. The results reported here reinforce the conclusion that an increase in the number of children in a household reduces household expenditure, and the cost of a child to the household exceeds the cost of an extra working or non-working adult.[26] The human capital variables yield one strong conclusion. In all countries, having a university-educated household head significantly improves household welfare; expenditures are higher in these households than in households with less educated heads. Other levels of education, relative to the benchmark of incomplete secondary schooling, do not consistently have a positive impact on material well-being. The effects of education dominate the effect of health on household consumption, but this may be due to the limited nature of the subjective measure of health that we use.

5. RELATION TO OTHER RESEARCH

Our findings about the importance of location, household composition, and education as explanations for variation in household expenditures per capita are consistent with other empirical work on formerly centrally planned economies, but the implications have not been clearly drawn out.

5.1 Location

The literature on earnings in eastern Europe has focused on labour market institutions, and the relationship between more or less regulated labour markets and the responsiveness of labour demand to changes in sales and of labour supply to changes in wages (Svejnar, 1999). The strength of the regional variables in our models for Central Asia suggests that national labour markets scarcely exist in these countries, or that people respond poorly to financial incentives to relocate; in either case, the Central Asian countries are much further from having a well-functioning market economy than are eastern European countries. This may reflect cultural factors such as the strength of the extended family (Buckley, 1998). Jovanovic (2001, 270), however, reports similar results for Russia, which suggests a common problem in the former Soviet Union due to economic obstacles such as poor infrastructure[27] or undeveloped housing markets, rather than features specific to Central Asian culture.

Previous analysis of changes over time in the Kyrgyz Republic suggests that, despite gradual improvement in the standard of living of households as the market economy developed, poverty reduction and improvement in household well-being may take many years. This could reflect the deep institutional obstacles to establishment of a market economy, or the awful physical infrastructure which sharply separates the regions of individual countries.[28] There is some evidence from applying human capital models over time that the market forces are taking firmer hold, but the fragmentation of national labour markets suggests that the process still has a long way to go in Central Asia.

The rural–urban division, while strongly related to poverty in simple cross-tabulations, is much subtler. In Kazakhstan there are distinctions between the disadvantaged rural south and relatively affluent rural areas in other regions with differing agrarian bases (cereals and livestock, rather than cotton). In the Kyrgyz Republic the rural disadvantage applies to all regions, but in Tajikistan rural locations in the south and north do relatively better. The Ferghana Valley comparison highlights a possible explanation of these variations; in very poor areas experiencing severe economic decline (as in the South of the Kyrgyz Republic and much of Tajikistan) a retreat to the rural economy is a coping mechanism, because self-sufficiency is preferable to destitution in economically decaying towns.

5.2 Household Composition

The increased cost of large households, and especially households with many children, is a recurring finding in the empirical transition literature. In part, this is explained by cutbacks in the real value of social assistance, but a striking feature is that pensioners have generally succeeded in maintaining their relative living standards, even when pension payments came to eat up a huge proportion of the government budget (Cangiano et al., 1998; Anderson and Becker, 1999).

The Soviet pension scheme related payments to the minimum wage and had generous coverage. During the early and mid 1990s many transition economies actually eased eligibility before the normal age of 60 for males and 55 for females, in order to cushion increased unemployment and other economic pressures, although the prevalence of payments arrears makes it difficult to assess the net impact.[29] One consequence was severe budget pressure as budgets came to account for a huge share of GDP – 15 percent in Poland in 1992–94 (Cangiano et al., 1998, 14) and over 10 percent in

Uzbekistan. Budgetary pressure contributed to the need for reform and major reforms have been introduced, including in Kazakhstan in 1997, but these changes occurred after the surveys on which our results are based.

The cost of children is more complex than pensioners, who are more or less non-working adults who receive a state subsidy. The cost of children is much more than their consumption minus child support payments (Falkingham, 2000b). In particular, parents have been hard hit by the sharp reduction in kindergarten availability and the increased private costs of schooling.[30] Cultural pressures not to send children to school in poor clothing or old shoes have added to these costs.[31] Reduction in freely available health services may also have impinged more on families with children.

5.3 Education

The existing literature on education in transition is mainly in terms of estimating returns to years of education, with little attempt to distinguish between types of education. The market rewards to human capital are well-established, but there has been little attempt to identify which types of skills are rewarded most. In the most thorough comparative study, Newell and Reilly (1999) use data from nine transition economies to estimate rates of return to an extra year of post-secondary schooling. In their table they distinguish between university and technical training, and the returns are generally higher to the former, but the evidence is spotty and the distinction between the two types of post-secondary education is not pursued in their analysis.

At the national level, estimates of Mincerian earnings functions have shown increases in the returns to education during transition to a market-oriented economy in, for example, the Czech Republic (Vecernik, 1995; Chase, 1998), East Germany (Krueger and Pischke, 1995), Hungary and Poland (Rutkowski, 1996; 2001), Slovenia (Orazem and Vodopivec, 1995), Russia (Newell and Reilly, 1996; Brainerd, 1998) and especially Estonia (Noorkiov et al., 1997). In Estonia employment of university-educated workers rose absolutely, even as overall employment declined substantially, and the skill premium for university-educated workers relative to workers with only primary education increased from 11 percent in 1989 to 69 percent in 1995; Noorkiov et al. (1997) suggest this is because labour market liberalization was especially drastic in Estonia, rather than focusing on the specific qualities of university education. Rutkowski (2001, 72) observes that in Hungary 'Surprisingly, skilled manual workers were the hardest hit as their wages fell by 14 percent' between 1992 and 1997, without discussing the redundant nature of skills acquired in pre-transition vocational training. Jovanovic (2001, 270) finds a larger and more consistently significant impact of university as opposed to technical education on household expenditure in Russia, but does not comment on it.

The clearest finding from Central Asian poverty studies, which is reproduced in our cross-country household expenditure analysis, concerns the importance of college education and the lack of evidence of positive returns to other forms of education. In the more detailed analysis of the Kyrgyz Republic, we also found that the return to university education increased while the returns to vocational training declined, and interpret this result as support for the idea that general purpose education becomes particularly valuable in disequilibrium situations (Schultz, 1975). The benefits of a non-specialized higher education would be especially apparent in dealing with the huge and unanticipated shocks associated with the dissolution of the USSR, but are also present in the uncertain world of a market economy – in contrast to the steady state of Soviet planning, where rules of thumb held good, initiative was not desired and education was undervalued. There must, however, be some prospect of benefiting from identification of profitable opportunities; the relatively unchanged, and desperately poor, economy of Tajikistan is the exception to our general finding. On the other hand, the fairly narrow vocational training offered in non-university post-secondary institutions in the USSR had very little economic value after the demise of central planning.

One corollary of these findings is that increased returns to education have benefited females at least as much as male workers, and the gender wage gap has generally narrowed since the end of central planning. Hunt (1998) has argued that in east Germany, where women's wages rose by 10 percentage points relative to men's wages, four-fifths of the reduction in the gap was due to a selection process whereby poorly qualified women withdrew from the labour force, but elsewhere there has been little difference between the decline in male and female labour force participation rates (for example, Ham et al., 1999, on the Czech and Slovak Republics).[32] In the next chapter, we find that better-educated female workers have been the biggest gainers from transition in the Kyrgyz Republic, despite fears that the position of women would decline in the Islamic countries of Central Asia.[33]

6. CONCLUSIONS

Analysis of the determinants of household living standards in the Central Asian transition economies during the second half of the 1990s indicates three strong relationships. Three variables are consistently significant across all four countries studied, and they have the largest role in determining household expenditure: location, children and university education. Location is very important, although whether this reflects specific cultural factors of the region or the time needed to create national labour markets in these economically least-developed parts of the former USSR is uncertain. The costs of large families, and in particular the higher (private) cost of children in a market economy than in a planned economy providing cradle to grave support, are also significant. Thirdly, we find that education brings greater material reward in the market economy, and that in the shift from central planning people with high-level general education have been best able to take advantage of new opportunities. Narrower technical education, by contrast, has left many with obsolete skills yielding zero returns in the market.

These findings are consistent with evidence from other formerly centrally planned economies, but their economic significance has not been emphasized in the transition literature. Failure to establish national labour markets even by the late 1990s in Central Asia highlights the lengthy process of institution building required for the effective functioning of a market economy. Secondly, the higher cost of children reflects the good record of the USSR in satisfying basic needs, but, unlike the elderly whose living standards have by and large been protected in transition, children suffered from the decline in many social services, which pushed costs on to their family. Higher returns to education were to be expected in a market economy, but few observers have distinguished between types of education; our findings support the view that in a market economy general purpose education is most valuable, while vocational training is relatively less valuable than in centrally planned economies (and this was exacerbated by the specificity of Soviet training).

The first two of these results may be of special significance to Central Asia, with its relative economic backwardness and high birth rate, but the importance of high-level general-purpose education appears to be a general but under-appreciated factor. Our findings have implications for inter-group distribution. Within Central Asia the regional inequality could be critical for internal social and political stability in light of the ethnic distribution of these countries' population. More universally, given that within the USSR and other centrally planned economies women tended to be directed relatively more into general as opposed to technical further education, the shift to a market economy may contribute to greater gender equity, at least among the better-off segments of the community.

NOTES

1. Turkmenistan is not considered, because although an LSMS survey was conducted in 1998 the results have not been publicized and the data are not available for analysis.

2. The EESU data are described in Coudouel (1998, 78–115). The more recent 1999 Fergana pilot survey from Uzbekistan and the 2001 Kazakhstan national survey have not yet been used in published research.
3. Akanov and Suzhikova (1998, 238) quote Asian Development Bank data on crude birth and death rates per thousand population: the CBR fell from 24.9 in 1985 to 21.0 in 1991 and 16.7 in 1995, while the CDR increased from 8.0 in 1985 and 1991 to 10.2 in 1995.
4. Ismail and Hill (1997) report on nutritional status, primarily using 1994 survey data from the Kzyl-Orda area. They find some negative impacts of transition (for example through changes in child care behaviour), but conclude that the links between socioeconomic indicators and nutritional status are not as strong in Kazakhstan as those found in other regions of the world.
5. The problem was exacerbated by the priority given to wage payments, which in the health sector crowded out spending on drugs and medical equipment almost to zero (Akanov and Suzhikova, 1998, 236–7).
6. Housing privatization is especially difficult to assess in Uzbekistan because rural housing was privately owned before independence and utilities remain free or heavily subsidized, so that the change in costs actually borne by households as a result of transition is unclear.
7. In Tashkent 71 percent of households have washing machines. In Fergana oblast, 53 percent of urban households and 22 percent of rural households have washing machines. In Karakalpakstan, 29 percent of urban households and 14 percent of rural households have washing machines (CER, 1997, 24).
8. The poor quality of Turkmenistan's statistics has frequently been noted. The World Bank stopped reporting the country's national accounts data in the mid 1990s, and the International Monetary Fund has also warned of the poor underlying data (IMF, 1998b, 15).
9. The GDP data in Table 3.1 paint a more dismal picture of the Turkmenistan economy's performance in the first half of the 1990s but the pattern of problems stored up, and then coming home to roost in 1996 and 1997 is apparent in all the sets of GDP estimates.
10. A similar conclusion is reached by Brainerd (1998, 1105), although her data set on wages of individuals appears inferior to the Kyrgyz Republic living standards data used in Chapter 4 above.
11. The administrative unit, equivalent to counties or provinces, in the USSR was the oblast. After independence the structure was maintained and, although new nomenclatures were adopted, oblast remains a universally recognized term. We use the names and jurisdictions at the time of the surveys and ignore administrative changes which occurred later (such as the relocation of Kazakhstan's capital from Almaty to Astana, the subdivision of the Osh oblast in the Kyrgyz Republic, or the renaming of the Leninabad oblast in Tajikistan).
12. This last change is implausibly large even allowing for the change in sample composition. The 1997 numbers for incomplete/complete secondary schooling appear more plausible than those for 1993, when compared to the shares in the neighbouring Fergana oblast. In the econometric estimation the coefficient for completed secondary education is not statistically significant apart from in the Kyrgyz Republic.

13. See the probit analysis results reported in Chapter 4.1. In general, ethnicity proves to be a poor explanatory variable once education, location and household size are allowed for, and ethnic variables are not included in the present chapter.

14. Expenditure is preferred to income because the arrears problem in former Soviet republics during the 1990s meant that income often came in lumps and many households reported zero income during the two-week survey period. We also expected under-reporting to avoid tax or other impositions to be less prevalent for expenditure. Non-purchased items, such as food grown on household plots, are valued and included in expenditure.

15. Tecnikum education is more academic, providing generic skills related to say computer science, rather than the narrower vocational training provided by PTUs. It includes artistic, music, medical, and technical education. PTU education is less general or professional and is linked to secondary education.

16. Almaty was the capital at the time of the LSMS survey, and is the manufacturing and financial centre of Kazakhstan. The South is the poorest part of Kazakhstan; it is an agricultural, cotton-growing region, and a manufacturing area producing intermediate goods. The North is the main wheat-producing area of the country, and also specializes in metallurgy and heavy industry such as steel. The Central region produces heavy metals such as chrome, lead and zinc, has coalmines, and grows wheat and other grains. In the East, hydroelectric power is important as well as the mining of light metals and the production of heavy equipment. The West is the oil-producing region.

17. The Gorna-Badakhshan region is sparsely populated and separated from the rest of the country by rugged mountains; it is the poorest region, and also culturally distinct. The Leninabad oblast, renamed Sughd in 2000, is the centre of much of Tajikistan's manufacturing, as well as lake areas for recreation. Khatlon is the centre of cotton production and a transit point for the illegal drug trade from bordering Afghanistan. In Dushanbe and the surrounding RRS, agricultural production is depressed, many state enterprises (cement, refrigerators, for example) have shut down or significantly reduced their production, and unemployment remains high in both the agricultural and non-agricultural regions, although the region is less poor than Khatlon or Leninabad.

18. The Ferghana Valley is the most fertile and most densely populated area of Central Asia. In the 1920s and 1930s the Ferghana Valley was divided between the Kyrgyz, Tajik and Uzbek republics of the USSR with economically meaningless borders.

19. The Uzbekistan pilot sample is too small for meaningful quantile regression analysis. The Tajikistan national survey is also ill-suited to quantile regression because a large proportion of households is in bad financial shape.

20. All of these percentage differences are relative to an identical household in the benchmark category. Note that for all of our regressions the constant term is positive, large and significantly different from zero, that is, omitted variables account for a positive household expenditure.

21. This may reflect national policies which have been especially harmful to cotton farmers in Uzbekistan (Pomfret, 2000b). It could also reflect the superior economic performance of Uzbekistan during the 1990s (Table 3.3) being reflected in relatively higher urban living standards. Anecdotal evidence from

the southern Kyrgyz Republic reports a return to the land due to depressed urban labour market conditions (Howell, 1996a, 1996b).

22. Use of an equivalence scale (such as $E^* = E/n^\theta$ where E is household expenditure and n is family size), allowing for lower consumption by children, would soften the main conclusion, but it is uncertain which equivalence scale would be appropriate. The numerical results are sensitive to the implicit assumption of no scale economies in the provision of household services, but similar studies have found that the qualitative results are not sensitive to this assumption. For example, Jovanovic (2001, 253n) reports that varying θ within a plausible range did not alter his results 'in any significant way'.

23. This is consistent with the evidence that Uzbekistan has been relatively successful in maintaining its social policies during the transition from central planning (Pomfret, 2000c) and that public service provision broke down in Tajikistan.

24. The independent impact of having a college-educated head is lower in the capital cities than in the country as a whole. The difference is small in Kazakhstan, but for Bishkek and Dushanbe the coefficient on the college graduate variable, although positive, is not significant at the 5 percent level.

25. The Uzbekistan estimate is especially striking in light of the smaller than the national average impact in the Ferghana region of Tajikistan and the absence of any significant effect of college education on household expenditure in the Ferghana region of the Kyrgyz Republic.

26. In all countries, an increase in the number of children in a household reduces household expenditure, and the cost of a child to the household exceeds the cost of an extra working or non-working adult. In the Kyrgyz Republic in 1997 and in the Ferghana regions of the Kyrgyz Republic and Tajikistan, pensioners cost the household less than working age adults, and in the Ferghana oblast of Uzbekistan the presence of an extra elderly adult significantly increases per capita household expenditure.

27. In the product market context, Aghion and Schankerman (1999) emphasize the role of improved infrastructure in reducing transactions costs and hence increasing competition, and their argument is supported by the convergence of infrastructure in Poland, Hungary and the Czech Republic towards western European standards; in all three countries the degree of competition appears to have been increasing. Similar causality works in labour markets; an oft-cited example is the impact of US road-building in eastern Thailand during the 1960s in creating a national labour market and contributing to the rapid economic growth in Thailand during the final quarter of the twentieth century.

28. The Soviet economy was planned without regard to republican borders. Train lines in the four southern republics converged on Tashkent (and thence to Russia) rather than creating national networks. Even roads between Bishkek and Osh (the two largest cities in the Kyrgyz Republic) or Dushanbe and northern Tajikistan (and hence to the country's main export markets) are shockingly poor and generally impassable in winter.

29. In Kazakhstan in the mid 1990s, according to de Castello Branca (1998), half of those receiving pensions were below the normal retirement age.

30. Kindergartens were often provided by enterprises and were one of the first non-core activities to be divested during transition (Klugman et al., 1997). This is especially important in view of the relatively late age to start formal schooling in the Soviet education system, normally seven. Many state schools started to charge unofficial fees during the 1990s to help provide even basic education.

31. Howell (1996a; 1996b) reports evidence from the south of the Kyrgyz Republic of the high costs which poor parents are willing to incur in order to send their children to school in a decent state.

32. Newell and Reilly (2001) report evidence from six eastern European economies and five former Soviet republics.

33. This is not to deny that some women have suffered during the transition from central planning, but the labour market evidence contradicts generalizations about the deteriorating relative position of women, as in Falkingham (2000a), Bauer, Boschmann and Green (1997), and Bauer, Green and Kuehnast (1997).

6. Women in the labour market in the Kyrgyz Republic, 1993 and 1997

The position of women in formerly centrally planned economies has been a source of widespread concern. The situation is often thought to be even worse in the Islamic former Soviet republics, where a major achievement of the Soviet era was the improvement in the economic status and access to education of women, which contrasted to the situation in Soviet Central Asia's southern neighbours (Afghanistan, Iran and Pakistan).[1] This chapter addresses the economic position of women in one Central Asian country, analysing 1993 and 1997 household survey data from the Kyrgyz Republic for differential impacts of transition on labour force participation, hours worked, and wages by men and women.

In the Soviet era gender equality was guaranteed in economic spheres, although western researchers found that women worked slightly fewer hours outside the home for lower wages than could be explained by human capital models.[2] In the political field, quotas ensured female representation, although as in the economic field a glass ceiling appears to have existed. In the social sphere, the Communist Party was especially active in Central Asia in promoting women's education and access to work outside the home and in discouraging practices such as female seclusion and the veil.[3] Measured by female participation and literacy rates, these policies were successful.[4] In 1989, the ratio of average female to average male wages in the Kyrgyz republic was 78 percent.[5]

Since the dissolution of the USSR at the end of 1991, women in the Kyrgyz Republic have faced erosion of their economic situation in several ways.[6] First, reassertion of pre-Soviet traditions might be associated with expectations that women will withdraw into the home. Such cultural pressures appear to be weaker in the north of the country, which is both closer to nomadic traditions and more russified, than in the south where Islam has a longer history and stronger hold. Second, the substantial economic decline during the first half of the 1990s, when real output fell by almost half, was associated with a return to home or non-market production which pulled more women than men out of the formal workforce.[7] Third, the erosion of public services, especially the drastic decline in kindergarten availability and increased costs to parents of elementary schooling, imposed greater private costs on families with children, which may fall disproportionately on women and lead them to withdraw from the labour market.[8]

There are also grounds for expecting the relative position of women to be improved by transition. Writers on the Soviet situation emphasized the downside of increased female labour force participation rates in a society which still expected women to do most of the household chores. The 'double burden' on Soviet women was likely to have been most severe in Central Asia where traditional gender roles within the household were most pronounced (Ubaidullaeva, 1982). In the Soviet economy, wage levels forced the participation of both marriage partners in the workforce if the family was to avoid poverty, and transition could increase the choice set for women deciding how to allocate their time between home and the workplace. The universal reduction in employment might hit men harder than women, even if more women became unemployed; female unemployment would reduce the double burden for women, while unemployment for men would be more dispiriting and contribute to the post-Soviet mortality crisis which has fallen disproportionately upon men (Becker and Bloom, 1998), although the drop in male life expectancy has been less sharp in the Kyrgyz Republic than in Russia or Kazakhstan.[9]

How these changes impact on women's economic status will depend upon many factors, including intra-household allocation of resources, which we do not address. We analyse changes within the workplace, focusing on participation and relative earning capacity of men and women, controlling for other relevant variables.[10] The literature on Soviet labour force participation suggests that behaviour was similar in Soviet and market economies, albeit responding to different conditions, so that we might expect responses to changed relative wages and job options during the transition to a market-based economy to be consistent with the predictions of established economic models.[11] Given that in most centrally planned economies women were at least as well-educated as men by the late 1980s, increased returns to education should not harm, and may benefit, women more than men. On the other hand, increased choice may encourage younger women to withdraw from the workforce in favour of spending more time at home.

Previous analysis of gender changes in the workplace during transition has been based primarily on evidence from eastern Europe or Russia. Increased returns to education after the end of central planning have driven reductions in the male–female gap in eastern Europe.[12] Orazem and Vodopivec (2000) found that in both the rapidly reformed Estonian labour market and the more regulated Slovenian labour market women were on average better educated than men and hence benefited from the increased returns to human capital, but in both countries women were less mobile than men and this was reflected in female unemployment increasing by more than male unemployment.

Hunt (1998) has analysed the large reduction in the gender wage gap in East Germany. During the first half of the 1990s, women's wages rose by 10 percentage points relative to men's wages, and Hunt ascribes four-fifths of this to a selection process due to the withdrawal of poorly qualified women from the labour force. Hunt (1999) analyses the large drop in labour force participation rates in East Germany after June 1990 and found that individuals over fifty and women have much longer non-employment durations, and better educated individuals and more experienced workers (as measured by their 1990 wage) have shorter non-employment spells. In the Czech Republic and Slovakia, however, there was little difference between the decline in male and female labour force participation rates (Ham et al., 1999).

Occupational segregation is another factor that may offset the positive effect on female/male wage ratios of increased returns to education. Ogloblin (1999), using 1994–6 data, concludes that the gender wage gap in Russia could not be explained by differences in education or experience and that most of the gap is attributable to occupational segregation inherited from the Soviet era. Jurajda (2000) finds some evidence of occupational segregation in the Czech Republic and Slovakia, but this only accounts for a third of the gender gap after allowing for education and experience, and two-thirds of the gap is unexplained. On the other hand, Orazem and Vodopivec (2000) found that the industrial distribution of female workers benefited them during the transition in Slovenia and Estonia, because women were over-represented in faster growing sectors.

Newell and Reilly (2000) run quantile regressions on a sample of eleven transition economies, and conclude that the transition has been approximately neutral to female/male pay differentials. Even in the former Soviet Union, where there have been large increases in wage inequality, the relative pay position of women has not worsened on average.[13] Newell and Reilly (2000) also conduct an extended decomposition analysis of Russia and Yugoslavia, where they find little evidence of anything other than minor movements in the observed gender pay gap. These results are broadly consistent with those reported above for Eastern Europe and those of Reilly (1999) and of Glinskaya and Mroz (2000) for Russia. They do, however, contrast with those of Brainerd (2000) who found a 'remarkable increase' in female relative wages in eastern Europe, but a substantial decline in Russia and Ukraine which she ascribes to the widening wage distribution in those two countries.[14]

Comparable analytical work on Central Asia is sparse. The evidence on increased returns to education during transition is less clear than in eastern Europe or Russia. Klugman (1998) finds that returns to education in Uzbekistan were similar to those in eastern Europe both before independence and in 1995, with a higher return to university education, especially to women, during transition.[15]   In the Kyrgyz Republic there is evidence of increased returns to college education and stronger evidence of lower returns to post-secondary vocational training (Chapter 4 above).   Klugman's dissertation is the only study to go further in analysing gender effects in Central Asian labour markets, but she is hampered by the limited data available for Uzbekistan and by conceptual difficulties.[16]   She finds some gender effects of transition, but allowing for education and experience and also for fixed effects associated with residence in the capital and with ethnicity leaves little unexplained 'discrimination' in the gender wage gap. The household survey data come from 1993, before significant economic transformation had taken place, and then annually since 1996 by which time important steps towards a market-based economy had occurred.

The first section of this chapter uses mean difference tests for gender differences in the variables described above. Over time, as the labour market in the Kyrgyz Republic has become more market-oriented, mean differences in hours of work, the wage, and monthly earnings have narrowed. This is consistent with the findings from eastern Europe, but in contrast to Brainerd's (2000) argument that the wage gap widened in Soviet successor states. To isolate the importance of gender and transition in the determination of these employment outcomes, we estimate multivariate models of labour force participation in Section 2, and of hours of work and monthly wages in Section 3 as in Anderson and Pomfret (2001a). The regression results are used in Section 4 as the basis for decomposition of the wage gap and the hours gap into a component explained by observed characteristics and an unexplained component, which includes discrimination by gender. We draw conclusions in Section 5.

1. DATA

The data used in this chapter are from the LSMS household surveys conducted in the Kyrgyz Republic during the fall of 1993 and of 1997.[17] The surveys do not contain panel data. We therefore cannot examine, within families, the dynamics of family interaction and work. However, we can examine cohorts of adults and evaluate changes in the behaviour of similar households over time.   For 1993, we have an analysis sample of 1909 households, and within these 1909 households we have usable data on 4997 adults aged 18 and older. For 1997, we have an analysis sample of 2577 households, and 7264 adults with usable data in the sample.[18]

Tables 6.1 and 6.2 present descriptive statistics on monthly wages, hours worked, human capital and employment characteristics of the adults in the

1993 and 1997 samples, by region and by gender. Within each region[19] and year, we test whether the mean differences in the human capital and employment characteristics differ between men and women. In general, we observe differences in the education, labour force status, job choice, and wages of women and men. Differences in hours of work are smaller.

In each year, men receive higher compensation per month than women (Table 6.1). Compensation includes money wages and the value of non-wage benefits or in-kind income received. In 1993, the female to male wage ratio is 0.66 but increases to 0.83 in 1997. One reason for the narrowing of the gender difference in monthly compensation is the narrowing in the gap in hours of work. In 1993, women report working about 45 hours per week, which is 85 percent of the hours of work reported by working men (52 hours per week). In 1997, men and women work fewer hours per week but women work, on average, 93 percent of the hours of working men, and this gender difference is statistically significant. If we compute the average hourly wage of men and women based on these mean differences in hours of work, we find that the hourly wage gap has also narrowed, from 0.78 in 1993 to 0.89 in 1997. Over time, as the labour market has become more market-oriented, mean differences in hours of work, monthly earnings and the hourly wage have all diminished.

We find the same general pattern of gender differences in the north and the south, and in rural and urban areas. In both the rural and urban north, the change in the gender gap in the hourly wage is smaller than the change in the gender gap in the monthly wage, indicating that the change in hours worked has led the reduction in gender wage differentials in the north. In the rural and urban south, the change in gender differences in hours per week is small, but there are significant reductions in the hourly wage gap (0.55 in 1993 to 0.93 in 1997 in the rural south and 0.69 to 0.88 in the urban south). This suggests that the patterns of changes in gender differentials are not influenced by cultural or religious factors.[20]

Education differences by gender are significant in 1997 but not in 1993; however, even in 1997, these differences are quite small (Table 6.2). Education is classified into four categories: incomplete secondary, completed secondary with no additional training, completed secondary with additional training, and college education. Women are more likely to be found in the lowest and highest education categories, while men are more likely to be found in the middle. The major changes in the education distribution over time, for both men and women, are that fewer persons report incomplete

Table 6.1. Gender differences in wages and hours of work, 1993–97*

Variables	1993		1997	
	Men	Women	Men	Women
All regions				
Hours of work	**52.347**	**44.751**	**46.892**	**43.709**
	[0.623]	[0.693]	[0.232]	[0.259]
Monthly compensation	**125.13**	**83.076**	**603.093**	**501.426**
	[4.896]	[3.290]	[27.148]	[16.675]
Urban north				
Hours of work	**48.44**	**41.058**	**48.2**	**46.353**
	[1.304]	[1.372]	[0.576]	[0.585]
Monthly compensation	**178.245**	**115.745**	**1197.072**	**841.006**
	[11.704]	[7.701]	[128.76]	[59.525]
Urban south				
Hours of work	48.411	45.344	**45.662**	**41.358**
	[1.387]	[1.751]	[0.661]	[0.799]
Monthly compensation	**99.049**	**64.113**	707.182	561.29
	[6.595]	[4.238]	[66.081]	[57.894]
Urban mountain region				
Hours of work	46.456	47.679	44.786	43.535
	[1.991]	[2.683]	[0.906]	[0.866]
Monthly compensation	**127.314**	**70.286**	**720.477**	**445.535**
	[14.979]	[10.050]	[58.844]	[23.445]
Rural north				
Hours of work	**51.553**	**44.115**	**53.267**	**47.142**
	[1.255]	[1.095]	[1.036]	[0.947]
Monthly compensation	**115.908**	**80.044**	821.091	589.234
	[10.369]	[5.867]	[121.991]	[42.157]
Rural south				
Hours of work	**56.329**	**49.402**	**44.201**	**41.888**
	[1.109]	[1.477]	[0.311]	[0.373]
Monthly compensation	**99.778**	**48.513**	**368.167**	**323.78**
	[10.804]	[3.387]	[11.448]	[9.084]
Rural mountain region				
Hours of work	**53.186**	**35.231**	**48.084**	**43.625**
	[2.818]	[1.977]	[0.481]	[0.643]

Table 6.1 continued

Monthly compensation	84.333	75.706	**366.561**	**324.448**
	[8.573]	[11.676]	[11.398]	[9.596]

Notes: *Mean values for hours worked and monthly wage in soms; the standard deviation is in parentheses. Boldface indicates gender differences are significant (5 percent level) for this variable.

Table 6.2 Gender differences in education and work, 1993–97

	1993		1997	
Variables	Men		Men	Women
Education				
Primary	32.4	34.6	**15.7**	**19.0**
Secondary	20.1	28.9	**49.5**	**46.5**
Other training	27.2	13.3	**9.5**	**5.6**
College	20.3	23.2	**25.3**	**28.9**
Labour force status				
Work	**66.6**	**50.8**	**58.8**	**39.6**
Unemployed	**10.8**	**6.7**	**7.0**	**4.7**
Not in labour force	**22.6**	**42.5**	**34.2**	**55.7**
Occupation				
White collar	**11.8**	**31.1**	**19.7**	**33.8**
Blue collar	**66.1**	**43.3**	**38.4**	**32.7**
Owner	**11.8**	**11.3**	**34.1**	**26.3**
Co-op member	**0.0**	**0.0**	**6.8**	**6.3**
Professional	**10.3**	**14.3**	**1.0**	**0.9**
Industry				
Produce goods	**7.5**	**2.3**	**7.5**	**6.0**
Produce agricultural goods	**29.3**	**37.1**	**55.6**	**42.2**
Construction	**13.0**	**1.5**	**4.1**	**1.9**
Sales	**1.8**	**4.9**	**4.9**	**6.6**
Transportation	**21.0**	**0.5**	**6.3**	**2.6**
Service	**27.4**	**53.7**	**21.6**	**40.7**

Notes: *Figures are percentages. Boldface indicates gender differences are significant (5 percent level) for this variable.

secondary education and more persons have obtained higher education by 1997.   Urban adults, especially in the north, are more likely to have completed higher education than people in rural areas.

Labour force status differs between men and women in most regions and at each point in time.   We classify labour force status as one of three categories: currently employed, unemployed but looking for work, and not in the labour force.   Women are less likely to report work or unemployment than men in both the 1993 and 1997 samples.

Occupational choices differ between men and women and change over time.   In the 1997 survey occupation is coded into five categories: blue-collar worker, white-collar worker, owner/employer, cooperative member and professional. For 1993 we assign workers to one of these categories based on their three-digit occupation code, which is not available in the 1997 survey.[21] Women are more likely to be found in white-collar jobs, while men are concentrated in blue-collar work or are owners of firms. For both genders there is a shift from blue collar to owner between 1993 and 1997, although this is more pronounced for males.   Professional employment declines over time for both men and women. While women are more likely than men to be in professional employment in 1993, professional employment is low but equally represented by men and women in 1997.

To evaluate changes in the industrial composition of the labour force over time, we code industry into the six categories in which the industry variable is divided in the 1997 survey: produces goods, produces agricultural products, construction, commerce, transportation and services. For 1993, no industry data are available except through the three-digit occupation codes. We are able to assign most workers to an industry based on their occupational information, but cannot assign an industry to 8 percent of 1993 workers with an occupation code. Among all workers, representation is highest in services and in agriculture, and this is especially true of women (91 percent in 1993 and 83 percent in 1997).   Few women are found in construction or transportation. These differences persist over time. In urban and rural areas, women are moving out of service jobs and into manufacturing. In rural areas, the proportion in agricultural employment increased between 1993 and 1997 for both sexes, but especially among men.

2. LABOUR FORCE PARTICIPATION

The labour force participation model is estimated using probit analysis over a sample of all adults reporting complete data on work and individual characteristics: 4997 people in 1993 and 7264 in 1997. The dependent variable is a dummy variable equal to one if the individual is either employed or unemployed and looking for a job and equal to zero if the individual is neither working nor looking.

Theoretically, labour force participation is affected by the difference between the market wage and the value of not working or reservation wage; the higher the market wage relative to the reservation wage, the more likely the individual is to work or seek work. Characteristics of the individual which likely affect labour force participation, therefore, are linked to either the market wage or the reservation wage. We assume that the market wage depends on the human capital of the individual, region, and demographic traits such as gender and ethnicity that may reflect differences in tastes for work or access to jobs. We expect labour force participation to increase with human capital. Determinants of the reservation wage include marital status and the number of children under the age of six. For women we expect labour force participation to decrease with marriage and the number of children under six; for men we expect positive effects of both variables on the decision to work or seek work. We expect men to work more than women, and we have no expectations about the effect of ethnicity on work.

Summary statistics on the variables included in this model are given in Table 6A1. Gender is equal to one if the adult is male and is equal to zero if she is female. Variables measuring the stock of human capital include education, health and experience of the worker. The education categories have been described above. The health variable is measured with a self-report of good health, and is equal to one if the adult reports good or very good health and is equal to zero otherwise. Experience in the labour market is proxied by age in a quadratic form. We expect labour force participation to increase at a decreasing rate with age. Ethnicity is measured with four dummy variables for Russian, Uzbek, other Slavic, and other ethnicity; the omitted category is Kyrgyz. The regional categories are described above; the omitted category in the analysis is rural north. In the pooled data we include a time dummy variable for 1997. Based on the descriptive analysis, we expect labour force participation to be higher in rural areas in 1993 than in the other regions and to decline over time.

The results of the probit estimation are given in Table 6.3. The cells in this table present the probit coefficients with the standard errors in brackets. The marginal effects of the independent variables on the probability of being in the labour force are in brackets below the standard errors. For each year and with pooled 1993 and 1997 data, we present results for all individuals and for men and women separately.

Allowing for all the other variables, women are less likely than men to be in the labour force. The marginal effect of gender is large, but decreases. In 1993 men are 29 percent more likely to work than women, while in 1997 they are 24 percent more likely to be in the labour force. In each year, the separate regressions for men and women are significantly different, indicating that the rewards for work relative to home production differ by gender.

In the pooled model, allowing for all other variables, between 1993 and 1997 labour force participation falls by 17 percent, with a slightly larger change over time for women than for men.   Labour force participation is highest in the north and in the rural south and lowest in the mountain region and urban south, and the regional differences are larger for men. Over time, the regional differences have grown in importance and, in general, men have experienced the largest reductions in labour market activity in most regions. Labour force participation has a nonlinear, quadratic relationship with age. The marginal effect of age is smaller in 1997 than in 1993, but the pattern is similar for men and women. The ethnic differences we measure indicate that Russians and Uzbeks have the highest participation rate and Kyrgyz have the lowest.[22]   Gender differences in the importance of ethnicity are small. Location, age and ethnicity all matter but without major gender dimensions.

Human capital characteristics that likely correlate with the market wage affect the decision to work. More education is associated with increased participation. In 1993 the probability of being in the labour force is 0.01 higher among workers with secondary education than among workers with incomplete secondary, 0.11 higher among workers with some vocational training, and 0.16 higher among those with college education. The marginal effects in 1997 are 0.13, 0.17 and 0.24. At the post-secondary levels of education, women are more responsive to education than men in their labour market activity. If a woman has completed higher education, labour force participation is more than twice as likely as for a comparable man. Comparing 1997 to 1993, educated adults are increasingly more likely to be in the labour market than the uneducated.

Health is associated with labour force participation; adults who self-report good health are more likely to be in the labour force, but men's behaviour is significantly more responsive to their own health than women's. We also find a small change over time in the importance of health, and men become more responsive to health than women.

The correlates of the reservation wage – marriage and number of young children – have a weaker impact than human capital variables. Marital status and number of children under six have significant negative coefficients for women's labour force participation in both years, although their marginal

Table 6.3 Probit models of labour force participation, 1993 and 1997*

Variables:	1993 and 1997			1993			1997		
	All	Men	Women	All	Men	Women	All	Men	Women
Constant	-3.249	-2.852	-3.040	-4.748	-5.109	-4.468	-3.303	-2.562	-3.320
	[0.134]	[0.208]	[0.179]	[0.256]	[0.415]	[0.349]	[0.165]	[0.253]	[0.222]
Gender (1=male)	0.647			0.762			0.620		
	[0.027]			[0.051]			[0.033]		
	{.250}			{.288}			{.243}		
Year (1=1997)	-0.435	-0.427	-0.460						
	[0.031]	[0.048]	[0.040]						
	{-0.17}	{-0.141}	{-0.18}						
Completed secondary	0.222	0.206	0.254	0.020	0.170	-0.030	0.320	0.273	0.398
	[0.042]	[0.062]	[0.059]	[0.069]	[0.116]	[0.091]	[0.057]	[0.079]	[0.085]
	{.088}	{.073}	{.091}	{.008}	{.048}	{-0.01}	{.126}	{.104}	{.136}
Secondary + non-college training	0.437	0.374	0.497	0.271	0.239	0.248	0.425	0.329	0.553
	[0.053]	[0.074]	[0.077]	[0.076]	[0.113]	[0.108]	[0.079]	[0.107]	[0.120]
	{.172}	{.127}	{.186}	{.105}	{.065}	{.09}	{.168}	{.124}	{.195}
Higher education	0.548	0.304	0.721	0.408	0.06	0.536	0.599	0.392	0.807
	[0.044]	[0.066]	[0.062]	[0.072]	[0.113]	[0.098]	[0.061]	[0.086]	[0.089]
	{.214}	{.105}	{.275}	{.155}	{.018}	{.203}	{.236}	{.146}	{.296}

Table 6.3 continued

Variable	1	2	3	4	5	6	7	8	9
Age in years	**0.198**	**0.199**	**0.199**	**0.302**	**0.335**	**0.32**	**0.164**	**0.155**	**0.164**
	[0.007]	[0.010]	[0.009]	[0.013]	[0.022]	[0.019]	[0.008]	[0.021]	[0.011]
	{.078}	{.067}	{.077}	{.117}	{.092}	{.118}	{.065}	{.057}	{.063}
Age squared	**−0.003**	**−0.003**	**−0.003**	**−0.004**	**−0.005**	**−0.005**	**−0.002**	**−0.002**	**−0.002**
	[0.000]	[0.000]	[0.000]	[0.000]	[0.000]	[0.000]	[0.000]	[0.000]	[0.000]
	{−0.001}	{−0.001}	{−0.001}	{−0.002}	{−0.001}	{−0.002}	{−0.001}	{−0.001}	{−0.001}
Health is good (=1)	**0.373**	**0.613**	**0.187**	**0.463**	**0.678**	**0.315**	**0.394**	**0.639**	**0.208**
	[0.052]	[0.081]	[0.069]	[0.095]	[0.144]	[0.130]	[0.064]	[0.099]	[0.084]
	{.148}	{.229}	{.071}	{.183}	{.226}	{.109}	{.155}	{.248}	{.077}
Marital status (1=married)	−0.061	0.078	**−0.169**	−0.063	0.119	**−0.273**	−0.069	0.074	**−0.148**
	[0.034]	[0.058]	[0.044]	[0.061]	[0.109]	[0.079]	[0.042]	[0.071]	[0.055]
	{−0.024}	{.026}	{−0.066}	{−0.025}	{.034}	{−0.102}	{−0.027}	{.027}	{−0.057}
Number of children < age 6	−0.051	0.001	**−0.104**	**−0.06**	0.009	**−0.125**	**−0.054**	−0.005	**−0.109**
	[0.014]	[0.021]	[0.019]	[0.025]	[0.043]	[0.032]	[0.017]	[0.026]	[0.245]
	{−0.020}	{0.000}	{−0.040}	{−0.023}	{.002}	{−0.046}	{−0.021}	{−0.002}	{−0.042}
Russian ethnicity	**0.244**	**0.200**	**0.284**	**0.321**	**0.296**	**0.372**	**0.238**	**0.224**	**0.248**
	[0.048]	[0.075]	[0.063]	[0.081]	[0.130]	[0.106]	[0.062]	[0.096]	[0.082]
	{.094}	{.066}	{.112}	{.121}	{.081}	{.141}	{.093}	{.076}	{.097}
Uzbek ethnicity	**0.16**	**0.368**	0.034	0.133	**0.355**	0.025	**0.209**	**0.398**	0.085
	[0.057]	[0.092]	[0.074]	[0.077]	[0.132]	[0.098]	[0.098]	[0.150]	[0.133]
	{.062}	{.115}	{.013}	{.052}	{.095}	{.009}	{.082}	{.128}	{.033}

Table 6.3 continued

Other Slavic ethnicity	0.152 [0.105] {.059}	0.059 [0.160] {.020}	0.213 [0.141] {.083}	0.194 [0.193] {.075}	0.207 [0.214] {.059}	0.199 [0.198] {.074}	0.253 [0.179] {.099}	0.156 [0.278] {.054}	0.34 [0.234] {.133}
Other ethnicity	0.042 [0.036] {.017}	0.146 [0.089] {.049}	−0.012 [0.074] {−0.005}	−0.058 [0.088] {−0.023}	0.224 [0.145] {.063}	−0.203 [0.115] {−0.068}	0.154 [0.076] {.061}	0.119 [0.118] {.042}	0.204 [0.102] {.079}
Urban north	−0.108 [0.053] {−0.042}	−0.168 [0.085] {.050}	−0.086 [0.069] {−0.033}	−0.287 [0.085] {−0.113}	−0.339 [0.138] {−0.101}	−0.288 [0.112] {−0.099}	−0.029 [0.071] {−0.012}	−0.155 [0.114] {−0.047}	0.047 [0.093] {.018}
Urban south	−0.323 [0.061] {−0.128}	−0.551 [0.096] {−0.186}	−0.183 [0.081] {−0.070}	−0.066 [0.095] {−0.026}	−0.227 [0.151] {−0.065}	0.018 [0.127] {.007}	−0.511 [0.086] {−0.201}	−0.79 [0.134] {−0.283}	−0.325 [0.114] {−0.116}
Urban mountain	−0.233 [0.064] {−0.092}	−0.435 [0.098] {−0.142}	−0.095 [0.086] {−0.037}	−0.019 [0.118] {.007}	−0.140 [0.182] {−0.038}	0.036 [0.159] {.013}	−0.305 [0.081] {−0.121}	−0.598 [0.124] {−0.207}	−0.080 [0.019] {−0.030}
Rural south	0.133 [0.051] {.050}	−0.069 [0.080] {−0.020}	0.306 [0.068] {.121}	0.165 [0.081] {.062}	0.162 [0.131] {.039}	0.187 [0.106] {.071}	0.143 [0.069] {.055}	−0.205 [0.107] {−0.064}	0.451 [0.091] {.178}
Rural mountain	−0.400 [0.052] {−0.158}	−0.482 [0.080] {−0.160}	−0.349 [0.070] {−0.129}	−0.202 [0.094] {−0.080}	−0.154 [0.147] {−0.043}	−0.190 [0.126] {−0.067}	−0.449 [0.068] {−0.178}	−0.627 [0.104] {−0.219}	−0.327 [0.092] {−0.117}

Table 6.3 continued

Sample size	12261	5781	6480	4997	2309	2688	7264	3472	3792
Chi-square	**4829**	**1927**	**2485**	**2799**	**1145**	**1541**	**2172**	**844**	**1064**
Pseudo R-square	0.292	0.275	0.277	0.44	0.464	0.42	0.217	0.189	0.204

Notes: Cells contain probit coefficients, [standard errors], and {marginal effects}. **Boldface** indicates significant at the 5 percent level.

effect is lower in 1997. For men, marital status and number of children under six have positive coefficients as expected, but they are not statistically significant in either year.

The labour force participation model has reasonable explanatory power in both years, supporting the hypothesis that behaviour was similar in Soviet and market economics. Surprisingly, however, the adjusted R^2 is lower in 1997 than in 1993. The main gender dimensions are the impact of marriage and young children, and the effect of education on labour force participation. The former variables reduce female participation, but their impact has declined, which does not support the hypothesis that with the shift to a more market-oriented system young married women will choose to substitute time spent at home for time in the workplace. The education variables have a stronger impact on the labour force participation decision, and especially striking is the differential behaviour of college-educated women, who have responded to the transition from central planning with disproportionately greater labour force participation than any other group.

3. WAGES PAID AND HOURS WORKED

In this section we estimate multivariate models of monthly wages and of hours worked. We have usable data on compensation received by 1162 workers in 1993 and 4855 in 1997 and on hours for 1987 workers in 1993 and for 5707 in 1997. The summary statistics are presented in Tables 6A.2 and 6A.3. We tested for non-randomness of the samples by estimating sample selection adjusted models (Heckman, 1979), assuming that selection is identified by marital status and number of children; in no case did we find evidence of non-random selection of workers. All equations are estimated by ordinary least squares in semi-log form.

In the first versions of the wages and hours models we include the human capital and demographic variables used in the previous section. Wages should increase with the stock of human capital, increase at a decreasing rate with experience, and may differ between men and women or across ethnic groups if gender and ethnicity reflect differential access to jobs. Hours of work should also increase with human capital, if the wage is positively affected by education and health and if the substitution effect of an increase in the wage dominates the income effect. Hours likely have a nonlinear relationship with experience, and we expect that women are more likely to choose part-time jobs than men. We have no priors on the effects of ethnicity on hours of work. The results are reported in Tables 6.4a (monthly compensation) and 6.5a (hours of work).

Table 6.4a Wage model, 1993 and 1997: occupation and industry excluded*

Variables	1993 and 1997			1993			1997		
	All	Men	Women	All	Men	Women	All	Men	Women
Constant	**3.65**	**3.784**	**3.655**	**2.681**	**3.357**	**2.61**	**4.268**	**4.231**	**4.401**
	[0.092]	[0.137]	[0.122]	[0.251]	[0.359]	[0.354]	[0.097]	[0.146]	[0.130]
Year (1=1997)	**0.484**	**0.348**	**0.609**						
	[0.028]	[0.040]	[0.038]						
Gender (1=male)	**0.214**			**0.495**			**0.149**		
	[0.020]			[0.045]			[0.022]		
Age in years	**0.016**	**0.021**	**0.013**	**0.052**	0.043	0.058	**0.013**	**0.019**	0.008
	[0.004]	[0.006]	[0.005]	[0.012]	[0.017]	[0.017]	[0.004]	[0.006]	[0.005]
Age squared (divided by 1000)	**-0.137**	**-0.221**	-0.075	**-0.58**	-0.501	-0.612	**-0.109**	**-0.196**	-0.034
	[0.042]	[0.065]	[0.055]	[0.052]	[0.210]	[0.223]	[0.045]	[0.071]	[0.058]
Health is good (=1)	0.0001	0.098	-0.065	0.143	0.112	0.119	-0.012	0.086	-0.09
	[0.038]	[0.063]	[0.055]	[0.052]	[0.164]	[0.135]	[0.045]	[0.071]	[0.058]
Completed secondary education	0.055	0.045	**0.097**	0.039	0.040	0.031	0.051	0.042	0.081
	[0.033]	[0.063]	[0.046]	[0.074]	[0.107]	[0.104]	[0.038]	[0.069]	[0.050]
Secondary education + non-college training	**0.099**	0.092	0.093	**0.134**	0.104	0.161	0.032	0.031	0.033
	[0.040]	[0.054]	[0.061]	[0.064]	[0.083]	[0.100]	[0.052]	[0.070]	[0.078]
Higher education	**0.253**	**0.296**	**0.25**	**0.255**	**0.245**	**0.276**	**0.236**	**0.288**	**0.217**
	[0.033]	[0.047]	[0.046]	[0.059]	[0.083]	[0.086]	[0.039]	[0.057]	[0.055]

Table 6.4a continued

Russian ethnicity	**0.078**	**0.176**	0.008	0.083	**0.142**	0.033	**0.093**	**0.197**	0.005
	[0.032]	[0.048]	[0.042]	[0.060]	[0.067]	[0.083]	[0.038]	[0.058]	[0.050]
Uzbek ethnicity	0.027	0.045	−0.028	**−0.194**	−0.107	**−0.294**	**0.129**	0.097	0.135
	[0.047]	[0.067]	[0.065]	[0.075]	[0.102]	[0.112]	[0.061]	[0.089]	[0.083]
Other Slavic ethnicity	0.024	0.071	0.002	0.113	0.219	0.020	−0.003	−0.065	0.055
	[0.082]	[0.127]	[0.104]	[0.122]	[0.174]	[0.171]	[0.110]	[0.181]	[0.136]
Other ethnicity	0.050	0.059	0.040	−0.029	−0.168	**0.222**	0.051	0.106	0.008
	[0.042]	[0.060]	[0.058]	[0.089]	[0.113]	[0.147]	[0.048]	[0.071]	[0.064]
Urban north region	**0.376**	**0.394**	**0.352**	**0.345**	**0.437**	**0.237**	**0.383**	**0.371**	**0.391**
	[0.037]	[0.054]	[0.049]	[0.065]	[0.093]	[0.091]	[0.044]	[0.066]	[0.058]
Urban south region	−0.061	−0.007	−0.109	0.002	0.026	−0.050	−0.066	0.008	−0.122
	[0.045]	[0.068]	[0.060]	[0.078]	[0.112]	[0.109]	[0.055]	[0.084]	[0.072]
Urban mountain region	0.0004	0.096	−0.115	0.015	0.159	−0.142	−0.002	0.062	−0.087
	[0.049]	[0.070]	[0.068]	[0.090]	[0.125]	[0.129]	[0.059]	[0.084]	[0.082]
Rural south region	**−0.412**	**−0.411**	**−0.408**	**−0.151**	−0.064	−0.222	**−0.454**	**−0.483**	**−0.412**
	[0.038]	[0.054]	[0.052]	[0.076]	[0.100]	[0.118]	[0.044]	[0.065]	[0.060]
Rural mountain region	**−0.362**	**−0.354**	**−0.346**	**−0.13**	−0.180	**−0.015**	**−0.379**	**−0.392**	**−0.345**
	[0.040]	[0.057]	[0.057]	[0.125]	[0.162]	[0.199]	[0.046]	[0.066]	[0.064]
Sample size	6017	3119	2898	1162	602	560	4855	2517	2338
F-statistic	**93.52**	**50.1**	**53.56**	**18.13**	**6.92**	**7.29**	**80.7**	**47.78**	**40.5**
R-square	0.21	0.205	0.229	0.202	0.152	0.167	0.211	0.223	0.202

Note: *Cells contain regression coefficients and [standard errors]. **Boldface** if significant at the 5 percent level.

Table 6.4b Wage model 1993 and 1997: occupation and industry included*

Variables	1993 and 1997			1993			1997		
	All	Men	Women	All	Men	Women	All	Men	Women
Constant	3.668 [0.090]	3.843 [0.137]	3.619 [0.120]	2.798 [0.250]	3.378 [0.360]	2.779 [0.353]	4.323 [0.095]	4.368 [0.146]	4.420 [0.126]
Year (1=1997)	0.490 [0.032]	0.397 [0.048]	0.551 [0.044]						
Gender (1=male)	0.193 [0.020]			0.404 [0.048]			0.148 [0.021]		
Age in years	0.015 [0.003]	0.018 [0.005]	0.014 [0.005]	0.045 [0.012]	0.034 [0.017]	0.050 [0.017]	0.010 [0.004]	0.168 [0.068]	0.005 [0.005]
Age squared (divided by 1000)	-0.128 [0.040]	-0.188 [0.063]	-0.097 [0.052]	-0.509 [0.150]	-0.399 [0.209]	-0.536 [0.223]	-0.082 [0.043]	-0.196 [0.071]	-0.007 [0.055]
Health is good (=1)	-0.014 [0.036]	0.087 [0.060]	-0.082 [0.045]	0.133 [0.102]	0.137 [0.162]	0.078 [0.134]	-0.035 [0.039]	0.062 [0.065]	-0.091 [0.048]
Completed secondary	0.046 [0.031]	0.026 [0.045]	0.089 [0.044]	0.036 [0.074]	0.065 [0.106]	-0.029 [0.105]	0.040 [0.036]	0.017 [0.051]	0.095 [0.051]
Secondary education + non-college training	0.042 [0.038]	0.026 [0.052]	0.065 [0.058]	0.076 [0.064]	0.072 [0.083]	0.161 [0.103]	0.015 [0.049]	-0.019 [0.066]	0.03 [0.074]
Higher education	0.202 [0.032]	0.220 [0.047]	0.211 [0.044]	0.199 [0.064]	0.187 [0.092]	0.208 [0.091]	0.172 [0.038]	0.201 [0.056]	0.174 [0.053]

Table 6.4b continued

	(1)	(2)	(3)	(4)	(5)	(6)	(7)	(8)	(9)
Russian ethnicity	0.036	**0.12**	−0.014	0.049	0.102	0.004	0.061	**0.138**	0.019
	[0.031]	[0.047]	[0.040]	[0.060]	[0.087]	[0.085]	[0.036]	[0.056]	[0.047]
Uzbek ethnicity	−0.017	−0.001	−0.049	**−0.167**	−0.087	**−0.295**	0.042	0.020	0.043
	[0.045]	[0.064]	[0.062]	[0.075]	[0.101]	[0.115]	[0.058]	[0.086]	[0.079]
Other Slavic ethnicity	0.02	0.076	−0.006	0.087	0.200	0.006	−0.018	−0.068	0.046
	[0.078]	[0.122]	[0.098]	[0.120]	[0.174]	[0.170]	[0.103]	[0.172]	[0.128]
Other ethnicity	0.032	0.013	0.046	−0.030	−0.139	0.193	0.035	0.045	0.013
	[0.040]	[0.058]	[0.055]	[0.087]	[0.112]	[0.146]	[0.045]	[0.068]	[0.060]
Urban north region	**0.252**	**0.237**	**0.265**	**0.307**	**0.413**	**0.196**	**0.200**	**0.143**	**0.272**
	[0.036]	[0.054]	[0.047]	[0.064]	[0.093]	[0.091]	[0.043]	[0.066]	[0.057]
Urban south region	**−0.179**	**−0.171**	**−0.167**	−0.015	0.042	−0.080	**−0.247**	**−0.28**	**−0.147**
	[0.044]	[0.066]	[0.057]	[0.077]	[0.111]	[0.109]	[0.043]	[0.083]	[0.069]
Urban mountain region	**−0.122**	−0.068	**−0.177**	−0.004	0.126	−0.139	**−0.181**	**−0.180**	**−0.167**
	[0.048]	[0.068]	[0.065]	[0.088]	[0.124]	[0.128]	[0.056]	[0.083]	[0.078]
Rural south region	**−0.340**	**−0.361**	**−0.314**	−0.128	−0.050	−0.155	**−0.400**	**−0.457**	**−0.244**
	[0.037]	[0.053]	[0.051]	[0.075]	[0.099]	[0.117]	[0.043]	[0.064]	[0.059]
Rural mountain region	**−0.256**	**−0.272**	**−0.218**	−0.082	−0.105	−0.019	**−0.311**	**−0.356**	**−0.246**
	[0.039]	[0.056]	[0.055]	[0.124]	[0.162]	[0.197]	[0.044]	[0.064]	[0.061]
White-collar worker occupation	**0.065**	**0.094**	**0.081**	−0.108	−0.059	−0.125	**0.150**	**0.150**	**0.160**
	[0.028]	[0.044]	[0.037]	[0.063]	[0.098]	[0.092]	[0.032]	[0.051]	[0.041]
Owner occupation	**0.285**	**0.280**	**0.318**	**0.184**	0.145	0.213	**0.317**	**0.308**	**0.341**
	[0.026]	[0.036]	[0.037]	[0.075]	[0.105]	[0.112]	[0.027]	[0.038]	[0.039]

Table 6.4b continued

Co-op member	**0.641** [0.050]	**0.565** [0.072]	**0.731** [0.069]				**0.676** [0.050]	**0.602** [0.073]	**0.759** [0.067]
Professional occupation	0.049 [0.053]	0.124 [0.078]	0.015 [0.071]	**0.165** [0.077]	0.192 [0.107]	0.165 [0.115]	**-0.477** [0.099]	-0.120 [0.144]	**-0.867** [0.134]
Missing occupation	-0.128 [0.089]	-0.165 [0.130]	-0.039 [0.121]				0.176 [0.119]	0.195 [0.161]	0.084 [0.178]
Industry produces goods	**0.333** [0.043]	**0.294** [0.061]	**0.341** [0.061]	0.211 [0.126]	0.264 [0.155]	0.170 [0.237]	**0.367** [0.045]	**0.322** [0.067]	**0.382** [0.061]
Industry produces agricultural products	**-0.346** [0.032]	**-0.354** [0.049]	**-0.329** [0.043]	-0.150 [0.089]	-0.237 [0.127]	-0.006 [0.131]	**-0.333** [0.036]	**-0.355** [0.054]	**-0.335** [0.047]
Construction industry	**0.529** [0.053]	**0.373** [0.067]	**0.846** [0.099]	**0.370** [0.106]	**0.311** [0.123]	**0.744** [0.311]	**0.575** [0.062]	**0.399** [0.081]	**0.867** [0.101]
Sales industry	**0.355** [0.044]	**0.354** [0.070]	**0.345** [0.056]	0.125 [0.133]	0.096 [0.225]	0.132 [0.169]	**0.426** [0.047]	**0.415** [0.076]	**0.414** [0.059]
Transportation[a] industry	**0.339** [0.046]	**0.302** [0.058]	**0.311** [0.089]	**0.235** [0.099]	**0.251** [0.114]		**0.367** [0.052]	**0.342** [0.069]	**0.307** [0.087]
Missing industry	**0.148** [0.044]	0.143 [0.066]	0.100 [0.060]	**0.195** [0.054]	**0.195** [0.083]	**0.217** [0.075]	**-0.310** [0.147]	**-0.537** [0.208]	-0.062 [0.214]
Sample size	6017	3119	2898	1162	602	560	4855	2517	2338
F-statistic	**87.01**	**43.41**	**49.63**	**14.22**	**5.85**	**6.08**	**79.72**	**41.27**	**45.02**
R-square	0.289	0.275	0.318	0.238	0.196	0.207	0.308	0.301	0.336

Notes: Cells contain regression coefficients and [standard errors]. **Boldface** if significant at the 5 percent level. [a]Transportation is collinear with other variables in 1993 for women; it is dropped.

We then estimate a second version of the wages and hours models including, as explanatory variables, all of the variables in the first version whether the missing data on these variables are non-randomly selected. The results of the estimation of the second version of the models are given in Table 6.4b (monthly wage) and 6.5b (hours of work).

3.1 Monthly Compensation

The explanatory power of the wage regressions is high; in the pooled model we explain about 21 percent of the variance in monthly wages. We find, as expected, gender differences in monthly wages, but the effect of gender falls significantly over time from 50 percent in 1993 to 15 percent in 1997 in Table 6.4a and from 40 percent to 15 percent in Table 6.4b. In the market economy, women have narrowed the wage gap. The male and female wage models are also significantly different.

Monthly wages are affected by location, and they change over the 1993–1997 period. Wages are highest in Bishkek and are lowest in the rural areas of the South and the Mountain region. Over time, we find little change in the Bishkek advantage (over the rural North), although residence in the rural areas of the South and the Mountain region has a larger negative effect in 1997 than in 1993. Regional differences have risen for both men and women. When we control for industry and occupation, the regional differences are narrower. In both Tables 6.4a and 6.4b a striking change is in the impact of residence in the urban north by gender. In 1993 the Bishkek effect was stronger for men, but in 1997 it was stronger for women. Women have gained most relatively in the best-developed labour market in the country.

Wages are significantly related to the human capital and demographic characteristics of the worker. Ethnicity effects in both models are small but suggest that Russian men earn about 18 percent more than other men, and this advantage increases slightly between 1993 and 1997. When we control for industry and occupation, the Russian advantage is smaller and only significant in 1997. There are no ethnic differences among women in the pooled data, but in 1993 Uzbek women earned 23 percent less than other women.

Human capital does affect monthly wages. The gender differences in returns to post-secondary education are small, and there is little change in these returns over time for either men or women. The returns to higher education are slightly greater for women than for men in 1993; this relationship is reversed in 1997. Age has a non-linear relationship with wages as expected; in 1993 it is significant for both sexes, but in 1997 only for men. Self-reported health has no effect on wages.

Finally, in Table 6.4b, we find that wages vary by occupation and industry. In 1993 professionals are paid significantly more than blue-collar workers, and there is no difference by gender. In 1997 wage differentials, as expected, have widened substantially, with white-collar workers, owners and co-op members all receiving significantly more than blue-collar workers. Surprisingly, however, professionals received significantly less than other occupations in 1997 and this is driven by the negative coefficient for professional women. Other things equal, professional women appear to have come off badly in the early years of transition.

Across the industry groups, the lowest paid workers are agricultural workers; their wages are 33 percent lower than the wages of service workers in 1997. Construction workers are the most highly paid with real wages that are 58 percent higher than service workers. Other workers (manufacturing, commerce, and transportation) receive real wages that are 36–43 percent higher than the wages of service workers. As with occupation, industrial differences in wages increased over time. With the exception of construction, the industry differences are similar for women and men by 1997.

3.2 Hours Worked

In this section we estimate multivariate models of labour supply or hours worked. Hours supplied to the market depend on the wage, consumer preferences (ethnicity, gender, location), and constraints on time in the market (marital status and number of children under the age of six). In the first version of the model, we estimate a reduced form version of the labour supply model that excludes the wage directly but includes the exogenous human capital correlates of the wage – education, experience, and health and occupation and industry. The reduced form results are given in Tables 6.5a and 6.5b. We then estimate a structural labour supply model including the wage. The wage is not exogenous to the determination of hours worked, and we instrument the wage with the predicted log wage obtained from the wage regression in Tables 6.4a and 6.4b. The coefficient on the log wage in this regression is our estimate of the labour supply elasticity. We identify the model by assuming that human capital (education, experience, and health) affect the wage but not hours of work. The estimated labour supply elasticities are given in the first row of Tables 6.5a and 6.5b.

First, we find that the labour supply is highly inelastic. In both 1993 and 1997, when we exclude occupation and industry from the estimation of the predicted wage, the elasticities for men and women are not significantly different from zero. When we include occupation and industry in the estimation of the predicted wage, the labour supply elasticity is only significant for women in 1993; the point estimate of 1.2 is not significantly different from one. Over time, the elasticity for women declines and is not different from zero in 1997.

Gender differences in hours of work are significant, but declining. Controlling for other variables, men work 14 percent more hours than women in 1993 and less than 10 percent more in 1997. The separate male and female models differ, but both models explain relatively little of the variance in reported hours of work. When we control for occupation and industry, the gender differential persists and is almost the same magnitude. The occupation and industry variables add slightly to the model's overall explanatory power, but have practically no impact on the gender dimension.[23] This suggests that occupational and industrial choices do not explain why women work fewer hours than men.

Location, ethnicity and education level all affect hours worked, but gender differences in their impact are minor. Workers in the North work longer hours, and Uzbeks longer and Russian workers shorter hours than Kyrgyz; gender differences and changes over time are small. Better-educated men tend to work shorter hours than other workers, but the difference is small. Self-reported health has no effect on hours worked. Older men work longer hours, but age is not a significant eterminant of the hours worked by women.

Women white-collar workers were working less than their male counterparts in 1993, but relatively more in 1997. Female professionals worked significantly fewer hours than other women in 1997, which was not true in 1993 and not true of male workers in either year. By 1997 female professionals work 32 percent fewer hours than blue-collar workers, while hours of work for all other categories of women workers increase. The largest negative impact of transition on hours worked has been for professional women.

Marriage and children affect hours of work only in 1997. Marriage lowers the hours of work of women, but has no effect on the hours of work of men. Young children, however, have no additional deterrent effect on women, but increase the hours of work of men.

Table 6.5a Models of hours of work, 1993 and 1997: occupation and industry excluded[a]

Variables	1993 and 1997			1993			1997		
	All	Men	Women	All	Men	Women	All	Men	Women
Wage elasticity	**1.579**	0.967	0.557	−0.110	−0.984	0.993	0.815	0.453	0.343
	[0.686]	[0.564]	[0.778]	[0.843]	[0.708]	[0.915]	[0.614]	[0.465]	[0.712]
Constant	**3.774**	**3.831**	**3.791**	**3.773**	**3.715**	**4.003**	**3.745**	**3.842**	**3.752**
	[0.044]	[0.059]	[0.060]	[0.133]	[0.164]	[0.203]	[0.044]	[0.055]	[0.070]
Year=1997	**−0.003**	**−0.020**	0.023						
	[0.012]	[0.014]	[0.019]						
Gender (1=male)	**0.109**			**0.137**			**0.098**		
	[0.009]			[0.023]			[0.010]		
Russian ethnicity	**−0.035**	**−0.047**	**−0.017**	−0.028	−0.078	0.028	**−0.029**	−0.025	−0.029
	[0.016]	[0.021]	[0.024]	[0.034]	[0.047]	[0.050]	[0.017]	[0.022]	[0.027]
Uzbek ethnicity	**0.121**	**0.09**	**0.151**	**0.088**	0.070	**0.124**	**0.097**	0.054	**0.138**
	[0.020]	[0.024]	[0.034]	[0.034]	[0.043]	[0.056]	[0.028]	[0.033]	[0.046]
Other Slavic ethnicity	−0.043	−0.045	−0.032	0.0004	0.002	0.017	−0.065	−0.09	−0.053
	[0.036]	[0.049]	[0.053]	[0.062]	[0.083]	[0.092]	[0.049]	[0.067]	[0.070]
Other ethnicity	**0.051**	0.045	0.060	**0.108**	0.087	**0.161**	0.011	−0.0007	0.029
	[0.019]	[0.024]	[0.031]	[0.042]	[0.051]	[0.073]	[0.022]	[0.026]	[0.034]
Health is good (=1)	−0.008	0.003	−0.007	−0.027	0.017	−0.055	0.005	0.004	0.006
	[0.019]	[0.027]	[0.026]	[0.052]	[0.077]	[0.072]	[0.018]	[0.025]	[0.027]

Table 6.5a continued

Age in years	0.002	0.005	0.00008	0.001	0.010	-0.009	**0.004**	**0.005**	0.002
	[0.002]	[0.003]	[0.003]	[0.007]	[0.009]	[0.010]	[0.002]	[0.002]	[0.002]
Age squared (divided by 1000)	-0.020	**-0.063**	0.005	-0.030	0.130	0.080	**-0.040**	**-0.066**	-0.014
Completed secondary education	-0.020	**-0.041**	0.001	-0.017	-0.073	0.036	-0.021	-0.035	-0.004
	[0.015]	[0.019]	[0.025]	[0.035]	[0.045]	[0.055]	[0.017]	[0.020]	[0.029]
Secondary education + non-college training	0.033	0.039	0.004	0.046	0.067	-0.040	0.005	-0.016	0.03
	[0.018]	[0.021]	[0.033]	[0.033]	[0.040]	[0.058]	[0.023]	[0.025]	[0.042]
Higher education	**-0.042**	**-0.062**	-0.022	-0.057	**-0.083**	-0.048	**-0.043**	**-0.064**	-0.018
	[0.015]	[0.019]	[0.025]	[0.032]	[0.042]	[0.050]	[0.018]	[0.021]	[0.029]
Urban north region	-0.017	-0.022	-0.013	-0.056	-0.01	-0.097	-0.012	**-0.047**	0.014
	[0.017]	[0.022]	[0.026]	[0.037]	[0.049]	[0.057]	[0.019]	[0.024]	[0.030]
Urban south region	**-0.134**	**-0.129**	**-0.14**	-0.061	-0.081	-0.044	**-0.159**	**-0.144**	**-0.174**
	[0.021]	[0.027]	[0.032]	[0.041]	[0.055]	[0.063]	[0.024]	[0.030]	[0.038]
Urban mountain region	-0.061	**-0.112**	0.003	-0.043	**-0.142**	0.055	**-0.08**	**-0.135**	-0.019
	[0.024]	[0.030]	[0.038]	[0.053]	[0.072]	[0.080]	[0.026]	[0.030]	[0.043]
Rural south region	**-0.091**	**-0.089**	**-0.086**	0.013	0.032	-0.034	**-0.136**	**-0.164**	**-0.103**
	[0.017]	[0.021]	[0.027]	[0.035]	[0.043]	[0.058]	[0.019]	[0.023]	[0.030]
Rural mountain region	-0.083	**-0.052**	**-0.116**	**-0.149**	-0.049	**-0.302**	**-0.092**	**-0.093**	**-0.097**
	[0.018]	[0.022]	[0.029]	[0.047]	[0.059]	[0.076]	[0.019]	[0.023]	[0.032]

Table 6.5a continued

Marital status (1=married)	−0.038	−0.0007	**−0.063**	−0.008	−0.008	−0.017	**−0.045**	−0.0005	**−0.071**
	[0.012]	[0.017]	[0.017]	[0.030]	[0.045]	[0.042]	[0.013]	[0.017]	[0.019]
Number of children < age 6	**0.014**	**0.012**	0.014	0.002	−0.002	0.010	**0.017**	**0.015**	0.016
	[0.005]	[0.006]	[0.008]	[0.012]	[0.014]	[0.021]	[0.005]	[0.006]	[0.009]
Sample size	7694	4081	3613	1987	1167	820	5707	2914	2793
F-statistic	**16.3**	**6.84**	**4.76**	**6.70**	**2.85**	**2.99**	**13.26**	**6.24**	**4.51**
R-square	0.039	0.029	0.023	0.058	0.04	0.06	0.04	0.035	0.027

Notes:

[a]Cells contain probit coefficients, [standard errors], and {marginal effects}. [b]Sample size determined by adults reporting non-zero hours worked. **Boldface** if significant at the 5 percent level.

Table 6.5b Models of hours of work, 1993 and 1997: occupation and industry included [a]

Variables	1993 and 1997			1993			1997		
	All	Men	Women	All	Men	Women	All	Men	Women
Wage elasticity	0.858	0.356	0.571	1.203	0.161	1.205	0.536	0.410	0.277
	[0.467]	[0.395]	[0.499]	[0.639]	[0.575]	[0.583]	[0.356]	[0.285]	[0.404]
Constant	3.723	3.785	3.744	3.659	3.575	3.985	3.680	3.795	3.676
	[0.045]	[0.060]	[0.069]	[0.131]	[0.174]	[0.199]	[0.046]	[0.058]	[0.072]
Year=1997	−0.062	−0.068	−0.052						
	[0.014]	[0.017]	[0.023]						
Gender (1=male)	0.098			0.143			0.087		
	[0.010]			[0.025]			[0.010]		
Russian ethnicity	−0.029	−0.038	−0.017	−0.034	−0.063	−0.005	−0.021	−0.022	−0.018
	[0.016]	[0.021]	[0.024]	[0.034]	[0.047]	[0.049]	[0.017]	[0.022]	[0.027]
Uzbek ethnicity	0.118	0.090	0.151	0.067	0.066	0.063	0.102	0.046	0.15
	[0.020]	[0.024]	[0.034]	[0.034]	[0.043]	[0.055]	[0.028]	[0.033]	[0.046]
Other Slavic ethnicity	−0.035	−0.037	−0.032	0.021	0.034	0.016	−0.061	−0.088	−0.055
	[0.036]	[0.049]	[0.053]	[0.060]	[0.082]	[0.090]	[0.048]	[0.066]	[0.070]
Other Ethnicity	0.047	0.037	0.06	0.071	0.064	0.113	0.011	−0.006	0.033
	[0.019]	[0.024]	[0.030]	[0.041]	[0.050]	[0.071]	[0.021]	[0.026]	[0.034]
Age in years	0.003	0.006	0.078	0.0002	0.011	−0.014	0.005	0.006	0.002
	[0.002]	[0.003]	[2.707]	[0.006]	[0.009]	[0.010]	[0.002]	[0.002]	[0.003]

Table 6.5b continued

Age squared (divided by 1000)	-0.026 [0.021]	-0.071 [0.031]	0.005 [0.031]	-0.013 [0.082]	-0.137 [0.109]	0.151 [0.123]	-0.044 [0.022]	-0.077 [0.029]	-0.012 [0.032]
Health is good (=1)	-0.012 [0.018]	-0.006 [0.026]	-0.009 [0.025]	-0.033 [0.051]	-0.014 [0.076]	-0.031 [0.069]	-0.0002 [0.018]	-0.002 [0.025]	0.0005 [0.027]
Completed secondary education	-0.019 [0.015]	-0.035 [0.019]	-0.005 [0.025]	-0.055 [0.035]	-0.091 [0.045]	-0.038 [0.054]	-0.024 [0.017]	-0.038 [0.019]	-0.009 [0.028]
Secondary education + non-college training	0.039 [0.018]	0.045 [0.021]	0.006 [0.033]	0.062 [0.032]	0.091 [0.040]	-0.050 [0.057]	0.008 [0.023]	-0.021 [0.025]	0.042 [0.041]
Higher education	-0.003 [0.016]	-0.026 [0.020]	0.015 [0.025]	0.023 [0.035]	-0.032 [0.047]	0.049 [0.052]	-0.025 [0.018]	-0.043 [0.021]	-0.002 [0.029]
Urban north region	0.013 [0.018]	0.010 [0.023]	0.013 [0.027]	-0.021 [0.037]	0.017 [0.049]	-0.057 [0.056]	0.007 [0.020]	-0.022 [0.025]	0.02 [0.031]
Urban south region	-0.103 [0.021]	-0.101 [0.027]	-0.101 [0.032]	-0.019 [0.041]	-0.043 [0.055]	0.002 [0.062]	-0.143 [0.025]	-0.129 [0.031]	-0.151 [0.038]
Urban mountain region	0.033 [0.024]	-0.080 [0.030]	0.026 [0.038]	-0.007 [0.052]	-0.104 [0.071]	0.072 [0.078]	-0.059 [0.027]	-0.114 [0.031]	-0.003 [0.044]
Rural south region	-0.119 [0.017]	-0.107 [0.021]	-0.127 [0.027]	-0.028 [0.034]	0.013 [0.043]	-0.128 [0.058]	-0.163 [0.019]	-0.183 [0.023]	-0.137 [0.031]
Rural mountain region	-0.094 [0.018]	-0.061 [0.022]	-0.130 [0.029]	-0.182 [0.046]	-0.071 [0.059]	-0.372 [0.075]	-0.102 [0.020]	-0.1 [0.023]	-0.108 [0.032]
White collar occupation	0.026 [0.014]	-0.0004 [0.019]	0.053 [0.021]	0.078 [0.034]	0.107 [0.05]	0.051 [0.051]	0.008 [0.015]	-0.042 [0.019]	0.048 [0.024]

Table 6.5b continued

Owner occupation	0.007	−0.00006	0.019	0.054	**0.114**	−0.01	0.023	0.002	**0.05**
	[0.013]	[0.015]	[0.021]	[0.037]	[0.05]	[0.058]	[0.013]	[0.014]	[0.022]
Co-op member	**0.080**	**0.078**	**0.079**				**0.112**	**0.109**	**0.115**
	[0.023]	[0.029]	[0.037]				[0.022]	[0.025]	[0.037]
Professional occupation	**−0.145**	**−0.092**	**−0.187**	−0.071	−0.027	−0.114	**−0.172**	−0.026	**−0.317**
	[0.026]	[0.033]	[0.040]	[0.042]	[0.057]	[0.064]	[0.050]	[0.058]	[0.084]
Missing occupation	0.078	0.002	0.162				0.087	−0.003	**0.173**
	[0.056]	[0.071]	[0.090]				[0.052]	[0.059]	[0.087]
Industry produces goods	0.027	−0.009	**0.064**	0.057	0.043	0.198	0.012	−0.031	0.051
	[0.021]	[0.026]	[0.036]	[0.066]	[0.076]	[0.150]	[0.022]	[0.025]	[0.036]
Industry produces agricultural products	**0.128**	**0.095**	**0.156**	**0.330**	**0.295**	**0.403**	**0.076**	**0.041**	**0.096**
	[0.015]	[0.020]	[0.024]	[0.038]	[0.052]	[0.059]	[0.017]	[0.021]	[0.026]
Construction industry	0.035	−0.003	0.091	0.028	0.025	−0.022	0.055	0.014	0.100
	[0.026]	[0.028]	[0.058]	[0.051]	[0.058]	[0.184]	[0.030]	[0.031]	[0.060]
Sales industry	**0.144**	**0.124**	**0.155**	0.092	0.126	0.123	**0.123**	**0.084**	**0.139**
	[0.024]	[0.033]	[0.034]	[0.082]	[0.138]	[0.103]	[0.024]	[0.031]	[0.036]
Transportation industry	**0.123**	**0.095**	**0.116**	**0.189**	**0.163**	0.309	**0.104**	**0.078**	**0.098**
	[0.023]	[0.025]	[0.052]	[0.047]	[0.054]	[0.279]	[0.026]	[0.027]	[0.052]
Missing industry	−0.001	−0.016	−0.004	**0.063**	0.059	0.066	0.031	−0.038	0.175
	[0.021]	[0.026]	[0.035]	[0.029]	[0.042]	[0.043]	[0.163]	[0.152]	[0.418]
Marital status (1=married)	**−0.038**	−0.005	**−0.061**	−0.013	−0.005	−0.02	**−0.045**	−0.007	**−0.068**
	[0.012]	[0.017]	[0.017]	[0.030]	[0.044]	[0.041]	[0.012]	[0.017]	[0.019]

Table 6.5b continued

Number of children < age 6	**0.012**	0.01	0.01	−0.008	−0.009	−0.007	**0.016**	**0.017**	**0.012**
	[0.005]	[0.006]	[0.008]	[0.012]	[0.014]	[0.020]	[0.005]	[0.006]	[0.009]
Sample size	7694	4081	3613	1987	1167	820	5705	2914	2793
F-statistic	**16.55**	**6.91**	**6.72**	**8.76**	**4.01**	**4.68**	**12.16**	**6.09**	**5.15**
R-square	0.061	0.047	0.052	0.095	0.084	0.105	0.059	0.056	0.05

Notes:
[a]Cells contain probit coefficients, [standard errors], and {marginal effects}. Sample size determined by adults reporting non-zero hours worked. **Boldface** if significant at the 5 percent level.

4. DECOMPOSITIONS

4.1 Decomposition of wage

To further examine the wage differential, we decompose the wage gap into explained and unexplained components. Assuming the log wage of person i in group j in year t (LnW_{ijt}) is equal to:

$$LnW_{ijt} = \beta_{jt} X_{ijt} + u_{ij} \tag{6.1}$$

where j=men (m), women (f), $t = 1993,1997$, and $E(u_{ijt} |X_{ijt}) = 0$, then the difference in the mean log wage of men and women in year t can be written as:

$$Ln\overline{W}_{mt} - Ln\overline{W}_{ft} = (\overline{X}_{mt} - \overline{X}_{ft})\beta_{mt} + (\beta_{mt} - \beta_{ft})\overline{X}_{ft} \tag{6.2}$$

The term $(\overline{X}_{mt} - \overline{X}_{ft})\beta_{mt}$ is the portion of the wage gap that is explained by the difference in average characteristics of men and women in year t, assuming that the regression model for men is the true or base wage model. The portion of the log wage gap that is not explained by differences in characteristics, $(\beta_{mt} - \beta_{ft})\overline{X}_{ft}$, captures differences in the male and female returns to these characteristics and is frequently the measure of wage discrimination, although it incorporates the effect of any omitted variables, including discrimination, on wage differentials. The decomposition can also be performed assuming that the female log wage regression is the base model.

The decomposition of wages is given in Table 6.6a for 1993 and 1997 using both the male and female models as the base model. We perform two decompositions for each year. The first decomposition is based on the log wage regression in Table 6.4a, and the second decomposition is based on the log wage regression in Table 6.4b, in which industry and occupation variables are included.

The log wage gap evaluated at the mean is equal to 0.42 in 1993.[24] If the male model without industry and occupation variables is the base model, the explained log wage gap in 1993 is −0.07; given their characteristics, the average log wage of women should exceed the average log wage of men. The unexplained portion of the gap is therefore 117 percent. If the female model is the base, the unexplained gap is also over 100 percent. In 1997, the log wage gap evaluated at the mean is equal to 0.119, significantly smaller than in 1993. The explained portion of the gap is still −0.07.[25] The wage decomposition shows that the actual wage gap declined over time, while the size of the gap explained by differences in characteristics remained constant between 1993 and 1997.

Our next task is to examine the change in the log wage gap over time and to illustrate the role played by the change in the wage distribution over time. Juhn et al. (1991) begin with (6.1) above, but rewrite $u_{ijt} = \sigma_t \theta_{ijt}$, where θ_{ijt} is the standardized error (u_{ijt}/σ_t) with mean 0 and variance 1, and σ_t is the standard deviation of u_{imt} in the male log wage model. The log wage gap evaluated at any point in the distribution at time t, assuming $E(u_{imt}|X_{imt}) = 0$ and with the male log wage model as the base is:

$$\Delta LnW_t = LnW_{mt} - LnW_{ft} = (\overline{X}_{mt} - \overline{X}_{ft})\beta_{mt} + \sigma(\theta_{mt} - \theta_{ft})$$

$$= (\overline{X}_{mt} - \overline{X}_{ft})\beta_{mt} + \sigma_t(-\theta_{ft}) \qquad (6.3)$$

The change in the gender log wage gap over time, from 1993 ($t=1$) to 1997 ($t=2$), assuming that the male log wage model for year 2 is the base model, is:

$$\Delta LnW_1 - \Delta LnW_2 = (\Delta \overline{X}_1 - \Delta \overline{X}_2)\beta_{m2} + \Delta \overline{X}_1(\beta_{m1} - \beta_{m2})$$

$$+ (\Delta\theta_1 - \Delta\theta_2)\sigma_2 + \Delta\theta_1(\sigma_1 - \sigma_2) \qquad (6.4)$$

Thus the change in the gap over time has four components:

A = $(\Delta\overline{X}_1 - \Delta\overline{X}_2)\beta_{m2}$ is the portion of the change in the log wage gap that is explained by change in the relative characteristics of men and women between 1993 $(\Delta\overline{X}_1)$ and 1997 $(\Delta\overline{X}_2)$ If $\Delta\overline{X}_i > 0$, then the characteristics of men are more positive in the labour market than the characteristics of women. If A > 0, then the characteristics of men relative to women are more positive in 1993 than in 1997.

B = $\Delta\overline{X}_1(\beta_{m1} - \beta_{m2})$ is the portion of the change in the log wage gap that is due to the change over time in returns to those characteristics through the male log wage model. If B > 0, then the returns to characteristics were higher in 1993 than in 1997.

C = $(\Delta\theta_1 - \Delta\theta_2)\sigma_2$ is the portion of the change in the log wage gap that is due to the change in the relative position of men and women in the residual distribution of 1997. If $\Delta\theta_t > 0$, then the average man in year t is positioned higher in the residual distribution than the average woman. If C > 0, then the relative position of women is worse in 1993 than in 1997 within this residual distribution.[26]

D = $\Delta\theta_J(\sigma_1 - \sigma_2)$ is the portion of the change in the log wage gap
that is due to the change in the residual log wage distribution over
time. If D > 0, then the variance in the residual distribution for men
in 1993 is larger than the variance in the residual distribution for men
in 1997.

We measure the change in the mean log wage gap between 1993 and 1997
and decompose this change (D93–97) into the four portions (A, B, C, D)
described above, using the male model with and without industry and
occupation variables as the base model. The results of this decomposition are
presented at the bottom of Table 6.6a.

The change in the log wage gap is positive; the wage gap was larger in
1993 than in 1997. In both the model without industry and occupation
variables and the model with these variables, the largest contributor to this
change in the wage gap is reflected in component C, changes in the residual
distribution (112 percent without industry and occupation, 75 percent with
them).[27] Because C is positive, within the residual distribution, the relative
position of women improved over time, which can represent a relative
improvement in the skills of women or a reduction in discrimination. This is
consistent with the results reported for each year at the top of Table 6.6a;
closer examination of the unexplained gap due to $\beta_m \neq \beta_f$ attributes the change
between 1993 and 1997 largely to movement within the distribution over
time. While the variance in the residual distribution (the distribution of skill
as interpreted by Juhn et al.) increased, the position of women relative to men
within that distribution improved, and this change explains most of the decline
in gender wage differences between 1993 and 1997.

Table 6.6a Decomposition of wage gap from 1993 to 1997

	1993		1997	
	Male	Female	Male	Female
No ind/occ				
Ln(wage) gap	0.423	0.423	0.119	0.119
Due to $X_m \neq X_f$	−0.073	−0.038	−0.073	−0.067
Due to $\beta_m \neq \beta_f$	0.496	0.461	0.192	0.186
Ind/occ				
Ln(wage) gap	0.420	0.420	0.139	0.139
Due to $X_m \neq X_f$	0.090	0.061	−0.078	−0.061
Due to $\beta_m \neq \beta_f$	0.417	0.365	0.217	0.200

1993– 97*

	D93–97	A	B	C	D
No ind/occ	0.304	−0.027	0.027	0.339	−0.055
		(−9%)	(9%)	(112%)	(−12%)
With ind/occ	0.285	0.021	0.066	0.214	−0.016
		(7%)	(23%)	(75%)	(−5%)

Note: *Number in brackets is the percentage of D93–D97 gap explained by this component.

Table 6.6b   Decomposition of hours gap from 1993 to 1997

	1993		1997	
	Male model	Female model	Male model	Female model
No ind/occ				
Ln (hours) gap	0.185	0.185	0.097	0.097
Due to $X_m \neq X_f$	0.040	0.009	−0.001	−0.012
Due to $\beta_m \neq \beta_f$	0.145	0.176	0.098	0.109
Ind/occ				
Ln (hours) gap	0.185	0.185	0.084	0.084
Due to $X_m \neq X_f$	0.025	0.021	0.008	−0.001
Due to $\beta_m \neq \beta_f$	0.160	0.164	0.076	0.085

1993– 97*

	D93–97	A	B	C	D
No ind/occ	0.088	0.014	0.027	−0.005	0.052
		(16%)	(31%)	(−6%)	(59%)
With ind/occ	0.101	0.016	0.001	0.028	0.056
		(16%)	(1%)	(28%)	(55%)

Note: *Number in brackets is the percentage of D93 – D97 gap explained by component.

4.2 Decomposition of hours

In Table 6.6b we analyse differences in the hours worked by men and women between 1993 and 1997 using the decomposition methodology described for wages.   First, for each year, we decompose the log hours gap into a component explained by differences in the characteristics of working men and women and an unexplained component (top panel of Table 6.6b).   In 1993, the log hours gap is equal to 0.19. The portion of this gap explained by the observable characteristics is small, 0.01 to 0.04. The residual 78–95 percent is unexplained, and is due to gender differences in the impact of these characteristics and to unmeasured characteristics. By 1997, the log hours gap shrinks to between 0.08 and 0.10. Given their characteristics women should work from one percent more to one percent fewer hours than men; thus, almost the entire observed hours gap in 1997 is unexplained by characteristics.

We next decompose the change in the gap between 1993 and 1997 into the four components described above (bottom panel of Table 6.6b). In contrast to the wage decomposition, we find that the change in the hours gap is largely explained by component D, the change in the residual hours distribution over time. The variance in residual hours declined between 1993 and 1997, and increased the hours of women relative to men. When we include controls for industry and occupation in the model, component C is also positive and important, indicating that over time women moved up the hours distribution relative to men. In general, however, the hours decomposition yields weaker results than the wages decomposition.

5. CONCLUSIONS

Transition to a market economy has not been accompanied by a deteriorating situation for women in the labour market. Although some women have undoubtedly suffered from loss of job security and from developments such as the well-publicized trafficking in women, on the whole women have fared no worse, and probably better, than men. This conclusion, supported by evidence from European economies in transition from central planning, is confirmed in this chapter in the Asian and Islamic setting of the Kyrgyz Republic. Gender differences in hours worked, wage rates and monthly earnings all narrowed between 1993 and 1997.

Women have benefited more than men from the transition for three reasons. First, the returns to formal education have increased. The centrally planned economies provided equality of access, and in many countries women's educational achievement was on average at least as high as men's by the end of the planning era. In the Kyrgyz Republic a specific exception is the group of professional women, whose labour force position declined markedly because of a large reduction in hours worked; whether that was a voluntary reduction or not cannot be answered from our data. Big losers during transition were people who had acquired vocational training specific to the planned economy or had moved up the hierarchy; returns to such 'experience' have fallen, and in the Kyrgyz Republic as in other transition economies this tended to harm men more than women. The other big losers were the unskilled, but this appears to be gender-neutral in terms of lost employment.

Second, greater choice over labour force participation and hours worked likely benefited women more than men. To be sure, the declining participation rates associated with transition were involuntary in many cases, but unemployment may have been more psychologically damaging to males than to females, who could turn to household work. The huge gender disparity in increased mortality rates in many transition countries lends some support to the hypothesis that men came under greater stress than women. If the hypothesis is correct, then even in countries where reduced employment of unskilled workers fell disproportionately on females, the impact on men may have been more negative.

Third, the unexplained gender wage gap narrowed. This was not due to less-educated women leaving the workforce in disproportionate numbers and creating a selection bias, and nor did patterns of industrial or occupational segregation work against women overall. Discrimination by gender appears to be less in a market-based economy than it was in centrally planned economies. The decompositions, however, suggest that discrimination, although less significant in 1997 than in 1993, may still account for much of the wage and hours gender gaps.

The evidence presented in this chapter strongly supports these conclusions. By 1997, six years after the dissolution of the Soviet Union and a decade after the Law on Enterprises which formally ended Soviet central planning, there is no evidence of deteriorating relative labour market status of women in the Kyrgyz Republic.

NOTES

1. See, for example, the article on trafficking in women in the 26th August 2000 issue of *The Economist* (London), and Bauer, Boschmann and Green (1997), and Falkingham (2000a) and Mee (2001) on Central Asia. The International Organisation for Migration estimates that up to 4000 women were recruited into prostitution abroad from Kyrgyzstan in 1999, mainly to the United Arab Emirates and Turkey ('The Rise in Vice', *The Economist*, 18 June 2001).
2. See for example Swafford (1978) and Ofer and Vinokur (1992). Work on the Soviet labour force, however, tended to rely on samples drawn primarily from the European Soviet republics (for example using interviews of Soviet émigrés, few of whom came from Central Asia).
3. Between 1921 and 1923 Soviet law was established as taking precedence over customary law. Marriage without consent and polygamy were banned, the minimum legal age for marriage was raised from nine to sixteen for brides and set

at eighteen for grooms, and women were guaranteed rights to divorce. Massell (1975) is the only detailed western study on female emancipation in Soviet Central Asia. On the 1927 mass unveiling campaign (*khudzhum*), see also Akiner (1997, 270–71).

4. The female participation rate in the Kyrgyz republic increased from 29 percent in 1940 to 48 percent in 1974 (Ubaidullaeva, 1982, 148). In 1990 83 percent of women in the Kyrgyz republic were in the official labour force. This was supported by public services such as day-care centres and kindergartens, accessible basic healthcare and extended maternity leave. The majority of the female population had completed secondary education and over a third of female students continued to vocational training or tertiary education. By contrast, in the 1897 census only 0.03 percent of Turkic people in the Russian empire had any education beyond elementary school (Lubin, 1984, 113). Within the area of modern Kyrgyzstan, literacy rates remained very low, and practically zero among women, until the 1920s.

5. Women also worked fewer hours than men, so the hourly wage gap was even smaller. The Kyrgyz ratio of female to male wages was above the Soviet average, perhaps because lower average incomes in the Kyrgyz republic meant that the minimum wage applied to more workers of both sexes than elsewhere in the USSR. In the USA in the late 1980s the ratio was 65 percent (figures from Atkinson and Micklewright, 1992).

6. Bauer, Green and Kuehnast (1997) provide an overview of the position of women in the Kyrgyz Republic since independence, based on interviews with officials from the government and non-governmental organizations.

7. Falkingham (1999, 383 and 386) reports on an ILO survey which found that nearly two-thirds of the jobs lost in the Kyrgyz Republic during the 1990s were women's.

8. In 1989 31 percent of 1–6 year-olds were in kindergarten, but in 1997 the proportion had fallen to 7 percent (UNICEF, 1999, 133). Heating of schools is a problem throughout the country, and in the Bel-Adoi region two-thirds of children did not attend school in the winter of 1994 for lack of winter clothes and shoes.

9. Reduction in time spent queuing for scarce goods and services in the planned economy has also benefited women more than men.

10. We restrict ourselves to economic variables. Some sociologists (for example Ashwin and Bowers, 1997, 34) provide anecdotal evidence of rapid and general downgrading of women in the post-Soviet workplace.

11. Gregory (1982) applied a Becker/Mincer/Schultz model of fertility and labour force participation to Soviet data and obtained similar results to those from western market economies.

12. Svejnar (1999, 2835–39) reviews the earlier literature applying Mincerian earnings function to eastern European transition economies, but his survey contains little on gender aspects of changes in labour markets in these countries. Increased returns to education have been found in Poland (Rutkowski, 1996), the Czech Republic and Slovakia (Chase, 1998), East Germany (Krueger and Pischke, 1995), and Russia (Newell and Reilly, 1996; Brainerd, 1998). In Romania Paternosto and Sahn (1999) found that increased returns to human

capital widened male/female wage differentials in rural areas. For China, Gustafsson and Li (2000) found that higher educational attainment of males explains a third of the slight increase in gender wage differentials, from 15.6 percent in 1988 to 17.5 percent in 1995, in urban areas. Chase (1998) and Flanagan (1998) both found that returns to experience gained in the planned economy of Czechoslovakia fell during the transition, but specifying returns to experience is subject to serious measurement problems.

13. Their sample included Kazakhstan, Latvia, Russia, Ukraine and Russia from the former Soviet Union, and Bulgaria, the Czech Republic, Hungary, Poland, Slovakia and Yugoslavia from eastern Europe. In a related exercise, Newell and Reilly (2001) find that the gender gap has on average not widened during transition, and the gap is wider at the top end of the wage distribution than at the bottom end.

14. Brainerd uses survey data from Bulgaria, the Czech Republic, Hungary, Poland and Slovakia, and from the Kyrgyz Republic, Russia and Ukraine. For the Kyrgyz Republic she only uses 1993 data survey data which she describes as post-transition, a characterization with which we disagree. We also had difficulty reconciling her summary statistic of a female/male wage ratio of 100 percent in 1993, with our ratio, drawn from the same data set, of around three quarters (Table 6A.3)

15. Klugman tests for, and rejects, sheepskin effects; it is the amount of education that matters, rather than receipt of formal qualifications.

16. Her post-transition data come from a 1995 survey of 1500 households in three districts (the capital city, the disadvantaged region of Karakalpakstan, and part of the Ferghana Valley). Her wage equations include an 'experience' term, which is complicated by the disrupted workforce participation of women; over 30 percent of women in the sampled households are on maternity leave. The problems due to high fertility rates in Uzbekistan are less pronounced in the Kyrgyz Republic. The total fertility rate has fallen in both countries but the Kyrgyz Republic is always below Uzbekistan: 4.07 in the Kyrgyz republic to 4.81 in the Uzbek republic in 1980, 3.67 to 4.17 in 1991, 3.30 to 3.81 in 1993, 3.31 to 3.59 in 1995, and 2.79 to 3.17 in 1997 (UNICEF, 1999, 116).

17. The analysis was also carried out using the fall 1996 LSMS survey, but the 1996 and 1997 results are similar, so we quote only the more recent year. The 1996 results are available upon request.

18. Some households and adults were deleted from these final analysis files because of missing information on variables included in our models.

19. Based on rural–urban status and oblast, we classify the regions as urban north (Bishkek and urban areas of Chyi), urban south (urban areas of Osh and Djalabad), urban mountain (urban areas of Narun, Talas and Issuk-kul), rural north (rural areas of Chyi), rural south (rural areas of Osh and Djalabad), and rural mountain (rural areas of Narun, Talas and Issuk-kul). The data on gender differences in education and work by region are available upon request.

20. The mountain region is the outlier. In the small urban mountain category, there is no significant change in hours of work but the gender difference in the hourly wage narrows (from 0.54 in 1993 to 0.64 in 1997). In the rural mountain area, women work more in 1997 than in 1993 relative to men, but their hourly wage,

which is higher than the hourly wage of men in 1993, seems to fall over time to parity with men (1.36 in 1993 to 0.98 in 1997).

21. There may be some error in the 1993 coding because the occupation questions are not identical to the 1997 questions.

22. Changes over time are difficult to assess because Russians and Uzbeks had opportunities to emigrate to Russia or to Uzbekistan; common estimates are of some 100 000 Russians and 10 000 Uzbeks having emigrated in the early and mid 1990s. We owe this point to Yelena Kalyuzhnova.

23. The main change in industrial patterns during transition is the erosion of the extra hours worked by agricultural workers in 1993. This applies to both sexes, but especially to women.

24. We compute the average log wage directly from each regression as $(\overline{X}_{jt'}\beta_{jt})$.

    Because of rounding error, the mean log wage from the regression without industry and occupation may differ from the mean log wage from the regression with industry and occupation variables.

25. When we add industry and occupation variables to the base model, the unexplained gap declines but is still large. In 1993, 86–98 percent of the log wage gap at the means of the characteristics is caused by gender differences in returns to these characteristics or to omitted variables. In 1997, the unexplained portion is 144–156 percent.

26. Component C can be the result of discrimination or changes in the skills of men and women. Juhn et al. (1991) assume that it is the result of the change in skill prices over time.

27. Component D is negative in our decomposition but relatively small. This indicates that the variance in the residual log wage distribution widened over time, and the increase in the variance widened the log wage gap because women were at a lower position in that distribution than men in 1993. Components A and B are both positive when industry and occupation are included, but their effects are relatively small.

APPENDIX 6A

*Table 6A.1 Descriptive statistics, 1993 and 1997: labour force participation model**

Variables	1993 and 1997			1993			1997		
	All	Men	Women	All	Men	Women	All	Men	Women
Labour force participation (=1)	0.595 [0.491]	0.705 [0.456]	0.498 [0.500]	0.667 [0.471]	0.774 [0.418]	0.575 [0.494]	0.546 [0.498]	0.658 [0.474]	0.443 [0.497]
Gender (1=male)	0.471 [0.499]			0.462 [0.499]			0.478 [0.500]		
Year (1=1997)	0.592 [0.491]	0.601 [0.490]	0.585 [0.493]						
Completed secondary education	0.385 [0.487]	0.378 [0.485]	0.392 [0.488]	0.247 [0.432]	0.201 [0.401]	0.287 [0.453]	0.480 [0.500]	0.495 [0.500]	0.465 [0.499]
Secondary education + non-college training	0.124 [0.330]	0.165 [0.372]	0.088 [0.283]	0.197 [0.398]	0.271 [0.445]	0.132 [0.339]	0.074 [0.262]	0.095 [0.293]	0.056 [0.229]
Higher education	0.25 [0.433]	0.233 [0.423]	0.265 [0.441]	0.218 [0.413]	0.202 [0.402]	0.232 [0.422]	0.271 [0.445]	0.253 [0.435]	0.289 [0.453]
Age in years	38.7 [16.3]	37.8 [15.5]	39.5 [16.9]	39.5 [16.8]	38.3 [15.9]	40.6 [17.5]	38.2 [15.9]	37.6 [15.3]	38.7 [16.5]
Health is good (=1)	0.903 [0.296]	0.929 [0.256]	0.879 [0.326]	0.904 [0.294]	0.932 [0.253]	0.881 [0.323]	0.902 [0.298]	0.928 [0.259]	0.878 [0.327]
Marital status (1= married)	0.699 [0.459]	0.735 [0.441]	0.666 [0.472]	0.712 [0.453]	0.752 [0.432]	0.677 [0.467]	0.690 [0.463]	0.724 [0.447]	0.658 [0.474]

Table 6A.1 continued

Number of children age									
<6	0.858	0.869	0.847	0.857	0.874	0.843	0.858	0.385	0.851
	[1.025]	[1.030]	[1.021]	[1.044]	[1.051]	[1.037]	[1.013]	[1.015]	[1.010]
Russian ethnicity	0.152	0.134	0.168	0.191	0.170	0.209	0.124	0.109	0.138
	[0.359]	[0.340]	[0.374]	[0.393]	[0.376]	[0.407]	[0.330]	[0.312]	[0.345]
Uzbek ethnicity	0.083	0.085	0.082	0.149	0.154	0.145	0.038	0.039	0.037
	[0.276]	[0.279]	[0.274]	[0.357]	[0.361]	[0.353]	[0.190]	[0.193]	[0.188]
Other Slavic ethnicity	0.021	0.019	0.023	0.037	0.035	0.038	0.010	0.008	0.012
	[0.143]	[0.135]	[0.150]	[0.188]	[0.184]	[0.191]	[0.100]	[0.088]	[0.111]
Other ethnicity	0.071	0.072	0.071	0.090	0.093	0.087	0.058	0.057	0.06
	[0.257]	[0.258]	[0.257]	[0.286]	[0.291]	[0.283]	[0.234]	[0.232]	[0.237]
Urban north region	0.171	0.153	0.186	0.182	0.165	0.197	0.163	0.145	0.179
	[0.376]	[0.360]	[0.389]	[0.386]	[0.371]	[0.398]	[0.369]	[0.352]	[0.383]
Urban south region	0.299	0.099	0.110	0.138	0.134	0.142	0.082	0.075	0.088
	[0.458]	[0.298]	[0.313]	[0.345]	[0.341]	[0.349]	[0.274]	[0.264]	[0.283]
Urban mountain region	0.073	0.072	0.075	0.060	0.061	0.059	0.083	0.080	0.086
	[0.261]	[0.259]	[0.263]	[0.237]	[0.239]	[0.235]	[0.276]	[0.271]	[0.280]
Rural south region	0.299	0.311	0.288	0.326	0.336	0.318	0.280	0.294	0.267
	[0.458]	[0.463]	[0.453]	[0.469]	[0.472]	[0.466]	[0.449]	[0.456]	[0.442]
Rural mountain region	0.230	0.245	0.218	0.126	0.135	0.118	0.302	0.318	0.288
	[0.421]	[0.430]	[0.413]	[0.332]	[0.342]	[0.323]	[0.459]	[0.466]	[0.453]
Sample size	12261	5781	6480	4997	2309	2688	7264	3472	3792

Note: Cells contain the mean of the variable with the standard deviation below it in brackets.

Table 6.2 Descriptive statistics, 1993 and 1997: hours of work model*

Variables	1993 and 1997			1993			1997		
	All	Men	Women	All	Men	Women	All	Men	Women
Hours of work per week	46.366 [15.694]	48.452 [15.746]	44.009 [15.300]	49.212 [21.035]	52.347 [21.293]	44.751 [19.838]	45.374 [13.202]	46.892 [12.540]	43.791 [13.682]
Gender (1=male)	0.530 [0.499]			0.587 [0.492]					
Completed secondary education	0.401 [0.490]	0.401 [0.490]	0.401 [0.490]	0.210 [0.407]	0.181 [0.385]	0.251 [0.434]	0.467 [0.499]	0.489 [0.500]	0.445 [0.497]
Secondary education + non-college training	0.126 [0.331]	0.161 [0.367]	0.086 [0.280]	0.260 [0.439]	0.317 [0.466]	0.179 [0.384]	0.079 [0.269]	0.098 [0.298]	0.058 [0.234]
Higher education	0.290 [0.454]	0.257 [0.437]	0.327 [0.469]	0.289 [0.454]	0.237 [0.426]	0.363 [0.481]	0.290 [0.454]	0.265 [0.442]	0.316 [0.465]
Age in years	37.5 [14.2]	36.9 [13.7]	38.1 [14.7]	35.9 [11.1]	35.9 [11.6]	35.9 [10.3]	38.0 [15.1]	37.2 [14.5]	38.8 [15.7]
Health is good (=1)	0.922 [0.269]	0.947 [0.224]	0.893 [0.309]	0.953 [0.211]	0.965 [0.184]	0.937 [0.244]	0.911 [0.285]	0.940 [0.238]	0.88 [0.325]
Russian ethnicity	0.152 [0.359]	0.130 [0.336]	0.177 [0.382]	0.211 [0.408]	0.173 [0.378]	0.265 [0.441]	0.132 [0.338]	0.113 [0.317]	0.151 [0.358]
Uzbek ethnicity	0.071 [0.258]	0.081 [0.273]	0.060 [0.238]	0.165 [0.371]	0.182 [0.385]	0.141 [0.349]	0.039 [0.193]	0.041 [0.199]	0.037 [0.188]
Other Slavic ethnicity	0.018 [0.131]	0.015 [0.120]	0.021 [0.143]	0.037 [0.189]	0.033 [0.178]	0.044 [0.205]	0.011 [0.103]	0.008 [0.087]	0.014 [0.117]

Table 6A.2 continued

Other ethnicity	0.069 [0.254]	0.071 [0.257]	0.067 [0.250]	0.085 [0.278]	0.098 [0.297]	0.066 [0.248]	0.064 [0.244]	0.06 [0.238]	0.067 [0.251]
Urban north region	0.184 [0.388]	0.161 [0.367]	0.211 [0.408]	0.187 [0.390]	0.163 [0.369]	0.222 [0.416]	0.183 [0.387]	0.160 [0.367]	0.208 [0.406]
Urban south region	0.102 [0.302]	0.095 [0.294]	0.108 [0.311]	0.148 [0.355]	0.136 [0.343]	0.165 [0.371]	0.085 [0.279]	0.079 [0.270]	0.092 [0.289]
Urban mountain region	0.055 [0.228]	0.056 [0.231]	0.054 [0.226]	0.055 [0.229]	0.049 [0.216]	0.065 [0.246]	0.055 [0.228]	0.059 [0.236]	0.051 [0.220]
Rural south region	0.342 [0.474]	0.350 [0.477]	0.334 [0.472]	0.343 [0.475]	0.373 [0.484]	0.300 [0.459]	0.342 [0.474]	0.341 [0.474]	0.343 [0.475]
Rural mountain region	0.191 [0.393]	0.214 [0.410]	0.165 [0.371]	0.084 [0.278]	0.087 [0.283]	0.079 [0.270]	0.228 [0.420]	0.265 [0.441]	0.190 [0.392]
White-collar worker	0.248 [0.432]	0.176 [0.381]	0.33 [0.470]	0.207 [0.405]	0.129 [0.336]	0.317 [0.466]	0.262 [0.440]	0.194 [0.396]	0.333 [0.471]
Owner occupation	0.250 [0.433]	0.269 [0.444]	0.229 [0.421]	0.109 [0.311]	0.095 [0.294]	0.128 [0.334]	0.300 [0.458]	0.339 [0.473]	0.259 [0.438]
Co-op member	0.047 [0.213]	0.047 [0.211]	0.048 [0.215]				0.064 [0.245]	0.065 [0.247]	0.063 [0.242]
Professional occupation	0.042 [0.200]	0.038 [0.192]	0.045 [0.208]	0.134 [0.341]	0.11 [0.313]	0.168 [0.374]	0.010 [0.098]	0.010 [0.099]	0.009 [0.096]
Missing occupation	0.007 [0.081]	0.007 [0.081]	0.007 [0.081]	0	0	0	0.009 [0.094]	0.009 [0.096]	0.009 [0.092]

Table 6A.2 continued

Industry produces goods	0.057 [0.233]	0.066 [0.248]	0.048 [0.214]	0.031 [0.173]	0.043 [0.203]	0.013 [0.115]	0.067 [0.250]	0.075 [0.263]	0.058 [0.234]
Industry produces agricultural products	0.417 [0.493]	0.453 [0.498]	0.377 [0.485]	0.206 [0.405]	0.199 [0.399]	0.217 [0.413]	0.491 [0.500]	0.555 [0.497]	0.424 [0.494]
Construction industry	0.039 [0.193]	0.058 [0.233]	0.017 [0.130]	0.061 [0.239]	0.098 [0.297]	0.009 [0.092]	0.031 [0.173]	0.042 [0.200]	0.02 [0.139]
Sales industry	0.047 [0.211]	0.037 [0.188]	0.058 [0.233]	0.018 [0.135]	0.011 [0.105]	0.029 [0.169]	0.056 [0.231]	0.047 [0.212]	0.066 [0.249]
Transportation industry	0.056 [0.229]	0.086 [0.281]	0.021 [0.144]	0.087 [0.281]	0.145 [0.352]	0.004 [0.060]	0.045 [0.207]	0.063 [0.243]	0.026 [0.160]
Missing industry	0.078 [0.268]	0.087 [0.282]	0.067 [0.250]	0.298 [0.458]	0.302 [0.459]	0.294 [0.456]	0.0009 [0.030]	0.001 [0.037]	0.0004 [0.019]
Sample size	7694	4081	3613	1987	1167	820	5707	2914	2793

Note: *Cells contain the mean of the variable with the standard deviation below it in brackets.

Table 6A.3 Descriptive statistics, 1993 and 1997: wage model*

Variables	1993 and 1997			1993			1997		
	All	Men	Women	All	Men	Women	All	Men	Women
Monthly compensation (soms)	141.4 [279.4]	156.0 [336.1]	125.7 [200.3]	104.9 [104.1]	125.1 [120.1]	83.1 [77.9]	150.2 [306.3]	163.4 [369.1]	135.9 [218.5]
Gender (1=male)	0.518 [0.500]			0.518 [0.500]			0.518 [0.500]		
Completed secondary education	0.404 [0.491]	0.415 [0.493]	0.393 [0.489]	0.145 [0.352]	0.12 [0.325]	0.173 [0.379]	0.466 [0.499]	0.485 [0.500]	0.446 [0.497]
Secondary education + non-college training	0.112 [0.315]	0.139 [0.345]	0.083 [0.276]	0.253 [0.435]	0.312 [0.464]	0.189 [0.392]	0.078 [0.268]	0.097 [0.296]	0.058 [0.233]
Higher education	0.305 [0.461]	0.275 [0.447]	0.338 [0.473]	0.35 [0.477]	0.294 [0.456]	0.411 [0.492]	0.295 [0.456]	0.271 [0.444]	0.321 [0.467]
Age in years	37.9 [14.4]	37.4 [14.0]	38.3 [14.8]	36.9 [11.1]	37.3 [11.6]	36.4 [10.5]	38.1 [15.1]	37.5 [14.5]	38.8 [15.6]
Health is good (=1)	0.920 [0.271]	0.943 [0.231]	0.895 [0.306]	0.952 [0.214]	0.963 [0.188]	0.939 [0.239]	0.912 [0.283]	0.938 [0.240]	0.885 [0.320]
Russian ethnicity	0.168 [0.374]	0.143 [0.350]	0.195 [0.396]	0.302 [0.459]	0.252 [0.435]	0.355 [0.479]	0.136 [0.343]	0.117 [0.321]	0.156 [0.363]
Uzbek ethnicity	0.064 [0.246]	0.070 [0.255]	0.059 [0.235]	0.157 [0.364]	0.178 [0.383]	0.136 [0.343]	0.042 [0.201]	0.044 [0.205]	,040 [0.196]

Table 6A.3 continued

Other Slavic ethnicity	0.016 [0.124]	0.013 [0.114]	0.018 [0.134]	0.038 [0.191]	0.035 [0.184]	0.041 [0.199]	0.010 [0.101]	0.008 [0.089]	0.013 [0.113]
Other ethnicity	0.068 [0.252]	0.069 [0.253]	0.068 [0.251]	0.074 [0.262]	0.091 [0.288]	0.055 [0.229]	0.067 [0.250]	0.064 [0.244]	0.071 [0.256]
Urban north region	0.223 [0.416]	0.194 [0.395]	0.254 [0.435]	0.296 [0.457]	0.264 [0.441]	0.330 [0.471]	0.205 [0.404]	0.177 [0.382]	0.235 [0.424]
Urban south region	0.112 [0.315]	0.104 [0.306]	0.119 [0.324]	0.204 [0.403]	0.203 [0.402]	0.205 [0.404]	0.089 [0.285]	0.081 [0.272]	0.099 [0.298]
Urban mountain region	0.063 [0.244]	0.066 [0.248]	0.061 [0.239]	0.086 [0.281]	0.085 [0.279]	0.088 [0.283]	0.058 [0.234]	0.062 [0.240]	0.054 [0.227]
Rural south region	0.310 [0.463]	0.319 [0.466]	0.300 [0.458]	0.177 [0.382]	0.209 [0.407]	0.143 [0.350]	0.342 [0.474]	0.346 [0.476]	0.338 [0.473]
Rural mountain region	0.180 [0.384]	0.209 [0.406]	0.148 [0.356]	0.038 [0.191]	0.045 [0.207]	0.030 [0.172]	0.214 [0.410]	0.248 [0.432]	0.177 [0.381]
White-collar worker	0.264 [0.441]	0.189 [0.392]	0.344 [0.475]	0.270 [0.444]	0.166 [0.372]	0.382 [0.487]	0.263 [0.440]	0.195 [0.396]	0.335 [0.472]
Owner occupation	0.287 [0.452]	0.313 [0.464]	0.259 [0.438]	0.113 [0.316]	0.096 [0.295]	0.130 [0.337]	0.329 [0.470]	0.364 [0.481]	0.290 [0.454]
Co-op member	0.044 [0.205]	0.043 [0.202]	0.046 [0.209]	0	0	0	0.055 [0.227]	0.053 [0.224]	0.056 [0.231]
Professional occupation	0.041 [0.198]	0.037 [0.189]	0.045 [0.208]	0.165 [0.372]	0.145 [0.352]	0.188 [0.391]	0.011 [0.106]	0.012 [0.107]	0.011 [0.105]

Table 6A.3 continued

Missing occupation	0.013 [0.112]	0.012 [0.108]	0.013 [0.115]	0	0	0	0.016 [0.124]	0.015 [0.120]	0.017 [0.128]
Industry produces goods	0.059 [0.236]	0.066 [0.249]	0.052 [0.222]	0.034 [0.180]	0.047 [0.211]	0.020 [0.139]	0.065 [0.247]	0.071 [0.257]	0.059 [0.237]
Industry produces agricultural products	0.387 [0.487]	0.439 [0.496]	0.331 [0.471]	0.090 [0.287]	0.088 [0.284]	0.093 [0.290]	0.458 [0.498]	0.523 [0.500]	0.388 [0.487]
Construction industry	0.037 [0.189]	0.054 [0.226]	0.018 [0.134]	0.054 [0.227]	0.095 [0.293]	0.011 [0.103]	0.033 [0.178]	0.044 [0.206]	0.02 [0.140]
Sales industry	0.060 [0.237]	0.050 [0.218]	0.070 [0.256]	0.030 [0.171]	0.020 [0.140]	0.041 [0.199]	0.067 [0.250]	0.057 [0.232]	0.077 [0.267]
Transportation industry	0.054 [0.226]	0.083 [0.276]	0.023 [0.149]	0.071 [0.258]	0.138 [0.345]	0	0.050 [0.218]	0.070 [0.256]	0.028 [0.166]
Missing industry	0.079 [0.269]	0.080 [0.271]	0.078 [0.268]	0.345 [0.582]	0.375 [0.484]	0.354 [0.479]	0.010 [0.010]	0.009 [0.093]	0.012 [0.107]
Sample size	6017	3119	2898	1162	602	560	4855	2517	2338

Note: *Cells contain the mean of the variable with the standard deviation below it in brackets.

7. Household non-farm business formation in the Kyrgyz Republic, 1993–97

The emergence of small and medium private enterprises is often seen as a key to successful transition from central planning to a market economy, although comparative evidence is limited due to the lack of data outside the more developed European transition economies.[1] This chapter draws on the LSMS-style household surveys in the Kyrgyz Republic to (1) describe the characteristics of small businesses in the Kyrgyz Republic's early transition years, (2) examine the determinants of small business creation, and (3) analyse the determinants of small business profitability.

All of the surveys contain a question asking whether households have non-farm businesses, and the positive responses to this question form the dataset for the analysis in this chapter. The reported household enterprises are small, although this approach will not capture all businesses considered small or medium-sized. The advantage of using the LSMS data, rather than trying to create a sample of small businesses, is that the sampling is nationwide and representative of all households, and the sample set involves no subjective judgment on the part of the researcher.

Evidence about the nature of household businesses in the Kyrgyz Republic in 1993, 1996 and 1997 is presented in Sections 2 and 3. Both the descriptive statistics and logit analysis provide strong results about characteristics of households reporting non-farm businesses. Such businesses tend to be in urban households with younger and better-educated heads. Households with businesses are less likely to be poor. Household businesses appear to have a short lifespan with an average age in all three surveys of about two years.

The fourth section addresses impediments to household enterprises' operation in the Kyrgyz Republic, as revealed by responses to questions in the 1996 and 1997 surveys. In these surveys households with businesses were invited to select from a list the main challenges faced by their business; the list included the main obstacles raised in the literature on small businesses in transition economies. In the Kyrgyz Republic, problems in output markets, the price of non-labour inputs, and red tape and other government-related issues are the most-cited challenges, while credit difficulties are rarely listed among the main challenges.

1. NEW ENTERPRISES IN FORMERLY PLANNED ECONOMIES

Privatization has proven far more difficult and complex than many foresaw at the start of the transition from centrally planned economies. Large-scale privatization was slower than anticipated even in the most committed reformers of eastern Europe and the former Soviet Union, and the nature of privatization mattered. Even measuring the share of the private sector in transition economies is difficult, given the many arrangements for 'golden shares' or other mechanisms by which states have retained effective control over formally privatized enterprises. In the poorer countries in transition, the issue is complicated by differing definitions of private agriculture. The rounded numbers in the EBRD estimates of private sector development, reported in Table 7.1, reflect these ambiguities and uncertainties. An analytical implication is that we should examine the various forms of private-sector activity separately, rather than in a heterogeneous aggregate.

Table 7.1 Privatization in Central Asian Economies*

	Kazakh.	Turkmen.	Uzbek.	Kyrgyz Republic	Tajik.
1990	5	10	10	5	10
1991	5	10	10	15	10
1992	10	10	10	20	10
1993	10	10	15	25	10
1994	20	15	20	30	15
1995	25	15	30	40	15
1996	40	20	40	50	20
1997	55	20	45	60	25
1998	55	30	45	70	25

Note: *Private sector output as a share of GDP, as reported in EBRD (1999).

The small enterprise sector has boomed since 1989 in the more successful Central European transition economies.[2] Konings et al. (1996) found that job creation in Poland during the early years of transition was located disproportionately in the private sector, where small firms were more dynamic than large firms. Bilsen and Konings (1998) reached similar conclusions on the basis of 1995–96 firm survey data from Bulgaria, Hungary and Romania. Although the ownership structure of new enterprises in China is more opaque, these findings parallel the emphasis usually placed on the township and village enterprises as the drivers of China's rapid development, especially during the first decade after the initiation of reforms in December 1978.[3]

In analysing the determinants of the emergence of new private enterprises, Green (1993) emphasizes the way in which the approach to privatization of state-owned enterprises affects the competitive position of new small firms. Green also mentions the capital constraints on new private enterprises, a point taken up by Pissarides (1998) and by Pissarides et al. (2000), and familiar from the wider literature on economic development. Bartlett and Bukvić (2001) finds in Slovenia that bureaucracy and the cost of credit are the main barriers to small and medium-sized enterprises' growth, and he emphasizes that, although the availability of finance matters, it is not the only thing. Brixiova et al. (1999) downplay the role of financial capital and emphasize human capital; in particular, the lack of skilled labour in transition economies limits entrepreneurship and the expansion of new firms.

In principle, the same constraints on new enterprise formation could obtain in manufacturing and service activities, but our knowledge is restricted because the studies of manufacturing enterprise formation are from the Central European countries characterized by relatively good governance and relatively smooth large-scale privatization. They are also the more affluent transition countries in which the human capital and own resources of potential entrepreneurs are likely to be more pronounced, not to mention the availability of domestic markets and proximity to large export markets.[4] Studies of service sector start-ups emphasize the potential of the state to block new enterprise formation if the grabbing hand of the state displaces the hidden hand of the market.[5] Ease of entry is critical to the success of service sector start-ups.[6] In all transition economies there was a large pent-up demand for restaurants and bars, taxis and other transport facilities, and other personal services. These are sectors in which entry barriers tend to be small, unless the state imposes such barriers or allows them to be imposed.[7]

There are definitional problems associated with identifying 'entrepreneurs' from surveys asking questions about self-employment, and these may be especially severe in Central Asia. Everywhere there is a dichotomous view of self-employment: 'A self-employed worker may be striving to grow wealthy by taking risks with new ventures, or she may be casting about desperately for any means to ensure survival' (Earle and Sakova, 2000, 579).[8] The positive entrepreneurial aspects of self-employment tend to be highlighted in studies of North American and western European labour markets, while the 'last resort' view of self-employment is more common in developing country studies, drawing on a long literature started by Arthur Lewis (1954) and by Harris and Todaro (1970). Within Central Asia, it is widely believed that new small enterprises were undertaken by the poorest members of society to eke out a living. Another widespread belief is that private entrepreneurs are often involved in dubious activities. Together these beliefs suggest a picture of shady dealings, rather than the more genuine entrepreneurship associated with new enterprises in countries like Poland.

2. DATA

Our dataset draws on the LSMS surveys conducted in the Kyrgyz Republic during the autumns of 1993, 1996 and 1997. For 1993 we have a sample of 1929 households, for 1996 a sample of 1951 households and for 1997 a sample of 2695 households. The stratified random samples covered about 0.25 percent of the country's total population in 1993 and 1996, and slightly more in 1997. Within the 6545 sampled households, 508 reported a non-farm business.[9] An additional 3940 reported self-employment income but not a non-farm business.

For these 508 observations we have data on the business type, use of family labour, length of operation, and fairly detailed revenue and expenditures, as well as information about the household (location, number and age of members, education levels, ethnicity, and so on). In the 1993 survey, individual adults were asked if they had a business or entrepreneurial income.[10] In the 1996 and 1997 surveys, the household was asked whether it had a non-farm business; information on a maximum of three non-farm businesses was collected. Detailed data on revenues, costs and assets were obtained for each business. Enterprises were defined as goods production, sales or services firms, and separate information was collected on each of these three types of businesses. We created a file that contained information on each business reported between 1993 and 1997; 185 enterprises in 1993, 160 in 1996, and 219 in 1997.

The totals implied by these numbers, that is, some 60–70 000 household-owned businesses in the country in 1996–97, are consistent with more recent official estimates of the number of active small and medium-sized enterprises (SMEs). The National Statistical Office reported the existence of 154 000 SMEs in the first quarter of 1999; farmers accounted for 34.2 percent, leaving some 100 000 non-agricultural businesses. The non-agricultural SMEs in these official data were small, with 24 percent of the
1 089 000 people employed in the SME sector (about 260 000 people) working in the 101 000 non-agricultural SMEs (Hubner, 1999). Ministry of Finance data on the regional structure of the SME sector report far smaller

numbers of SMEs, although they confirm the regional concentration in Bishkek and Chyi found in the LSMS survey data (Table 7.2).

Table 7.2 Regional pattern of SMEs in the Kyrgyz Republic, March 1998

Region	Population	SMEs	People employed by SMEs
Bishkek	619 900	13 178	75 607
Chyi	769 600	2 866	46 646
Osh	1 539 100	3 490	57 285
Jalalabad	887 200	1 518	24 400
Issyk-kul	434 900	1 397	22 284
Naryn	269 000	554	8 940
Talas	212 000	507	7 318

Source: Hubner (1999, 8–9), based on information from the Center for Social and Economic Reforms at the Ministry of Finance.

3. CHARACTERISTICS OF NEW ENTERPRISES IN THE KYRGYZ REPUBLIC

3.1 Four Waves of Small Enterprise Creation

The process of non-state enterprise creation in Central Asia has passed through four waves since the Stalinist era. During the destalinization process from the mid 1950s through the 1960s, gaps in provision of consumer goods and services were filled by the non-state sector, which provided food from private plots and services like car and house repairs. A second wave occurred during the Gorbachev era when cooperative and individual entrepreneurship was encouraged, and especially after 1988 when such activities were granted a legal status. In Central Asia these developments were important because of the existence of surplus labour and it was hoped that the non-state sector would provide a safety valve for the underemployed, but this phenomenon was probably less significant in the Kyrgyz republic than in the Uzbek republic or Kazakhstan (Abazov, 1997). The extent of the non-state sector by the time of the dissolution of the USSR in late 1991 is unknown, although the process of local economic reforms and experiments which occurred in other Soviet republics in the twilight of the Soviet Union was generally absent from Central Asia.

Associated with the Kyrgyz Republic's declaration of independence in 1991, the government's privatization programme moved rapidly to privatize 85 percent of the state's 4700 enterprises between 1991 and 1994. These, mostly small and medium-sized enterprises, represent a third wave of small enterprise creation. The remaining 15 percent of state enterprises were turned into joint stock companies sometimes going to workers and also private investors, although in most cases the state and the workers hold the majority shareholding.   The privatized enterprises did not experience significant increases in efficiency, and allegations of corruption and price-rigging have undermined public perceptions of the fairness of the privatization process (Tursunkhodjaev, 2000, 35).

Thus, although the Kyrgyz government moved relatively quickly to privatize the state sector, it has created a public atmosphere towards private activity that is suspicious, or at best neutral. In other aspects of the reform process, the outcome during the first decade has been at best mixed. Despite a reputation as the most reformist regime in Central Asia, many areas of the market economy and supporting institutions remain poorly developed, whether from poor implementation or from underlying factors such as the relative poverty of the country and lack of existing manufacturing base. Within this environment the fourth wave of small enterprise creation has been occurring as entrepreneurs identify market opportunities and open new businesses.

The size of the private sector remains difficult to assess, and how much entrepreneurial activity has actually been taking place is difficult to sort out from the aggregate figures. The EBRD estimates the share of private sector output in the Kyrgyz Republic's 1998 GDP at 70 percent, second only to Armenia among former Soviet republics despite a slow start in 1992 (Table 7.1).   This record fits with the Kyrgyz Republic's reputation for rapid economic reform. Yet as in all transition economies there are question marks about the true ownership of agriculture and of large enterprises. Moreover a single foreign invested enterprise, the Kumtor goldmine, has played a huge role in the Kyrgyz Republic (see the first section of Chapter 3).

3.2 Small Businesses in the LSMS Surveys

The crude figures from the LSMS surveys, reported in Table 7.3, indicate a dichotomy between 1993 on the one hand and 1996 and 1997 on the other. This probably reflects the fact that the transition from central planning had only just begun in 1993. The initial years following independence were dominated by nation building and fighting hyperinflation. The national currency was only issued in May 1993 and macroeconomic control was not established until 1995, when annual inflation first fell below fifty percent. By 1996 and 1997 the Kyrgyz Republic had a market-based economy, even if it was not functioning smoothly.   In fall 1993 the average life of the businesses was just under two years; 70 percent of the businesses had been in existence for one year or less and 12 percent for between one and two years (Figure 7.1).[11] This suggests that many of them were the results of the first wave of privatization, which began in 1991 and involved small enterprises. The average age in 1996 and 1997 was just over two years.

Table 7.3 Summary characteristics of businesses in the Kyrgyz LSMS
surveys

		1993	1996	1997
1	Number of households	1929	1959	2678
2	Number of businesses reported	185	160	219
3	2 as a percentage of 1	9.6	8.2	8.2
4	– produces goods (% of 2)	17	8	7
5	– produces services (% of 2)	27	20	23
6	– sells goods (% of 2)	56	66	68
7	Average years in operation	1.98	2.38	2.12
8	Uses family labour (% of 2)	38	92	89
9	Number of workers	7.97	1.80	1.59

In fall 1996, 63 percent had reported ages of two years or less, and in fall 1997 the age of 82 percent of the non-farm businesses was three years or less. Thus, most of the household businesses were founded after the first wave of privatization, which was more or less completed in 1994 and are new, rather than formerly state-owned, enterprises. A corollary is that many of the privatized small state enterprises did not survive.

In 1993 one-sixth of the reported businesses produced goods. By 1997 the goods-producing household enterprises have practically disappeared; only sixteen, 7 percent of the total, are goods-producing and the remainder are in service activities.[12] There are also major differences in the use of family labour and in the average number of workers. Only 38 percent of businesses reported using family labour in 1993, compared to 92 percent in 1996 and 89 percent in 1997. The average number of workers fell from around eight in 1993 to less than two in 1996 and 1997.

(a) Which households had businesses?

Table 7.4 presents summary statistics on characteristics of households that have small businesses or that report self-employment income in 1993, 1996 and 1997. Most of these characteristics differ significantly among households with no business or self-employment income, households with a family

(a) 1993

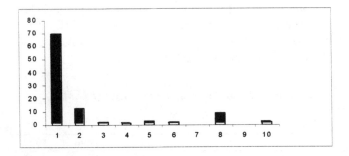

(b) 1996

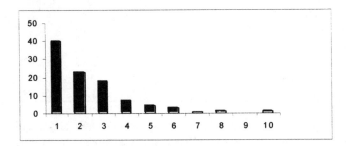

(c) 1997

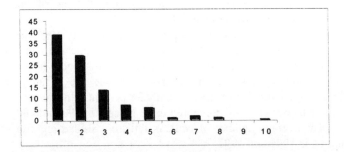

Note: Vertical axis is the proportion of the total; horizontal axis is the number of years in operation (1 = up to and including one full year, etc.; 10 = at least nine years in operation).

Figure 7.1 Age distribution of household non-farm businesses*

business, and households with other self-employment income; exceptions are male head of household and number of children in the household.

First, we examine the relationship between education and the presence of a family business. Education is a categorical variable with four categories measuring completed education of the household head: higher education, completed secondary plus some other non-college training, completed secondary education with no post-secondary training, and less than completed secondary education. We find that households with a family business are, on average, more educated than other households. Fifty-six percent of these households have heads with post-secondary training or higher education while 43–44 percent of other households have highly educated heads. The household head is also younger in households with a family business than in other households; the average age is 37 in business households, 41 in other households.

Second, ethnic differences are evident across households. Ethnicity is a categorical variable with four categories: Kyrgyz, Russian and other Slavic, Uzbek, and other ethnicity of the household head. Households with a family business are less likely to be Kyrgyz than other households. Fifty-one percent of business households are Kyrgyz, and 28 percent are Russian or other Slavic. In households with other self-employment income, 59 percent are Kyrgyz, and 24 percent are Slavic. In households with no self-employment income, 69 percent are Kyrgyz, and 21 percent are Slavic. These ethnic differences are large and strongly significant.

Third, households with a family business or other self-employment income report more working-age adults than other households but have fewer pensioners in the household. The presence of children does not differentiate business households from households without self-employment income.

Fourth, family businesses are more likely to develop in Bishkek and other urban regions of the country while households with other self-employment income are more likely to be found in rural areas. Thirty-one percent of households with a business are in Bishkek, and 37 percent are found in other urban areas. In contrast, only 17 percent of households with other self-employment income are located in Bishkek, and 20 percent are in other urban areas, while 14 percent of other households are located in Bishkek and 24 percent in other urban areas. Family business is primarily an urban enterprise.

Finally, we examine the link between self-employment and the poverty status of the household , using measures of whether the household is below a poverty line based on per capita food expenditures and whether the household is in extreme poverty.[13] We find that households with a family business are less likely to be poor or in extreme poverty than other households. There is no difference in the poverty or extreme poverty rate of households reporting other self-employment income and households without self-employment

Table 7.4 Summary statistics: household characteristics and business status*

Variables	No business	Small business	Other self-employed
Bishkek	**0.141**	**0.314**	**0.166**
	(0.348)	(0.465)	(0.372)
Other urban region	**0.236**	**0.366**	**0.198**
	(0.424)	(0.482)	(0.399)
Rural region	**0.623**	**0. 320**	**0.636**
	(0.485)	(0.467)	(0.481)
Kyrgyz ethnicity	**0.687**	**0.507**	**0.591**
	(0.464)	(0.500)	(0.492)
Slavic ethnicity	**0.214**	**0.276**	**0.239**
	(0.410)	(0.416)	(0.427)
Uzbek ethnicity	**0.040**	**0.084**	**0.087**
	(0.195)	(0.329)	(0.282)
Other ethnicity	**0.059**	**0.133**	**0.083**
	(0.236)	(0.340)	(0.276)
Less than secondary education	**0.170**	**0.121**	**0.237**
	(0.376)	(0.327)	(0.425)
Secondary education	**0.383**	**0.322**	**0.337**
	(0.486)	(0.468)	(0.473)
Some post-secondary education	**0.132**	**0.153**	**0.169**
	(0.339)	(0.360)	(0.374)
Higher education	**0.315**	**0.404**	**0.257**
	(0.465)	(0.491)	(0.437)
Male head	0.833	0.853	0.852
	(0.373)	((0.355)	(0.355)
Age of head	**41.295**	**37.484**	**41.219**
	(14.276)	(10.373)	(13.647)
Number of children in household	1.972	1.946	2.057
	(1.713)	(1.537)	(1.734)
Number of working-age adults in household	**2.178**	**2.537**	**2.449**
	(1.407)	(1.285)	(1.624)
Number of pensioners in household	**0.536**	**0.302**	**0.531**
	[.0747]	(0.592)	(0.737)
Poor household	**0.532**	**0. 316**	**0.532**
	(0.499)	(0.465)	(0.499)
Very poor household	**0.191**	**0.054**	**0.196**
	(0.393)	(0.226)	(0.397)

Table 7.4 continued

Year = 1997	**0.745**	**0.421**	**0.227**
	(0.436)	(0.494)	(0.419)
Year = 1996	**0.175**	**0.298**	**0.363**
	(0.380)	(0.458)	(0.481)
Year = 1993	**0.080**	**0.281**	**0.410**
	(0.271)	(0.441)	(0.492)
Sample size	2097	508	3940
Sample share	0.319	0.082	0.599

Note: *Mean (standard deviation). **Boldface** indicates significant difference at the 5 percent level.

income.   Thirty-two percent of business households are in poverty in comparison to 53 percent of other households.   These results suggest that family business may help keep households out of poverty.   We test the implications of these descriptive statistics in the section below.

(b) Characteristics of the businesses

Table 7.5 presents summary statistics describing the characteristics for the sample of small businesses reported in the three years.   The availability of information varies across the three years.   In 1993, 1996 and 1997, we know whether the firm produced goods, sold goods and services, or produced services.   In 1997, services are classified as café or restaurant, automobile, home appliances repair, and other services.   In each year, we know the total revenues and expenditures of each firm.   The 1996 and 1997 surveys provide more detail on these revenues and expenditures, and we report information on labour, maintenance, raw materials, utilities and fuel, taxes and license fee expenditures in addition to total firm expenditures.   We adjust expenditures, revenues, and profits in 1996 and 1997 for inflation using the consumer price index with 1993 as the base year.[14]

Business type changes over time.   In each year, most firms are retail firms and report primarily selling goods.   In 1993, 17 percent of firms produce goods and 56 percent sell goods.   By 1996–97, the percentage of firms producing goods falls to 7–8 percent and the percentage of firms selling goods increases to 66–68 percent.   The production of services falls slightly between 1993 and 1996–97, but the major change is the decline in goods production.

Table 7.5. Characteristics of small businesses*

Variables	1993	1996	1997
Business type			
Produces goods	0.173	0.081	0.074
	(0.379)	(0.274)	(0.261)
Sells goods	0.562	0.656	0.684
	(0.497)	(0.476)	(0.466)
Produces services	0. 265	0. 200	0.228
	(0.442)	(0.401)	(0.421)
– café or restaurant			0.060
			(0.240)
– automobile services			0.060
			(0.240)
– home appliance repair			0.140
			(0.351)
– other services			0.620
			(0.490)
Business characteristics			
Years in business	1.981	2.379	2.122
	(3.647)	(3.772)	(1.860)
Uses family labour	0.351	0.563	0.699
	(0.479)	(0.498)	(0.460)
Number of workers	0.384	0.919	0.886
	(0.488)	(0.274)	(0.319)
Real total revenues	7.972	1.796	1.592
	(74.658)	(1.908)	(1.510)
Real total expenditure	1,175.427	924.115	724.138
	(3813.674)	(4081.522)	(1666.851)
Expenditures on business			
Labour	1113.286	1785.143	1093.633
	(3605.975)	(4826.740)	(2101.972)
Maintenance		260.471	35.486
		(1410,253)	(149.673)
Raw materials		15.847	20.268
		(75.416)	(74.982)
Utilities and fuel		201.545	115.535
		(1159.987)	(911.465)
Taxes		159.654	62.145
		(1129.497)	(262.582)

Table 7.5 continued

Licenses		185.834	15.337
		(2074.792)	(111.421)
Profitability			
Firm is profitable		9.409	10.261
		(23.675)	(25.212)
Real total profit	0.730	0.406	0.393
	(0.445)	(0.493)	(0.489)
	62.141	-861.028	-369.495
	(4293.682)	(5364.529)	(2112.416)
Sample size	185	160	219

Note: *Mean (standard deviation)

Among firms reporting service production in 1997, most are in the 'other' category (62 percent). Six percent of firms report restaurant or automobile service production, and 14 percent report appliance repair. We cannot determine from our data whether there is a shift in the type of services produced by family businesses over the transition period.

The ownership of these firms changes dramatically over time. In 1993, only 35 percent of these firms report full ownership of the business. By 1996, 56 percent of these firms are fully owned and this percentage rises to 70 percent in 1997. This increase in the family's ownership of business capital is positively correlated with the use of family labour. The number of workers employed by family firms declines over time, but households are significantly more likely to use family labour in 1996–97 than in 1993. In 1993, only 38 percent of household businesses use family labour, and the average number of workers is eight. In 1996–97, 89–92 percent of businesses used family labour, and the average number of workers declines to less than two.

Even with these dramatic changes in the use of family inputs, we find that family businesses struggle to survive. Real expenditures rise from 1113 soms in 1993 to 1785 soms in 1996; they fall to 1094 soms in 1997. Labour, raw materials, and utilities and fuel expenses account for the largest share of these expenditures in 1996 and 1997, and almost all of these expenditures are higher in 1996 than in 1997. Real revenues on average are not able to keep up with the increase in expenditures. Real revenues fall from 1175 soms in 1993 to 924 soms in 1996 and 724 soms in 1997. The result is a large drop in firm profit over time. In 1993, the average firm is able to cover its costs, and profit is 62 soms. By 1996–97, expenditures are greater than revenues for the average firm, and reported profit is negative at 861 soms in 1996 and 369 soms in 1997. Only 39–40 percent of these businesses report positive profit in 1996–97, a decline from 73 percent in 1993. In the analysis below, we try to determine which households and regions are most likely to experience financial problems over the transition period.

3.3 Models of Family Business Development

In this section, we develop models to explain the decision by households to start a family business. We assume that the decision by a household to develop a business (Y_i) depends on the characteristics of the household and the region of the country in which the household is located. The characteristics of the household that likely influence the business decision are the human capital of the household (X_h), the family composition of the household (X_c), the demographic characteristics of the household (X_d), and its location (X_r). We measure human capital with the education and age (experience) of the household head. We expect businesses to form in households with more adult members relative to dependent children, because adults have more human capital and real world experience and are more productive in employment than children. We also expect to find more businesses in urban environments where the retail market is larger. We control for ethnicity and gender of the head of household, but we have no priors as to the effects of these characteristics on business development.

We estimate the model above using the pooled household data for 1993–97. We control for the fixed year effects with dummy variables for 1997 and 1996. We first assume that Y is a categorical variable equal to one if the household reports a family business and equal to zero if the household reports other self-employment income or no self-employment income. We estimate this model using maximum likelihood logit. The likelihood function is:

$$\text{Ln L} = \sum_{j=1}^{k} w_j \ln F(x\beta) + \sum_{j=k+1}^{\tau} w_j \ln[1 - F(x_j\beta)] \tag{7.1}$$

where k households report a business, $T - k$ households do not report a business, and $F(x_j\beta) = e^{x_j\beta} / (1 - e^{x_j\beta})$.[15] In the first column of Table 7.6, we report the logit coefficient (β) and its standard error; statistically significant coefficients are boldfaced. We also compute and report in square brackets the marginal effect of each variable on the probability of having a family business. For dummy variables, this marginal effect is the difference between the predicted probability of having a business if the dummy variable is equal to one and the predicted probability of having a business if the dummy variable is equal to zero: $P(Y = 1) - P(Y = 0)$. For continuous variables, the marginal effect is the change in the predicted probability if the independent variable increases by one unit. All marginal effects are evaluated at the mean values of the other variables.

In our second model, we look at the decision of households to have self-employment income but not have a family business. Y in this case is equal to one if other, self-employment income is reported and is equal to zero if the household has a family business or has no self-employment income. We estimate this model with logit and report the results in Table 7.6, column (3).

Finally, we assume that the household has three choices – to form a business, to receive self-employment income from other sources, or to have no self-employment income. Y in this case is equal to 1 if the household has no self-employment income, is equal to 2 if the household has a family business, and is equal to 3 if the household has other self-employment income. These choices are not ordered. We estimate a set of coefficients, β, for each Y category using multinomial logit (Greene, 2000, 859–62):

$$P(Y_i = k) = \frac{\exp\left(\sum_{j=0}^{p} x_{ij}\beta_{jk}\right)}{\sum_{m=1}^{T}\exp\left(\sum_{j=1}^{p} x_{ij}\beta_{jm}\right)} \qquad (7.2)$$

where $P(Y_i = k)$ is the probability that household i chooses k ($k = 1$, 2, or 3), p is the number of X variables in the model, and T is the number of choices. To identify the model, β is set equal to 0 for one of the choices (no self-employment income) and is estimated for the other two (having a household business or having other self-employment income). The coefficients and standard errors from the multinomial logit estimation are reported in columns (2) and (4) of Table 7.6. The marginal effects of a unit change in the independent variable on the probability of choosing outcome Y are reported in brackets.

Turning to the results of the small business and other self-employment estimation, we find that education does have a strong effect on the business decision but has no significant effect on other self-employment. If the head has completed higher education, the probability of starting a business is 0.036 higher relative to less educated households. Completing secondary education also has a positive effect on business start-up but completing post-secondary, non-college training does not affect the business decision. Education has no effect on the decision to have other forms of self-employment.

Age of the head, our other measure of human capital, has a significant effect on the development of family business, but the effect is negative. This is consistent with the descriptive results. Younger heads are more likely to be in households that have a business.[16] Age has no effect on other forms of self-employment.

Consequences of creating a market economy

Table 7.6 Logit models of business selection: pooled data 1993–97*

Variables	Small Business		Other Self-employed	
	Logit	Multinomial Logit	Logit	Multinomial Logit
Constant	**–3.069**	**–1.503**	**1.247**	**1.684**
	(0.293)	(0.148)	(0.176)	(0.198)
Year = 1997	0.136	**–1.851**	**–2.450**	**–2.929**
	(0.125)	(0.148)	(0.081)	(0.098)
	[0.009]	[–0.010]	[–0.512]	[–0.510]
Year = 1996	0.092	**–0.716**	**–0.697**	**–0.957**
	(0.132)	(0.159)	(0.085)	(0.104)
	[0.006]	[–0.007]	[–0.112]	[–0.110]
Head has higher	**0.558**	**0.511**	–0.171	–0.082
education	(0.162)	(0.178)	(0.093)	(0.103)
	[0.035]	[0.036]	[–0.032]	[–0.037]
Head has secondary	0.256	0.139	–0.161	–0.165
education +	(0.186)	(0.206)	(0.108)	(0.121)
other training	[0.014]	[0.014]	[–0.030]	[–0.035]
Head has secondary	**0.392**	**0.498**	0.085	0.170
education only	(0.0 23)	(0.187)	(0.094)	(0.104)
	[0.035]	[0.023]	[0.015]	[0.011]
Russian and	0.216	**0.314**	0.090	0.140
other Slavic	(0.140)	(0.154)	(0.088)	(0.097)
ethnicity	[0.014]	[0.014]	[0.017]	[0.013]
Uzbek ethnicity	**0. 726**	**0.985**	0.203	**0.555**
	(0.163)	(0.197)	(0.125)	(0.151)
	[0.042]	[0.046]	[0.037]	[0.052]
Other non-Kyrgyz	**0.752**	**0.999**	0.072	**0.353**
ethnicity	(0.156)	(0.181)	(0.114)	(0.132)
	[0.060]	[0.061]	[0.013]	[0.010]
Number of adults in	**0.114**	**0.182**	**0.048**	**0.089**
household of	(0.037)	(0.042)	(0.023)	(0.026)
working age	[0.009]	[0.009]	[0.009]	[0.008]
Number of	**–0.357**	**–0.296**	**0.134**	**0.087**
pensioners in	(0.081	(0.087)	(0.042)	(0.046)
household	[–0.021]	[–0.020]	[0.025]	[0.027]
Number of	0.024	**0.100**	**0.099**	**0.116**
children in	(0.0 35)	(0.038)	(0.020)	(0.022)
household	[0.002]	[0.002]	[0.018]	[0.017]

Table 7.6 continued

Bishkek	**1.370**	**1.534**	–0.150	**0.258**
	(0.137)	(0.154)	(0.090)	(0.102)
	[0.102]	[0.101]	[–0.027]	[0.030]
Other urban	**1.176**	**0.992**	**–0.494**	**–0.277**
	(0.123)	(0.134)	(0.077)	(0.085)
	[0.080]	[0.079]	[–0.092]	[–0.095]
Male head	0.075	0.124	0.079	0.114
	(0.145)	(0.159)	(0.089)	(0.098)
	[0.005]	[0.004]	[0.015]	[0.016]
Age of head	**–0.024**	**–0.025**	0.004	–0.002
	(0.005)	(0.005)	(0.003)	(0.003)
	[–0.002]	[–0.001]	[0.001]	[–0.001]
Sample size	6466	6466	6466	6466
Pseudo R-square	0.089	0.184	0.180	0.184
Chi square	**314.85**	**2058.97**	**1556.84**	**2058.97**

Note: *Cells contain logit coefficients with standard errors in parentheses underneath the coefficient, and the marginal effect in square brackets beneath the standard errors. **Boldface** indicates coefficients significantly different from zero at the 5% level.

Household composition affects family business formation. The more working-age adults in the household, the more likely is the household to have a business or to report self-employment income. The marginal effect of one adult in the household on the probability of family business is equal to the marginal effect on the probability of other self-employment (0.009). However, households with pensioners are less likely to have a family business and more likely to have other self-employment income, while children have no effect on family business but also have a positive effect on other self-employment. The positive effects of children and elderly household members on the probability of other self-employment are stronger than the marginal effect of prime-age adults. Family size is important to self-employment in the household, but only prime-age adults matter in the formation of a business.

Ethnic differences are measured in our probability models. Consistent with the summary statistics, we find that Slav, Uzbek, and other non-Kyrgyz households are more likely to form businesses than Kyrgyz households. The marginal effect (relative to Kyrgyz) is 0.014 for Slav households, 0.046 for Uzbek households, and 0.061 for other households. Ethnic effects are weaker in the receipt of other self-employment income. We find no Kyrgyz–Slavic differences, but Uzbeks and other households are more likely to report other self-employment income.

Finally, region and time affect the formation of family business. As expected, households in urban areas are more likely to form businesses. The probability of having a business is 10 percent higher in Bishkek and 8 percent higher in other urban centres than in rural areas. In contrast, other self-employment is less likely in Bishkek or other urban centres than in the rural areas. Consistent with the descriptive statistics, family business is primarily an urban activity. We also measure significant change in the formation of businesses over the transition period. From our multinomial logit model, we estimate a significant decline in 'other self-employment' over the transition period with the largest changes in 1997. The relative declines in other self-employment were 11 and 51 percent respectively in 1997 and 1996 in comparison to 1993. The changes in business formation are relatively small.[17]

3.4 The Effect of Business Formation and Self-employment on Living Standards

We next examine the impact of business formation and self-employment on the well-being of households. We estimate logit models of poverty and extreme poverty (Y) as a function of the household characteristics above and self-employment status. The model is assumed to be fully recursive. The results from the estimation of these two models are given in Table 7.7.

Households with self-employment income are less likely to be poor or in severe poverty, and the presence of a family business has a larger negative effect on poverty than the availability of other self-employment income. For households with a non-farm business, the probability of being poor is 15 percent lower than for other households, and the probability of being in severe poverty is 14 percent lower. In comparison, households with other self-employment are 4 percent less likely to be poor or in severe poverty. These results suggest that family businesses are associated with higher family living standards on average.

In summary, we find that human capital, location, and family composition affect business formation and self-employment. Businesses are more likely to form in the urban areas of the country and in households with well-educated heads and mostly prime-age adult members. Ethnic differences in business formation are also quite large. We also find that non-farm business has a positive effect on the well-being of the average household. Households with a non-farm business or other self-employment income are less poor than other households. Policy which encourages the formation of family enterprises may be important to an overall poverty reduction strategy.

Table 7.7 Logit models of family business, self-employment and poverty, 1993–97*

Variables	Poor	Very Poor
Constant	**−0.384**	**−1.075**
	(0.180)	(0.223)
Non-farm business	**−0.795**	**−1.280**
	(0.123)	(0.216)
	[−0.152]	[−0.136]
Other self-employed	**−0.197**	**−0.272**
	(0.072)	(0.083)
	[−0.038]	[−0.038]
Year = 1997	−0.057	**−0.800**
	(0.082)	(0.099)
	[−0.012]	[−0.107]
Year = 1996	**0.925**	**−0.376**
	(0.079)	(0.093)
	[0.173]	[−0.056]
Head has higher education	**−0.529**	**−0.758**
	(0.090)	(0.118)
	[−0.104]	[−0.089]
Head has secondary school + other training	0.030	**−0.294**
	(0.101)	(0.124)
	[0.006]	[−0.039]
Head has secondary education only	**0.215**	0.180
	(0.0 91)	(0.106)
	[0.042]	[0.027]
Russian and other Slavic ethnicity	**−0.318**	**−0.687**
	(0.085)	(0.128)
	[−0.062]	[−0.086]
Uzbek ethnicity	**−0. 354**	**−0.513**
	(0.111)	(0.137)
	[−0.069]	[−0.067]
Other non-Kyrgyz ethnicity	**−0.8142**	**−1.282**
	(0.113)	(0.190)
	[−0.159]	[−0.136]
Number of adults in household of working age	**0.135**	**0.069**
	(0.022)	(0.024)
	[0.026]	[0.009]
Number of pensioners in household	**0.179**	0.048
	(0.042)	(0.049)
	[0.034]	[0.006]

Table 7.7 continued

Number of children in household	**0.328**	**0.232**
	(0.021)	(0.022)
	[0.068]	[0.032]
Bishkek	**−1.527**	**−1.430**
	(0.099)	(0.187)
	[−0.303]	[−0.142]
Other urban region	**−0.226**	**−0.322**
	(0.072)	(0.096)
	[−0.047]	[−0.044]
Male head	−0.128	−0.057
	(0.088)	(0.119)
	[−0.024]	[−0.007]
Age of head	−0.002	0.003
	(0.002)	(0.003)
	[−0.001]	[0.001]
Sample size	6466	6466
Pseudo R^2	0.187	0.135
Likelihood ratio chi^2	**1677.47**	**833.69**

Note: *Cells contain logit coefficients, standard errors in brackets underneath the coefficient, and the marginal effect in square brackets. **Boldface** indicates coefficients significantly different from zero at the 5 percent level.

3.5 Business Profitability

Our final analyses address business performance in 1993–97. We examine the pooled sample of 558 firms and estimate, to the extent possible, whether these firms are able to cover their costs in each year. The dependent variable in these models (Y) is equal to one if total revenues are greater than total costs and is equal to zero if the revenues are less than or equal to expenditures.[18] We estimate the effects of household characteristics, region, and time on the probability of reporting a positive profit using logit estimation.[19]

These models of profitability have low explanatory power, but the models are significant. However, we find that only two of the independent variables – number of children in the household and urban residence – have any effect on the outcome in 1993 and 1996. The most important factor in profitability seems to be transition itself. We find that firms are less profitable in 1996 and 1997 than in 1993, and the differences are large. Profitability is about 30 percent lower in each year relative to 1993. There are no effects of human capital or experience in the business on the probability of making a profit. We can draw no implications about business management from these models.

3.6 How Comprehensive a Picture do the Surveys Provide?

The survey responses provide a useful picture of change during the transition process. The surveys are not a panel but they are sufficiently similar in coverage and questions to possess properties of consistency. The picture of the privatized small and medium-sized enterprises of the 1990s having a limited lifespan, especially in manufacturing, and of the emergence of new private enterprises in service sectors once the transition process was further established, is a plausible one.

The survey data are less convincing in providing a comprehensive picture of small-scale entrepreneurial activity at a point in time, and the omission may have become more serious as the transition progressed during the second half of the 1990s. James Anderson's more focussed single-period survey of 770 'informals' in Mongolia, mainly in the capital city, suggests some likely omissions from the Kyrgyz surveys. Major groupings in Anderson's study were in the retail and transport sectors, and many of these informals did not actually consider themselves to be entrepreneurs or to have businesses. The description of taxis would fit Bishkek:

> A 'taxicab' in Ulaanbaatar means simply a vehicle that will carry a passenger for money. In the early part of the 1990s, formal taxicabs (i.e. vehicles clearly painted or marked as taxis) were virtually non-existent. However, anyone who could afford it only had to wave to passing vehicles for a moment or two before one would stop to pick them up. At any point in time, there exists a fare per kilometre that is widely known and accepted by both drivers and passengers. Every vehicle in Ulaanbaatar is a potential taxicab. (Anderson, 1998, 31–2)

Of Ulaanbaatar's taxi drivers 72 percent were moonlighters with other 'primary' jobs, even though income from taxi driving almost certainly dominated other income.[20]

In answering questions about whether they had a business, respondents to the Kyrgyz LSMS surveys may have under-reported activities such as taxi driving, food selling or trading.[21] Some of these under-reported activities, such as the sad scenes of peasants selling a few fruit or vegetables by the roadside, involve poor people supplementing an inadequate income, but given the need for capital (a car for taxiing or working capital for retailing) most of these under-reported activities are likely to be undertaken by better off members of society. However, if the Mongolian parallels apply, size limits are imposed by the tendency of 'informals' to be individual, or at most family, concerns.

4. CHALLENGES FACING NON-FARM HOUSEHOLD ENTERPRISES[22]

The short average lifespan of the businesses in our sample and anecdotal reports of the difficulties of small enterprises suggest that despite the Kyrgyz Republic's reputation for liberalism there are obstacles to entrepreneurial activity. Data on perceived challenges to the operation of an enterprise are available in the 1996 and 1997 surveys. For each household business, the respondent is asked to list the three most significant challenges the business faced during the past year. These business challenges include: high input prices, the lack of inputs, high interest rates on credit, the lack of credit, high taxes, low demand for the product, high cost of labour, difficulty finding good (skilled) workers, extortion, low production capacity, difficulty getting a legal licence to operate the business, violence, and other reasons. In 1996 139 businesses out of 160 report at least one challenge to the business, and 214 businesses out of 219 in 1997 report at least one

Table 7.8 The most important challenge to the operation of a non-farm household business in the Kyrgyz Republic, 1996 and 1997*

Business challenge	1996	1997	Total
High input prices	14 (10.07)	51 (23.83)	65 (18.41)
Lack of inputs	14 (10.07)	8 (3.74)	22 (6.23)
High interest rates	3 (2.16)	11 (5.14)	14 (3.97)
Lack of credit	6 (4.32)	7 (3.27)	13 (3.68)
High taxes	47 (33.81)	75 (35.05)	122 (34.56)
Low product demand	32 (23.02)	41 (19.16)	73 (20.68)
High labour cost/low quality	0	0	0
Extortion	7 (5.04)	7 (3.27)	14 (3.97)
Low capacity	1 (0.72)	3 (1.40)	4 (1.13)
Licence difficulty	4 (2.88)	1 (0.47)	5 (1.42)
Other	11 (7.91)	10 (4.67)	21 (5.95)
Sample size	139	214	353

Note: *Numbers in parentheses are column percentages. Differences in the challenges in 1996 and 1997 are statistically significant; Pearson chi-square statistic (11 degrees of freedom) = 22.825.

Table 7.9 The second most important challenge to the operation of a non-farm household business in the Kyrgyz Republic, 1996 and 1997*

Business challenge	1996	1997	Total
High input prices	3 (2.48)	20 (12.50)	23 (8.19)
Lack of inputs	3 (2.48)	4 (2.50)	7 (2.49)
High interest rates	0	3 (1.88)	3 (1.07)
Lack of credit	0	6 (3.75)	6 (2.14)
High taxes	32 (26.45)	39 (24.38)	71 (25.27)
Low product demand	36 (29.75)	48 (30.00)	84 (29.88)
High labour cost	2 (1.65)	0	2 (0.71)
Lack of good labour	0	1 (0.62)	1 (0.36)
Extortion	20 (16.53)	16 (10.00)	36 (12.81)
Low capacity	3 (2.48)	1 (0.62)	4 (1.42)
Licence difficulty	11 (9.09)	6 (3.75)	17 (6.05)
Other	11 (9.09)	16 (10.00)	27 (9.61)
Sample size	121	160	281

Note: *Numbers in parentheses are column percentages. Differences in the challenges in 1996 and 1997 are statistically significant; Pearson chi-square statistic (11 degrees of freedom) = 26.042.

Table 7.10 The third most important challenge to the operation of non-farm household business in the Kyrgyz Republic, 1996 and 1997*

Business challenge	1996	1997	Total
High input prices	5 (4.59)	8 (6.67)	13 (5.67)
Lack of inputs	5 (4.59)	4 (3.33)	9 (3.93)
High interest rates	0	4 (3.33)	4 (1.75)
Lack of credit	1 (0.92)	6 (5.00)	7 (3.06)
High taxes	10 (9.17)	9 (7.50)	19 (8.30)
Low product demand	11 (10.09)	19 (15.83)	30 (13.10)
High labour cost	1 (0.92)	1 (0.84)	2 (0.87)
Lack of good labour	2 (1.83)	1 (0.84)	3 (1.31)
Extortion	13 (11.93)	27 (22.50)	40 (17.47)
Low capacity	8 (7.34)	1 (0.83)	9 (3.93)
Licence difficulty	9 (8.26)	15 (12.50)	24 (10.48)
Other	44 (40.36)	25 (20.83)	69 (30.13)
Sample size	109	120	229

Note: *Numbers in parentheses are column percentages. Differences in the challenges in 1996 and 1997 are statistically significant; Pearson chi-square statistic (11 df) = 27.506.

challenge. Table 7.8 reports the distribution of the most important challenge reported by businesses in 1996 and 1997, while Tables 7.9 and 7.10 tabulate the distribution of the second and third challenges in each year; the differences between 1996 and 1997 are statistically significant in all three tables.[23]

High taxes, low product demand and high input (non-labour) costs are the three most cited main challenges to operation of a household business in both 1996 and 1997. As their most important challenge, 35 percent of businesses list high taxes, 21 percent of businesses list low product demand, and 18 percent list high, non-labour input costs.   While the 1996 and 1997 distributions in Table 7.8 differ, the percentages reporting these three as their main challenge are not significantly different between 1996 and 1997. These three challenges are also relatively important in Tables 7.9 and 7.10.   In addition, when we expand our analysis to include the second and third challenges to business, extortion, violence, and difficulty obtaining a legal licence to operate the business are also significant business concerns. Among those reporting a second challenge to business, 13 percent of firms report extortion problems and 6 percent report problems obtaining a licence. Among those reporting a third challenge to business, 17 percent report extortion and 10 percent report difficulty obtaining a licence. In 1996, when violence was included as a separate category, 8 percent of firms listed it as their second challenge and 20 percent reported violence as their third challenge.

In Table 7.11, we tabulate whether the challenge to business was reported as one of the three major problems, and report tests of whether the reporting of each challenge differs between 1996 and 1997.   High taxes and low product demand are the most cited challenges to business in both years, and the reporting incidence for these challenges does not differ between the two years.   Sixty percent of businesses report that taxes are too high and 52 percent report low product demand. Twenty-nine percent of businesses report that input prices are too high and the difference between the percentage reporting this problem in 1996 and 1997 is statistically significant; 16 percent report this problem in 1996, but 37 percent report it in 1997. Extortion is reported by 25 percent of all firms, with no significant difference in the percentage between 1996 and 1997.   Violence was reported as a major challenge by 24 percent of firms in 1996, but not identified separately in 1997. Licence difficulties are reported by 13 percent of all firms.

Table 7.11 Business challenges reported in 1996 and 1997*

Business Challenge	1996	1997	Total
High input prices	**22** (15.83)	**79** (36.92)	**101** (28.61)
Lack of inputs	**22** (15.83)	**16** (7.48)	**38** (10.76)
High interest rates	3 (2.16)	**18** (8.41)	21 (5.95)
Lack of credit	7 (5.04)	19 (8.88)	26 (7.37)
High taxes	89 (64.03)	123 (57.48)	212 (60.06)
Low product demand	76 (54.68)	107 (50.00)	183 (51.84)
High labor cost	3 (2.16)	1 (0.47)	4 (1.13)
Lack of good labour	2 (1.44)	2 (0.93)	4 (1.13)
Extortion	39 (28.06)	50 (23.36)	89 (25.21)
Low capacity	**12** (8.63)	**5** (2.34)	**17** (4.82)
Licence difficulty	24 (17.27)	22 (10.28)	46 (13.03)
Other	**63** (45.32)	**51** (23.83)	**114** (32.29)
Sample size	139	214	353

Note: *If the difference in reporting a challenge in 1996 and 1997 is statistically significant at the five percent level, then the frequency is in boldface. Numbers in parentheses are column percentages; the column totals sum to over 100 percent because up to three challenges are recorded for each enterprise.

The problems facing household businesses in the Kyrgyz Republic do not seem to be related to input availability, credit availability, or capacity concerns. Labour costs are also not a significant challenge to business management, although this may be related to the dominance of family labour in 1996–97 reported in the previous section. Problems reported by business are related to the product market, both low output demand and high non-labour input prices, and to government (that is, taxes, licencing, corruption, and breakdown of law and order).[24]

How does the evidence from the Kyrgyz Republic relate to broader debates about obstacles to new enterprises in formerly centrally planned economies? Our knowledge of obstacles to new enterprises is restricted, because most existing studies deal with Central European countries characterized by relatively good governance and relatively smooth large-scale privatization. These are also the more affluent transition countries in which the human capital and own resources of potential entrepreneurs are likely to be more pronounced, not to mention the availability of domestic markets and proximity to large export markets.

The Kyrgyz Republic is one of the poorer economies in transition, and as mentioned in the introduction the nature of our data places the focus on small, rather than medium-sized, enterprises. The disruption caused by the massive shocks of dissolution of the USSR, new state formation and hyperinflation during the early 1990s ensured that the disorganization identified by Blanchard and Kremer (1997) as a feature of transition was especially pronounced in Central Asia, and might explain the continuing concerns about input prices and output demand in 1996–97.[25]   High input prices were not due to trade barriers, because the Kyrgyz Republic already had a liberal trade regime with low and fairly uniform tariffs and in 1998 would become the first Soviet successor state to accede to the World Trade organization.[26] The reliance on family labour meant that high labour costs and lack of labour do not feature among the reported challenges to household businesses.

Limited opportunities help to explain the phenomenon of household businesses being associated with educated household heads.   College-educated people have been better able to identify new opportunities in the massive economic disequilibria of the 1990s (Chapter 4 above), and although they do not require university training taxi-driving and similar family businesses may have yielded a higher income than any alternative activity open to university-educated people in Bishkek in the mid 1990s.   This contrasts with mixed findings from Eastern Europe, where well-educated people could access better opportunities and small enterprises are often run by people without university degrees.

Our finding that credit availability is not a concern to household businesses in the Kyrgyz Republic may reflect their small family-labour nature, and the fact that the household businesses covered in this chapter are primarily engaged in service sector activities. The finding is, however, consistent with other empirical studies, especially of poorer Asian transition economies. Financial constraints on new enterprises appear to have been minor in China and Vietnam, both of whose economies have been characterized by financial repression.[27]

Concerns about the grabbing hand are echoed in entrepreneurs' emphasis on high taxes, licence difficulties, extortion, and the breakdown of law and order as the main challenges facing them in the Kyrgyz Republic. The fact that about a quarter of the Kyrgyz Republic respondents include extortion, and similar numbers report violence in 1996, among their three main challenges is extraordinary. From the survey instruments it is not entirely clear what these categories include; high taxes and licence difficulties clearly involve the grabbing hand of the state, but extortion and violence may be at the hands of customs officers, local officials, police, or private sector criminal elements.   Anecdotal evidence could be cited in support any of these interpretations and the survey data itself cannot resolve the issue. Other sources suggest that the Kyrgyz Republic is not an extreme case; in the Business Environment and Enterprise Performance survey of firms in twenty transition countries (EBRD, 1999), for example, the percentage of firms in the

Kyrgyz Republic reporting that they bribe frequently (27 percent) is below the 20 country average (and remarkably similar to the extortion results reported in Table 7.4) and the average bribe as a percentage of firm's revenue (5.5 percent) is above the average, but neither is far from the mean.[28] Nevertheless, the implied breakdown of law and order is substantial and belies the Kyrgyz Republic's image as a peaceful little market-friendly country.[29]

5. CONCLUSIONS

Based on survey data from the Kyrgyz Republic for 1993, 1996 and 1997, we conclude that:

1. The widely reported categories of small business entrepreneurs and 'self-employed' are not identical. As found by Earle and Sakova in eastern Europe, the latter group are rarely entrepreneurs – although we do find that they are also not among the poorest groups.
2. The privatized small enterprises are a distinct group from the new private enterprises of the transition era. The latter are smaller, rely more on family labour, and are more totally concentrated in service activities.
3. Households with small businesses tend to be urban, with better educated and younger heads, fewer pensioners, and are not Kyrgyz.

Although reported profitability was very low, especially in 1996–97, and we had little success analysing the determinants of profitability, the small businesses were not associated with poverty, but rather appear to be associated with characteristics of economically more dynamic members of the community. The picture from the Kyrgyz Republic clearly supports the view of new private enterprises as dynamic phenomena, rather than desperate measures to cope with poverty.[30]

We also used household survey data from 1996 and 1997 to analyse the challenges facing non-farm household businesses in the Kyrgyz Republic. The nature of the data source means that we are primarily dealing with small businesses and relying on the household's own interpretation of what is in fact a business. The challenges too are as reported by the households themselves. Allowing these caveats, the picture is a clear one. High taxes, low product demand and high input prices are the three most cited challenges, implying that the general economic environment is tough for these new enterprises. The frequent mention of licence difficulties and extortion, in addition to high taxes, indicates that the grabbing hand of the government is perceived as a major obstacle to private businesses. The government is also failing to maintain law and order, to the extent that about a quarter of the businesses report extortion and violence among their three main challenges.[31]

NOTES

1.   The importance of encouraging new enterprises is one of the two central themes (the other theme is the need to discipline the old state enterprises, whether privatized or not) of the World Bank's assessment of the first ten years of transition from central planning in eastern Europe and the Soviet Union (World Bank, 2002).

2.   For a sceptical review of the literature on small enterprise development in Central and Eastern Europe during the 1990s, see the second section of the survey by Bateman (2000).

3.   Naughton (1995), however, in his analysis of China's rapid growth during the 1980s emphasizes the significance of competition between pre-existing state enterprises and new enterprises.

4.   Using survey data from two eastern European and four CIS countries, Dutz et al. (2001) find a significantly positive relationship between entrepreneurship and higher education in Poland and Croatia, a weaker relationship in Ukraine and Armenia, and no statistically significant relationship in Russia and the Kyrgyz Republic.

5.   The terminology derives from the comparison of small traders in Warsaw and Moscow made by Frye and Shleifer (1997). The success of the new enterprises in China is also associated with jurisdictions in which officials were willing to take a hands-off approach, while provinces and cities with more interventionist regimes experienced less new enterprise formation. In Vietnam the absence of many supportive institutions for the private sector has been met by innovative responses (McMillan and Woodruff, 1999b), implying that the absence of a helping hand from the state is less significant than the presence of a grabbing hand.

6.   See, for example, the analysis of 770 informal enterprises in Mongolia by James Anderson (1998).

7.   Prevention of such enterprise formation is usually a tragedy of the anti-commons. Too many individuals or agencies are able to tap the potential rent from enterprise formation by levying taxes, charging bribes for authorizations, demanding protection money, and so forth. These all reflect poor governance because the state apparatus is weak or authority is diffused. The consequence is that sub-optimally few enterprises actually emerge.

8.   In their study, based on 1993 survey data from Bulgaria, the Czech Republic, Hungary, Poland, Russia and Slovakia, Earle and Sakova (2000) found the own account self-employed sharing characteristics, and earnings levels, of the unemployed rather than of small-scale employers, but they recognize significant difficulties in separating the categories. The finding that small business owners/workers differ from other self-employed is confirmed by our data from the Kyrgyz Republic (see Table 7.4).

9. Some households and adults were deleted from the analysis files because of missing information on variables included in our models.
10. Since this information was obtained for the individual and not the household, we compared the information given by different members of the household. If adults within the household gave identical information on a family business, we assumed it was the same business and included the information only once in our firm file. If adults gave different information on family enterprises, we assumed that they were describing different family businesses and included the information on all of these businesses in our firm file.
11. The average age is pulled up by a few outliers in the 'over nine years' category: in 1993 they are aged 10, 12, 13 and 36, in 1996 the two businesses aged over nine are 25 and 38 years old, and in 1997 the outlier is 14 years old.
12. We cannot determine from our data whether there is a shift in the type of services produced by family businesses over the transition period, because services are only broken down into subcategories in 1997. Among household firms reporting service production in 1997, most are in the 'other' category (62 percent). Six percent of firms report restaurant or automobile service production, and 14 percent report appliance repair.
13. The nutrition-based poverty line developed by Barry Popkin (1994) for the World Bank is described in Chapter 4.
14. The CPI for 1996 is 321, and the CPI for 1997 is 369. The CPI was obtained from the European Bank for Reconstruction and Development Transition Reports.
15. This is similar to the probit model used in Chapters 4 and 6, apart from that the logit model assumes a logistic rather than a normal distribution for $F(x\beta)$. The logit model gives greater weight to the tails of the distribution, although in practice results from the two models tend to be similar (Greene, 2000, 815). We use logit in this chapter for comparability with Earle and Sakova (2000) and because the multinomial model is easier to estimate as a logit.
16. Dutz et al. (2001) find that an age 26–35 variable is the only significant correlate of being an entrepreneur in the Kyrgyz Republic. Their higher education variables had positive, but not significantly different from zero, coefficients. Overall, the explanatory power of their Kyrgyz Republic regression was low (pseudo R^2 of 0.004), perhaps because they only used a single year of data, 1997.
17. The coefficients on 1996 and 1997 in the business model are negative but the marginal effects of each year are small and positive. This is because the negative effects on other self-employment are very large and swamp the effects of business choice.
18. The 1996 and 1997 surveys include detailed information on expenditures so that measures of variable costs can be constructed. For 1993, however, only total business expenditures were reported and some of these expenditures were fixed capital expenses. Because we cannot separate fixed costs from variable costs for 1993, we include fixed expenditures in our 1996 and 1997 total expenditure measures so that we can compare 1996–97 to 1993. Profit is, therefore, equal to total revenues minus total fixed and variable costs, and the report of profit is based on this profit calculation.

19. These results are available upon request.
20. The 308 taxi drivers surveyed by Anderson in February 1997 reported an average monthly income of almost 200 000 togrog, by far the highest of any informal sector in Mongolia and over 50 per cent higher than the salary of the President of Mongolia.
21. In 1993 question 34 on the survey asked whether the respondent engaged in any kind of entrepreneurial activity regardless of whether the enterprise was registered or not. The printed question mentions producing equipment and tools, making clothes, shoes, wood products or other goods, providing medical services or tutoring, working privately as a hairdresser or cobbler. In other words it tries to be wide-ranging, although how this was transmitted by the enumerators and received by the interviewees is unclear. The wording in 1996 and 1997 differed, but had similar intent.
22. This section draws on research reported in greater detail in Anderson and Pomfret (2001c).
23. Violence is listed separately in 1996 but not in 1997. For comparative and statistical purposes violence is included in the 'other' category in the tables. The remaining categories are identical in the two years.
24. A World Bank project on private sector development in rural areas of the Kyrgyz Republic (Musaeva et al., 2000) reports some similar findings on the basis of anecdotal evidence. New businesses took at least two to three months to pass through the licensing bodies, and many businessmen were unhappy with the size of the fees required. Once in operation businessmen reported a multiplicity of checks for tax payments, of financial statements, for sanitary standards, for fire safety requirements, and for compliance with a host of other regulations, and the 'scornful attitude of officials' during compliance checks was sometimes accompanied by ungrounded faultfinding, bribery and extortion. The report states that 44 out of 148 firms reported having had to make illicit payments and that in terms of key challenges tax payments rank first, but these results are difficult to assess given the non-random sampling and low response rate (due to fears that interviewers were in some way related to tax assessment).
25. Similar concerns are voiced in neighbouring countries. Khalmurzaev (2000, 290–91) writing about Uzbekistan, lists lack of capital as the number one problem for small and medium-sized enterprises, followed by marketing of output, access to materials, and contacts with tax authorities, but he also acknowledges that for enterprises in the service sphere 'it is much easier to find money'. Although Khalmurzaev mentions a survey conducted by a market research company, he gives no details and so it is difficult to assess the evidence upon which these conclusions are based.
26. The small domestic market may still have permitted monopoly pricing, especially of non-traded inputs. It may also be that the responses capture perceptions of high input prices, based on historical standards which after half a decade of high inflation were out of touch with reality.
27. In China there is some evidence of financial sector innovation and new financial institutions emerging in response to the new non-state enterprises' demand as those enterprises expanded beyond their original small and medium scale; see the study by Cheng et al. (1998) and other papers in the special issue

of *MOCT-MOST: Economic Policy in Transitional Economies* on financial reform in China. On Vietnam, see McMillan and Woodruff (1999a).

28.   The BEEP survey was conducted in June/August 1999, and in the Kyrgyz Republic involved 132 firms. Hellman et al. (2000) break down the services provided in return for the bribes; in the Kyrgyz Republic, 54 percent of the bribes were paid to deal with taxes (more than 10 percentage points higher than the share devoted to tax-related matters in any of the other nineteen countries) and tax collection and 15 percent were paid to obtain licences and permits. Although the BEEP sample was not representative and included 25 state and 57 ex-state enterprises as well as 50 new private enterprises, the priority given to tax issues and to a lesser extent licences is strikingly consistent with our results for household enterprises.

29.   In the early years after independence, the Kyrgyz Republic was promoted as the 'Switzerland of Asia' (Pomfret, 1995, 106–18). By 1996 and 1997, it was becoming clear that the government was having increasing difficulty enforcing the rule of law, especially in the face of the burgeoning narcotics trade based on production in Afghanistan and the location of Osh (the second city of the Kyrgyz Republic) as the railhead for shipments to Europe.

30.   This is consistent with the finding of Dutz et al. (2001, 9–10), based on five transition economies, that entrepreneurship is associated with higher consumption although ironically their finding was supported by data from Armenia, Croatia, Russia and Ukraine, but not by the Kyrgyz Republic data.

31.   This chapter draws on research in Anderson and Pomfret (2001a, 2001b).

8. Conclusions

All of the new independent Central Asian countries suffered a large negative economic shock with the end of central planning and the dissolution of the USSR. Traditional supply chains and guarantees of economic security suddenly became unreliable, and national expenditure dropped sharply as intra-USSR transfers dried up between 1991 and 1993 and real GDP fell. The extent of the shock varied from country to country, but in none of the five countries had real GDP returned to its 1989 level by the end of the 1990s.

Living standards declined, but changes in average living standard were accompanied everywhere by increasing inequality and shifts in households' positions within the distribution. The evidence is most plentiful for the Kyrgyz Republic, which moved most rapidly to establish a market-oriented economy and experienced a sharp increase in inequality and in the number of people in poverty by 1993. During those initial years, however, the determinants of households' place in the income distribution appear to have changed little, with households in the capital city and with well-educated heads faring best; the only positive correlates of poverty reflected pre-existing rural–urban and regional distinctions. Between 1993 and 1996 the aggregate picture stabilized somewhat, but the determinants of household living standards changed, with the variables entering in the human capital model usually fitted to market economies' earnings distributions assuming greater explanatory power. Tertiary education, in particular, became more important as a positive determinant of household expenditures, while the number of dependents (especially children) became increasingly closely related, negatively, to a household's position in the distribution.

The data are less satisfactory for the other Central Asian countries but similar trends appear to be at work. Kazakhstan has followed a similar strategy to the Kyrgyz Republic, and living standards appear to have followed a similar path, although the incidence of poverty is much less in view of the higher initial living standards and endowments of natural resources. Uzbekistan has pursued a more gradual transition strategy which seems to have mitigated the increase in inequality and poverty, but many of the changes in the determinants of the household's place in the distribution are similar to those observed in the Kyrgyz Republic. Turkmenistan resisted economic change, at least until the disastrous economic performance of 1997–98, and although living standards declined their determinants may have changed little. Tajikistan has been disrupted by civil war.

The main implications for the welfare system are that a social safety net needs to be erected to protect those hurt by transition, but the old universal policies are poorly suited to the new environment. In view of the limited administrative capacity in the new independent states, detailed means testing is scarcely feasible and simpler targeting methods are needed. The evidence on living standards suggests that a prime target for assistance should be households with many dependents, especially children and possibly the elderly, although, especially with the elderly, simple tagging may lead to support going to the non-poor or perverse incentive effects. Some combination of tagging and local administration may be an appropriate approach to this dilemma. Given the importance of human capital formation, it may also be a most effective means of assisting families with many children for the state to subsidize education and health-care for children.

1. GROUPS AT RISK: IMPLICATIONS FOR THE WELFARE SYSTEM

Women, children and the elderly are often considered to be especially at risk in situations of extensive poverty. The evidence from Central Asia is, however, rather mixed and on the whole more positive than might be expected.

A more or less universal finding from economies in transition is that families with many children suffered much more during transition than families with many pensioners. At least in the early years pensioners were relatively well-protected; Anderson and Becker (1999) document this for the Kyrgyz Republic. Eligibility was extended in some cases to cushion increased unemployment and other economic pressures; in Kazakhstan in the mid-1990s, half of pensioners were receiving early retirement pensions (de Castello Branca, 1998). Maintenance of the generous Soviet pension schemes, however, placed heavy burdens on public finances. These were addressed by stop-gap measures such as delayed payments,[1] by more fundamental changes such as cutting pension payments, raising the retirement age and eliminating special categories, and in Kazakhstan by replacing the old pay-as-you-go system by a defined benefits scheme. In the Kyrgyz Republic, an increase in the pension receipt age is being phased in.

Some women have undoubted suffered in the new market economy. One of the first service sectors to flourish was prostitution and many newspaper reports have documented how poorly informed women became involved in trafficking for the sex trade. Unemployment has been heaviest among women, although this may be a misleading indicator in the transition context. The negative developments have been extensively documented for Central Asian countries in Bauer, Green and Kuehnast (1997), Bauer, Boschmann and Green (1997) and Falkingham (2000a). The household survey data, however, reveals a more complex picture than these anecdotal data. Educated women have been among the biggest beneficiaries of the move to a market economy. More generally, within the workplace there is no evidence from wages paid, hours worked or labour force participation that Central Asian women have on average suffered more than men.

Children are a different matter. The deteriorating situation in Kazakhstan and the Kyrgyz Republic is reviewed and supported by anecdotal evidence in Bauer et al. (1998). The household survey data analysis confirms that families with many children have been hard hit by the collapse of the Soviet state and the move to a market economy. Cuts to education and primary healthcare have exacerbated the risks facing poor children. This is a serious problem not only for immediate humanitarian reasons, but also because failure to provide for large numbers of children is eroding the countries' human capital which is a major source of future growth potential.

In the context of pre-existing universal entitlements and poor administrative capacity for targeting welfare programmes, a first step for transition economies could be to use easily measurable indicators of poverty, rather than income, to tag deserving recipients (Akerlof, 1978; Barr, forthcoming). Where indicators are highly correlated with poverty and easily observable, tagging is accurate and administratively undemanding and, as long as the indicator is exogenous, disincentive effects are weakened. Thus, targeting age or number of children could be an appropriate strategy, although simple indicators may be flawed insofar as they fail to take into account household circumstances, for example single pensioners may be more at risk than the elderly in extended families. Decentralization could also help if tags can vary geographically, and in general local authorities may be more adept at identifying the poor, but distribution across regions is difficult.

The analysis of Kyrgyz households' income reported in Chapter 4 suggests that region and number of children are easy tagging criteria. Thus, poverty relief should be targeted on the southern parts of the country. Similar regional patterns appear in other Central Asian countries,[2] or in the company town phenomenon in Kazakhstan. Targeting poor regions is a way to reach those most hurt by transition, but it risks discouraging the labour mobility which must emerge as part of a healthier market economy. The Kyrgyz data also reveal a dynamic problem, illustrated by the mountain region's displacement in the mid 1990s by the south as the poorest part of the country; poverty relief targeted at mountain pastoralists in the early years of independence may have been inappropriate as such groups were better placed to weather the changing conditions than the southern sedentary farmers. Any targeting based on analysis of past household survey data risks being outdated. One message of the regional results may be that the appropriate policy response should focus less on targeting poor regions than on improving mobility through investment in transport infrastructure, information spreading about jobs, creation of a well-functioning housing market, and so forth.[3]

A general finding about formerly centrally planned economies is that the (private) cost of large families, and especially the cost of having many children, has increased during the transition to a more market-oriented system (Cornia, 1995; Milanovic, 1998, 101–4). However, in their empirical study of seven transition economies, including Kazakhstan and the Kyrgyz Republic, Lanjouw et al. (1998) show that the relative importance of the number of children and of pensioners is highly sensitive to assumptions about economies of scale in household size. During transition these scale economies have increased with housing privatization and diminishing public support for maintenance and utilities, although some countervailing forces (for example the reduced provision of kindergarten services) have increased the marginal cost of children. Greater economies of scale make it less likely that additional dependents will reduce household living standards significantly, but economies of scale in the household increase the relative deprivation of pensioners who live alone or in small households.[4] The treatment of economies of scale in the household is rather opaque in the empirical studies cited in the previous three sections, so that although the balance of the evidence leans towards large numbers of children being the major correlate of poverty in Central Asia a question mark remains over the robustness of this conclusion.

The Kyrgyz data suggest that age in itself is a poor tagging variable, even though some groups of the elderly, such as single women living in the capital, are high-risk groups when it comes to poverty. This is a classic example of the need to recognize household circumstances rather than simply tagging age. If household circumstances are recognized, however, perverse incentives may be created, because key attributes are not exogenous. For example, if pensioners living alone are targeted for special assistance, the elderly may be encouraged to leave the more caring environment of the extended family in response to the financial incentives to be a single pensioner.[5]

Social spending has followed different national patterns. In the Kyrgyz Republic substantial foreign assistance enabled the government to maintain the share of public spending going to health and education, especially as donors encouraged investment in human capital, although the real amounts dropped with the decline in GDP.[6] In Kazakhstan, health care was one of the first casualties of independence, as the share of government spending going to health fell by about a third in 1992 and the percentage of GDP spent on health fell from 4 percent to 2 percent where it stayed in subsequent years (Brooks and Thant, 1998, 249). In Turkmenistan and Tajikistan social spending also declined as governments devoted diminishing aggregate public funds to pet projects in the one case and to military spending in the other. Uzbekistan stands out as the exception where the government has maintained domestically-generated social spending (Pomfret and Anderson, 1997) and introduced innovative measures to target social assistance (Coudouel and Marnie, 1999).

2. LOOKING AHEAD: IMPLICATIONS FOR FUTURE ECONOMIC DEVELOPMENT

Short- and medium-term considerations have tended to dominate debates over the transition from central planning. In particular, should the government introduce distortionary microeconomic policies to assist the poor, or will these policies anger the politically powerful upper classes? In the longer term, the best strategy for reducing poverty is economic growth. This book has emphasized the importance of education for determining household performance during the 1990s, and also as an instrument for promoting gender equity and entrepreneurship.

NOTES

1. Delayed pension payments became serious in Kazakhstan, whose government initiated a reform in 1996 based on a Chilean-type system of mandatory, privately-managed, competitively-funded pensions (Baldridge, 1999).
2. For evidence on Uzbekistan see Falkingham et al. (1997, 100–17).
3. The UNDP is sponsoring an innovative project in the Kyrgyz Republic tracking changes in human development indicators, which should help to cast more light on dynamic aspects of relative poverty.
4. Female-headed households also appear much more likely to be among the poorest when significant scale economies are assumed, because female-headed households are typically small.
5. Child benefits could also create perverse incentives if parents had more children in order to receive child support payments, but there is a longer time lag and the decision to bring an extra child into the household is less readily reversible than moving an elderly person out of the household.
6. There is also anecdotal evidence of regional disparities as the northern regions are treated better than the southern regions. Conditions in the two southern oblasts are described by Howell (1996a). Center for Preventive Action (1999, 180–1) quotes from a 1997 official report on Djalalabad oblast that 'Since 1990, the education sector has had to cope with a severe cutback in financing. There have been virtually no allocations from the domestic budget for textbooks, school equipment or building maintenance. Teachers' salaries have fallen dramatically in real terms. Teacher morale and performance has been

further undermined by the substantial delays in salary payments which are typically 2–4 months in arrears'.

Appendix: the LSMS data

The data used in this study were obtained from household surveys modelled after the World Bank's Living Standards Measurement Study (LSMS) surveys. The World Bank established the LSMS in 1980 to explore ways of improving the type and quality of household data collected by government statistical offices. The first two surveys were fielded in 1985 (in Côte d'Ivoire and Peru). Both were considered successful in gathering data that would allow detailed study of household behaviour and provide operational inputs into policy formation. Since these initial LSMS surveys, the World Bank has not provided sole funding nor led implementation of surveys, although it does maintain a unit to support implementation.

With the transition from central planning in Europe and the dissolution of the USSR, countries with formerly centrally planned economies wishing to supplement or replace their Household Budget Surveys (HBS) by more sophisticated household surveys could draw on the LSMS experience. The World Bank initially contracted out the technical assistance for surveys fielded in Russia (1991/2), the Kyrgyz Republic (1993) and Romania (1994/5). These surveys are better designed than the household budget surveys inherited from the Soviet era and still widely used in the former Soviet republics.

The great advantages of LSMS data over HBS data are the superior sampling techniques and the comparable sets of questions, which outweigh the drawback of the irregular collection and lack of a panel data set. The Kyrgyz Republic's LSMS surveys for 1993 and spring and fall 1996 had slightly different questionnaires, which undermine comparability across time on some issues (for example health), but the 1993 survey is the pioneer in the region and the only LSMS survey which could be considered substantially pre-transition.

The Kyrgyz LSMS surveys are typical in their sampling techniques. Nationally representative, stratified random samples of households were drawn from the Kyrgyz Republic's population during the fall of 1993, and the spring and fall of 1996.[1] The Kyrgyz Republic's National Statistical Office conducted annual surveys in 1997 and 1998, comparable to the fall 1996 survey. The World Bank supported the initial LSMS survey with $3.5 million as a rapid response to the need to design a programme of targeted social assistance, and contributed to the $3.7 million cost of the two 1996 rounds and 1997 and 1998 surveys (Blank and Grosh, 1999, 212–3). These subventions enabled hiring and training of enumerators in sufficient numbers to handle the intensive period of interviewing.[2] All of the surveys included around 2000 households and just under 10 000 individuals, and community surveys are available for all except fall 1996. Since 1997 the National Statistical Office has switched to random sampling for its regular household budgets surveys. Since 2000 the Kyrgyz HBS have included some 3000 households, and are of sufficiently high quality that they have superseded and precluded the need for special LSMS surveys.

The survey instruments were not identical in the three years; the 1996 and 1997 surveys were the most similar, and were closer to the LSMS model than the 1993 survey. For all persons in the household at the time of the survey, data were collected on demographic characteristics, work, income, health, education and training. Adults answered questions for children, and the survey instruments on education and health differed for adults and children. The surveys differed in the content of the information collected on income and work, but there is sufficient overlap in information on adults to make comparisons over time possible. The surveys do not contain panel data. A different random sample of households was selected each year. We therefore cannot examine, within specific households, the dynamics of living standards, employment, entrepreneurship, and so forth. However, we can examine cohorts of adults and evaluate changes in the behaviour of similar households over time.

Table A1 lists the LSMS surveys completed in Central Asia during the 1990s. For LSMS surveys in Kazakhstan (1996) and Uzbekistan (aborted), the technical assistance was allocated as a result of international competitive bidding. The LSMS history in the Kyrgyz Republic illustrates one weakness of the outside contractor model, which helped to bring expertise into the country, but led to outcomes of varying quality. In the Kyrgyz Republic, the spring 1996 survey is generally considered to have been less carefully conducted than that of 1993 or later surveys. Conflicts between the host nation, the contractor and the funding bodies also arose with respect to Uzbekistan's LSMS survey, leading to its abandonment before completion (and rendering it practically useless). In all cases, the World Bank and other contractors work in conjunction with the national statistical institute, which retains control over the process and its outputs.[3]

Table A1   LSMS-style surveys conducted during the 1990s

Kyrgyz Republic (fall 1993)
Kyrgyz Republic (spring 1996)
Kyrgyz Republic (fall 1996, 1997 and 1998)
Kazakhstan (spring 1996)
Turkmenistan (spring 1998)
Tajikistan (spring 1999)

The second Central Asian country to complete a LSMS survey was Kazakhstan in 1996. It includes both a household data set, for 1996 households containing 7223 individuals, and a community survey. The Committee on Statistics and Analysis conducted a second national survey in 2001 using a data set of 12 000 households selected on the basis of the 1999 national census, and this updated sample set will form the basis of subsequent quarterly surveys.

Turkmenistan's LSMS data set, from a survey conducted in February–April 1998, is not yet in the public domain, although some summary statistics have been reported in national and World Bank publications. The survey was done by the National Institute for Statistics and Forecasting in conjunction with the Research Triangle Institute of North Carolina, USA, and included 2094 households. The poverty line used was $2.15 at PPP, estimated to be 1914 manat per day or 57 000 manat per month, and the poverty headcount was 7 percent.

The Tajikistan LSMS survey conducted in May 1999 also contains a community survey. It covered 2000 households containing 141 423 individuals from 125 *jamats*.[4] The State Statistical Committee is intending to field a second LSMS survey in spring 2002 with support from the Asian Development Bank

As mentioned above, the LSMS survey begun in Uzbekistan was aborted. We do, however, have some sub-national data of comparable quality. First, researchers from the European University Institute and Essex University conducted a household survey in June 1995 which covered three oblasts in Uzbekistan: Karakalpakstan, Fergana and Tashkent. There are data on household income, but no expenditure or community data in the survey.[5] Second, within the context of redesigning the national HBS, a pilot project, conducted in the Fergana oblast in February 1999, tested a questionnaire to be used in a countrywide survey after April 2000. The pilot survey covered 542 households and 3238 individuals. Expenditure and income data are available, but no information on communities.

Table A2 presents some summary statistics from the five LSMS surveys used most extensively in this book, focusing on variables used in the comparative analysis of Chapter 5.

The LSMS-style surveys have come under some criticism. Deniz Kandiyoti (1999a, 1999b) argues that they use categories which are ambiguous in the Central Asian context. Basic concepts such as household, employment, access to land, income and expenditure invoke different meanings for Central Asian respondents to those commonly understood by statisticians, economists and other potential users of the survey data.[6]

While analysts must always take care, these obstacles are not insuperable. The extended family means that intra-household transfers are likely to be especially important in Central Asia, but that does not invalidate analysis of the household or individual data. Most studies use expenditure rather than income as a variable to be explained, because of problems of delayed wage payment during the 1990s and a reluctance to report income that may be seized by tax authorities, even though it is recognized that underreporting may also apply to expenditure and that valuation of home production is difficult.[7]

For the first decade since independence the LSMS data sets are by far the best available source on material living standards and other social phenomena. As with all survey instruments, the data need to be treated with care, but as nationally representative surveys for four of the countries and partially representative for the other, the LSMS surveys are far richer than the ongoing HBS or other more limited surveys.

In the early years of the twenty-first century the data situation is improving rapidly in the Kyrgyz Republic and Kazakhstan, which have both moved towards using superior sampling techniques for their regular household surveys. Uzbekistan has improved its HBS more incrementally, and still has a protective attitude towards all economic and social data. Turkmenistan too is unwilling to release raw data for analysis, even though it has conducted a full LSMS survey, and there is little information about the status of the HBS. Tajikistan, with a second LSMS slated for 2002, is the only Central Asian country still in the basic LSMS era of data collection.

NOTES

1.   For a description of household selection in the LSMS, see Grosh and Glewwe (2000). The 1993 Kyrgyz Republic survey was conducted under the direction of researchers from the University of North Carolina, Paragon Research International Inc., and the Institute of Sociology of the Russian Academy of Sciences, under contract with the World Bank, and is described in Pomfret and Anderson (1999). A different consulting firm (Research Triangle Institute, 1996) advised the state statistical agency (Goskomstat) in Bishkek on the design and

evaluation of the spring 1996 survey, and Goskomstat, with consultation from the World Bank, managed the collection of the fall 1996 and 1997 data.

2.   The surveys typically cover consumption over a two-week period. Deaton (1997, 25) quotes evidence from Ghana that reported household expenditures fell by an average 2.9 percent for every day added to the reporting period. Researchers working with budget surveys from the former USSR frequently claim that amounts are significantly higher in the second week of the two-week reporting period than the first. Synchronization of interviews is important to avoid seasonal biases.

3.   The World Bank encourages the national authorities to make the data available to external researchers, but practices vary. The Kyrgyz and Kazakhstan data have generally been released for a small handling fee. The Tajikistan data are freely available on the World Bank's LSMS website. The Turkmenistan data are unavailable.

4.   The sampling technique was a two-stage random probability design. In the first stage, 125 primary sampling units (*jamats*) were randomly selected out of the country's 362 *jamats* mapped during the 2000 Census, using probability proportionate to size. In the second stage, 16 households in each *jamat* were randomly selected and interviewed. The security situation posed special problems in Tajikistan. The opposition provided assistance by nominating local enumerators in villages where central government control was insecure, and helicopters were used to reach villages cut off by insurgents or for other reasons. Only two *jamats* had to be changed from the original selection, and the survey's managers believe this had no detrimental effect on the representativeness of the sample. See Falkingham (2000c) for details.

5.   Coudouel (1998) and some of the contributors to Falkingham et al. (1997) use the 1995 survey.

6.   Falkingham (1999a) also analyses pitfalls of the Central Asian LSMS data.

7.   In the Tajikistan 1999 LSMS survey 45 percent of the consumption of rural households came from household plots, and this may be downward biased because the survey was conducted in spring (World Bank, 2000, 59). In Tajikistan, income measures are especially understated because of the importance of remittances from the up to a million Tajik workers abroad, which are almost all sent through unofficial channels as cash.

*Table A2: Summary statistics**

Variables	Kazakhstan (1996)	Kyrgyz Rep (1993)	Kyrgyz Rep (1997)	Tajikistan (1999)	Uzbekistan (1999)
Per capita expenditure (national currency units)	4863.76 (3515.27)	144.61 (140.26)	782.00 (921.11)	15,636 (13,095)	4099.36 (3869.45)
Male head (%)	61.6	81.8	86.9	91.3	93.9
Head is married (%)	72.1	77.5	77.3	85.5	90.8
Age of head (years)	46.326 (14.218)	41.337 (13.722)	39.751 (12.642)	39.850 (11.047)	38.760 (10.444)
Head is college graduate (%)	18.2	25.1	32.7	14.8	14.4
Head has post-secondary education (%)	23.2	24.5	10.8	34.6	29.4
Head has other post-secondary training (%)	10.6				
Head has completed secondary (%)	25.5	16.9	43.8	36.0	45.3
Head has incomplete secondary (%)	22.5	33.5	12.7	14.6	10.9
Head is in good health (%)	28.9	90.7	90.5	69.3	
Rural community (%)	43.6	57.1	62.6	72.8	71.5
Capital city (%)	9.4	18.4	15.1	8.9	
Region 1 (%)	20.7	22.7	13.9	4.0	
Region 2 (%)	18.1	39.1	35.0	21.5	
Region 3 (%)	8.5	19.8	36.0	30.4	

Table A2 continued

Region 4 (%)	22.3			35.2	
Region 5 (%)	21.0				
Number of children in household	1.263	1.822	2.239	3.515	2.850
	(1.228)	(1.690)	(1.740)	(2.071)	(1.601)
Number of elderly in household	0.414	0.511	0.507	0.492	0.492
	(0.676)	(0.731)	(0.732)	(0.733)	(0.742)
Number of non-elderly in household	1.914	2.603	2.846	3.065	2.643
	(1.119)	(1.800)	(1.472)	(1.812)	(1.395)
Sample size (households)	1890	1926	2618	1983	541

Note: *Standard deviations of continuous variables are in parentheses. For Kazakhstan post-secondary education is divided between Tecnikum and PTU. The regions are: Kazakhstan 1 = Central, 2 = South, 3 = West, 4 = North, 5 = East (excluding Almaty); Kyrgyz Republic 1 = Chyi, 2 = South, 3 = Mountain; Tajikistan 1 = Gorna Badakhshan, 2 = RSS, 3 = Leninabad, 4 = Khatlon.

References

Abazov, Rafis (1997): 'Formation of the Non-state Sector and Privatization in Kazakhstan and Uzbekistan', *Communist Economies and Economic Transformation*, 9(4), 431–48.

Ackland, Robert, and Jane Falkingham (1997): 'A Profile of Poverty in Kyrgyzstan', in Jane Falkingham et al. (eds), *Household Welfare in Central Asia*. Macmillan, Basingstoke UK, 81–99.

Aghion, Philippe, and Mark Schankerman (1999): 'Competition, Entry and the Social Returns to Infrastructure in Transition Economies', *Economies of Transition*, **7(1)**, 79–101.

Akanov, Aikan, and Balzhan Suzhikova (1998): 'Kazakstan', in Douglas Brooks and Myo Thant (eds), *Social Sector Issues in Transitional Economies of Asia*, Oxford University Press for the Asian Development Bank, Oxford UK.

Akerlof, George (1978): 'The Economics of "Tagging" as Applied to the Optimal Income Tax, Welfare Programs and Manpower Planning', *American Economic Review*, **68**, 8–19.

Akiner, Shirin (1997): 'Between Tradition and Modernity: The Dilemma facing Contemporary Central Asian Women', in Mary Buckley (ed.), *Post-Soviet Women: From the Baltic to Central Asia,* Cambridge University Press, Cambridge UK, 261–304.

Anderson, James (1998): 'The Size, Origins, and Character of Mongolia's Informal Sector during the Transition', *Policy Research Working Paper 1916*, World Bank, Washington DC, May.

Anderson, Kathryn, and Charles Becker (1999): 'Post-Soviet Pension Systems, Retirement and Elderly Poverty: Findings from the Kyrgyz Republic', *MOCT-MOST: Economic Policy in Transitional Economies*, **9(4)**, 459–78.

Anderson, Kathryn, and Richard Pomfret (2000): 'Living Standards during Transition to a Market Economy: The Kyrgyz Republic in 1993 and 1996', *Journal of Comparative Economics*, **26(3)**, 502–23.

Anderson, Kathryn, and Richard Pomfret (2001a): 'Gender Effects of Transition: The Kyrgyz Republic', paper presented at the American Economics Association conference in New Orleans, 5–7 January 2001 – available as *Adelaide University School of Economics Working Paper 00-8*.

Anderson, Kathryn, and Richard Pomfret (2001b): 'Development of Small and Medium Enterprises in the Kyrgyz Republic, 1993–1997', in Faculty of Economics, Split (eds), *Enterprise in Transition* (University of Split, Croatia, 2001), p.400–401 (summary in hard copy, full text on accompanying cd-rom).

Anderson, Kathryn, and Richard Pomfret (2001c): 'Challenges facing Small and Medium-sized Enterprises in the Kyrgyz Republic, 1996–7', *MOCT-MOST: Economic Policy in Transitional Economies*, **11(3)**, 205–19.

Anderson, Kathryn, and Richard Pomfret (2002a): 'Living Standards in Central Asia 1991–2001', paper presented at the American Economics Association conference in Atlanta on 3–6 January – an earlier version circulated as 'Relative Living Standards in New Market Economies: Evidence from Central Asian Household Surveys', *Adelaide University School of Economics Working Paper 01-10*.

Anderson, Kathryn, and Richard Pomfret (2002b): 'Business Start-ups in the Kyrgyz Republic', mimeo, Vanderbilt University, Nashville, TN.

Ashwin, Sarah, and Elain Bowers (1997): 'Do Russian Women want to Work?', in Mary Buckley (ed.), *Post-Soviet Women: From the Baltic to Central Asia,* Cambridge University Press, Cambridge UK, 21–37.

Atkinson, Anthony, and Andrew Brandolini (2001): 'Promise and Pitfalls in the Use of "Secondary" Data-Sets: Income Inequality in OECD Countries as a Case Study', *Journal of Economic Literature*, **39(3)**, 771–99.

Atkinson, Anthony, and John Micklewright (1992): *Economic Transformation in Eastern Europe and the Distribution of Income*, Cambridge University Press, Cambridge UK.

Baldridge, W. (1999): 'Pension Reform in Kazakhstan', in United Nations Development Programme *Central Asia 2010* (United Nations, New York), 176–81.

Barr, Nicholas (forthcoming): 'Reforming Welfare States in Post-Communist Countries', in Leszek Balcerowitz (ed.), *Ten Years After: Transition and Growth in Postcommunist Countries.*

Bartlett, Will, and Vladimir Bukvić (2001): 'Barriers to SME Growth in Slovenia, in Faculty of Economics', Split (eds), *Enterprise in Transition* (University of Split, Croatia), 198–201 (summary in hard copy, full text on accompanying cd-rom).

Bateman, Milford (2000): 'SME Development and the Role of Business Support Centres in the Transition Economies of Central and Eastern Europe', *Small Business Economics*, **14(4)**, 275–98.

Bauer, Armin, Niña Boschmann and David Green (1997): *Women and Gender Relations in Kazakstan: The Social Cost,* Asian Development Bank, Manila.

Bauer, Armin, David Green and Kathleen Kuehnast (1997): *Women and Gender Relations: The Kyrgyz Republic in Transition,* Asian Development Bank, Manila.

Bauer, Armin, Niña Boschmann, David Green and Kathleen Kuehnast (1998): *A Generation at Risk: Children in the Central Asian Republics of Kazakstan and Kyrgyzstan,* Asian Development Bank, Manila.

Becker, Charles, and David Bloom (eds) (1998): 'Special Issue: The Demographic Crisis in the Former Soviet Union', *World Development*, **26(11)**, November.

Bilsen, Valentijn, and Jozef Konings (1998): 'Job Creation, Job Destruction, and Growth of Newly Established Private Firms in Transition Economies: Survey Evidence from Bulgaria, Hungary, and Romania', *Journal of Comparative Economics*, **26(3)**, 429–45.

Blanchard, Olivier (1997): *The Economics of Post-Communist Transition*, Clarendon Press, Oxford UK.

Blanchard, Olivier, and Michael Kremer (1997): 'Disorganization', *The Quarterly Journal of Economics*, **112(4)**, 1091–1126.

Blank, Lorraine and Margaret Grosh (1999): 'Using Household Surveys to Build Analytic Capacity', *The World Bank Research Observer*, **14(2)**, 209–27.

Bloem, Adriaan, Paul Cotterell and Terry Gigantes (1998): 'National Accounts in the Transition Countries: Balancing the Biases', *Review of Income and Wealth*, **44(1)**, 1–24.

Brainerd, Elizabeth (1998): 'Winners and Losers in Russia's Economic Transition', *American Economic Review*, **88(5)**, 1094–1115.

Brainerd, Elizabeth (2000): 'Women in Transition: Changes in Gender Wage Differentials in Eastern Europe and the Former Soviet Union', *Industrial and Labor Relations Review*, **54**, 138–162.

Brixiova, Zuzana, Wenli Li and Tarik Yousef (1999): 'Skill Acquisition and Firm Creation in Transition Economies', *IMF Working Paper WP/99/130*, International Monetary Fund, Washington DC.

Brooks, Douglas, and Myo Thant (1998): *Social Sector Issues in Transitional Economies of Asia*, Oxford University Press, for the Asian Development Bank, Oxford UK.

Brownstone, David, and Camilla Kazimi (2001): 'Applying the Bootstrap', in James Heckman and Edward Leamer (eds), *Handbook of Econometrics*, vol.5, Elsevier, Amsterdam NL.

Brownstone, David, and Robert Valletta (2001): 'The Bootstrap and Multiple Imputations: Harnessing Increased Computing Power for Improved Statistical Tests', *Journal of Economic Perspectives*, **15(4)**, 129–41.

Buchinsky, Moshe (1998): 'Recent Developments in Quantile Regression Models', *Journal of Human Resources*, **33**, 88–126.

Buckley, Cynthia (1998): 'Rural/Urban Differentials in Demographic Processes: The Central Asian States', *Population Research and Policy Review*, **17(1)**, 71–89.

Buckley, Robert, and Eugene Gurenko (1997): 'Housing and Income Distribution in Russia: Zhivago's Legacy', *World Bank Research Observer*, **12(1)**, 19–32.

Cangiano, Marco, Carlo Cottarelli, and Luis Cubeddu (1998): 'Pension Developments and Reforms in Transition Economies', *IMF Working Paper WP/98/151,* International Monetary Fund, Washington DC, October.

CER (1997): 'Methods and Applications of Poverty Analysis: Case of Uzbekistan', *CER Report 1997/4*, Centre on Economic Research, University of World Economy and Diplomacy, Tashkent.

Center for Social and Economic Research in Kyrgyzstan (2001): *Kyrgyz Economic Outlook.*

Center for Preventive Action (1999): 'Calming the Ferghana Valley: Development and Dialogue in the Heart of Central Asia', *Preventive Action Reports,* vol. 4, The Century Foundation Press, New York.

Chase, Robert (1998): 'Markets for Communist Human Capital: Returns to Education and Experience in the Czech Republic and Slovakia', *Industrial and Labor Relations Review*, **51(3)**, April, 401–23.

Cheng, Enjiang, Christopher Findlay and Andrew Watson (1998): 'We're not Financial Organisations! Financial Innovation without Regulation in China's Rural Cooperative Funds', *MOCT-MOST: Economic Policy in Transitional Economies*, **8(3)**, 41–55.

Cornia, Giovanni Andrea (1995): 'Ugly Facts and Fancy Theories: Children and Youth during the Transition', *Innocenti Occasional Papers, Economic Policy Series No. 47*, UNICEF International Development Centre, Firenze.

Cornia, Giovanni Andrea (1996): 'Transition and Income Distribution: Theory, evidence and initial interpretation', *Research in Progress 1*, United Nations University World Institute for Development Economics Research, Helsinki.

Coudouel, Aline (1998): *Living Standards in Transition: The case of Uzbekistan*, PhD Thesis, Department of Economics, European University Institute, Firenze.

Coudouel, Aline, Alastair McAuley and John Micklewright (1997): 'Transfers and Exchange between Households in Uzbekistan', in Jane Falkingham et al. (eds), *Household Welfare in Central Asia,* Macmillan, Basingstoke UK, 202–220.

Coudouel, Aline, and Sheila Marnie (1999): 'From Universal to Targeted Social Assistance: An Assessment of the Uzbek Experience', *MOCT-MOST: Economic Policy in Transitional Economies*, **9(4)**, 443–58.

De Broeck, Mark, and Vincent Koen (2000): 'The Great Contractions in Russia and the other Countries of the Former Soviet Union: A view from the supply side', *IMF Working Paper WP/00/32*, International Monetary Fund: Washington DC.

De Castello Branca, Marta (1998): 'Pension Reform in the Baltics, Russia and Other Countries of the Former Soviet Union', *IMF Working Paper WP/98/11*, International Monetary Fund, Washington DC.

Deaton, Angus (1997): *The Analysis of Household Surveys: A Microeconometric Approach to Development Policy,* Johns Hopkins University Press, for the World Bank, Baltimore MD.

Dmitrieva, Oksana (1996): *Regional Development: The USSR and After,* St. Martin's Press, New York.

Dutz, Mark, Celine Kauffmann, Serineh Najarian, Peter Sanfey and Ruslan Yemtsov (2001): 'Labour Market States, Mobility and Entrepreneurship in Transition Economies', *EBRD Working Paper No. 66,* European Bank for Reconstruction and Development, London UK.

Earle, John, and Zuzana Sakova (2000): 'Business Start-ups or Disguised Unemployment? Evidence on the Character of Self-employment from Transition Economies', *Labour Economics,* 7, 575–601.

EBRD (1996): *Transition Report 1996,* European Bank for Reconstruction and Development, London UK.

EBRD (1997a): *Transition Report 1997,* European Bank for Reconstruction and Development, London UK.

EBRD (1997b): *Transition Report Update, April 1997,* European Bank for Reconstruction and Development, London UK.

EBRD (1998): *Transition Report 1998,* European Bank for Reconstruction and Development, London UK.

EBRD (1999): *Transition Report 1999,* European Bank for Reconstruction and Development, London UK.

EBRD (2000): *Transition Report 2000,* European Bank for Reconstruction and Development, London UK.

EBRD (2001): *Transition Report Update, April 2001,* European Bank for Reconstruction and Development, London UK.

Efron, Bradley and Robert Tibshirani (1993): *An Introduction to the Bootstrap,* Chapman & Hall, New York NY.

Esentugelov, Arystan (2000): 'The Kazak Regions in the Transition Process', *Kazakstan Economic Trends,* January–March (Berlin: German Institute for Economic Research, for the European Union's Tacis programme).

Falkingham, Jane (1999a): 'Measuring Household Welfare: Problems and pitfalls with household surveys in Central Asia', *MOCT-MOST: Economic Policy in Transitional Economies,* **9(4),** 379–93.

Falkingham, Jane (1999b): 'Welfare in Transition: Trends in Poverty and Well-being in Central Asia', *CASE Paper 20,* Centre for Analysis of Social Exclusion, London School of Economics, London UK, February.

Falkingham, Jane (2000a): *Women in Tajikistan,* Asian Development Bank, Manila.

Falkingham, Jane (2000b): 'From Security to Uncertainty: The impact of economic change on child welfare in Central Asia', *Innocenti Working Papers,* no.76, UNICEF, Innocenti Research Centre, Florence, Italy – also forthcoming in Tim Smeeding and Koen Vleminckx: *Child Well-being,*

Child Poverty and Child Policy in Modern Nations: What do we know? The Policy Press, Bristol.

Falkingham, Jane (2000c): 'A Profile of Poverty in Tajikistan', ESRC Centre for the Analysis of Social Exclusion Discussion Paper No. 39, London School of Economics, London UK.

Falkingham, Jane, Jeni Klugman, Sheila Marnie and John Micklewright (eds) (1997): *Household Welfare in Central Asia,* Macmillan, Basingstoke UK.

Finkel, Eugen, and Helen Garcia (1997): 'Rehabilitating the Kyrgyz Republic's Power and District Heating Services', in Michael Cernia and Ayse Kudat (eds), *Social Assessments for Better Development: Case studies in Russia and Central Asia,* World Bank, Washington DC, 187–97.

Fischer, Stanley, Ratna Sahay and Carlos Vegh (1996): 'Stabilization and Growth in Transition Economies: The Early Experience', *Journal of Economic Perspectives,* **10(2)**, 45–66.

Flanagan, Robert (1995): 'Wage Structures in the Transition of the Czech Economy', *IMF Staff Papers,* **42(4)**, 836–54.

Flanagan, Robert (1998): 'Were Communists good Human Capitalists? The Case of the Czech Republic', *Labour Economics,* **5(3)**, 295–312.

Foster, James, J. Greer and Eric Thorbecke (1984): 'A Class of Decomposable Poverty Measures', *Econometrica,* **52**, 761–5.

Frye, Timothy, and Andrei Shleifer (1997): 'The Invisible Hand and the Grabbing Hand', *American Economic Review, Papers and Proceedings,* **87**, 354–8.

Glinskaya, Elena, and Thomas Mroz (2000): 'The Gender Gap in Wages in Russia from 1992 to 1995', *Journal of Population Economics,* **13(2)**, 353–86.

Green, David, and Richard Vokes (1997): 'Agriculture and the Transition to the Market in Asia', *Journal of Comparative Economics,* **25**, 250–80.

Green, Edward (1993): 'Privatization, the Entrepreneurial Sector, and Growth in Post-Comecon Economies', *Journal of Comparative Economics,* **17**, 407–17.

Greene, William (2000): *Econometric Analysis,* 4th ed., Prentice Hall, Upper Saddle River NJ.

Gregory, Paul (1982): 'Fertility and Labor Force Participation in the Soviet Union and Eastern Europe', *Review of Economics and Statistics,* **64(1)**, 18–31.

Griffin, Keith, ed. (1996): *Social Policy and Economic Transformation in Uzbekistan,* International Labour Office, Geneva.

Grootaert, Christiaan, and Jeanine Braithwaite (1998): 'Poverty Correlates and Indicator-based Targeting in Eastern Europe and the Former Soviet Union', ms. *Poverty Reduction and Economic Management Network,* World Bank, May.

Grosh, Margaret, and Paul Glewwe (1998): 'Data Watch: The World Bank's Living Standards Measurement Study Household Surveys', *Journal of Economic Perspectives,* **12**, 187–96.

Grosh, Margaret and Paul Glewwe (2000): 'Making Decisions on the Overall Design of the Survey' in Margaret Grosh and Paul Glewwe (eds). *Designing Household Survey Questionnaires for Developing Countries: Lessons from 15 Years of the LSM Study,* vol.1, World Bank, Washington DC, 21–41.

Gürgen, Emine, Harry Snoek, Jon Craig, Jimmy McHugh, Ivailo Izvorski, and Ron van Rooden (1999): 'Economic Reforms in Kazakhstan, Kyrgyz Republic, Tajikistan, Turkmenistan, and Uzbekistan', *Occasional Paper 183,* International Monetary Fund, Washington DC.

Gustafsson, Björn, and Shi Li (2000): 'Economic Transformation and the Gender Earnings Gap in Urban China', *Journal of Population Economics,* **13(2)**, 305–29.

Ham, John, Jan Svejnar and Katherine Terrell (1999): 'Women's Unemployment during Transition: Evidence from Czech and Slovak Micro-data', *Economics of Transition,* **7(1)**, 47–78.

Harris, J. and Michael P. Todaro (1970): 'Migration, Unemployment, and Development: a Two Sector Analysis', *American Economic Review,* **60(1)**, 126–42.

Heckman, James (1979): 'Sample Selection Bias as a Specification Error', *Econometrica,* **47**, 153–61.

Heleniak, Timothy (1997): 'Mass Migration in Post-Soviet Space', *Transition,* **8(5)**, 15–18.

Hellman, Joel, Geraint Jones, Daniel Kaufmann and Mark Schankerman (2000): 'Measuring Governance and State Capture: The Role of Bureaucrats and Firms in Shaping the Business Environment – Results of a Firm-Level Study across 20 Transition Economies', *EBRD Working Paper No. 51,* European Bank for Reconstruction and Development, London UK.

Horowitz, Joel, and N.E. Savin (2001): 'Binary Response Models: Logits, Probits and Semiparametrics', *Journal of Economic Perspectives,* **15(4)**, 43–56.

Horowitz, Joel (2001): 'The Bootstrap', in James Heckman and Edward Leamer (eds), *Handbook of Econometrics,* vol.5, Elsevier, Amsterdam NL.

Howell, Jude (1996a): 'Poverty and Transition in Kyrgyzstan: How some households cope', *Central Asian Survey,* **15(1)**, 59–73.

Howell, Jude (1996b): 'Coping with Transition: Insights from Kyrgyzstan', *Third World Quarterly,* **17**, 53–68.

Hubner, Wojciech (1999): 'Technical Assistance to SME in Kyrgyzstan: Building the Regional Network', paper prepared for the OECD/UNIDO FEED Forum, Istanbul June 8–10, 1999.

Hunt, Jennifer (1998): 'The Transition in East Germany: When is a Ten Point Fall in the Gender Pay Gap Bad News?', *CEPR Discussion Paper Series in*

Transition Economies No.1805, Centre for Economic Policy Research, London UK.

Hunt, Jennifer (1999): 'Determinants of Non-employment and Unemployment Durations in East Germany', *NBER Working Paper 7128*, National Bureau of Economic Research, Cambridge MA, May.

IMF (1998a): 'Republic of Tajikistan: Recent Economic Developments', *IMF Staff Country Report No.98/16*, International Monetary Fund, Washington DC, February.

IMF (1998b): 'Turkmenistan: Recent Economic Developments', *IMF Staff Country Report No.98/81*, International Monetary Fund, Washington DC, September.

IMF (1998c): *World Economic Outlook, May 1998*, International Monetary Fund, Washington DC, May.

IMF (2000a). 'Republic of Kazakhstan: Selected Issues and Statistical Appendix', *Staff Country Report No.00/29*, International Monetary Fund, Washington DC, March.

IMF (2000b): '*World Economic Outlook, October 2000: Focus on Transition Economies*', International Monetary Fund, Washington DC, October.

IMF (2001). 'Tajikistan: Second Review Under the Third Annual Arrangement Under the Poverty Reduction and Growth Facility and Request for Waiver of a Performance Criterion – Staff Report and News Brief on the Executive Board Discussion', *Staff Country Report No.01/115*, International Monetary Fund, Washington DC, July.

Ismail, Suraiya, and Hereward Hill (1997): 'Nutritional Status in the Kzyl-Orda Area of Kazakhstan', in Jane Falkingham et al. (eds), *Household Welfare in Central Asia*, Macmillan, Basingstoke UK, 141–60.

Jovanovic, Branko (2001): 'Russian Roller Coaster: Expenditure Inequality and Instability in Russia, 1994–98', *Review of Income and Wealth*, **47(2)**, 251–71.

Juhn, Jinhui, Kevin Murphy and Brooks Pierce (1991): 'Accounting for the Slowdown in Black-White Wage Convergence', in Marvin Kosters (ed.), *Workers and their Wages,* AEI Press, Washington DC, 107–43.

Jurajda, Štepán (2000): 'Gender Wage Gap and Segregation in Late Transition', *William Davidson Institute Working Paper No.306*, University of Michigan, Ann Arbor MI, May.

Kalyuzhnova, Yelena (1998): *The Kazakstani Economy: Independence and Transition*, Macmillan, Basingstoke UK.

Kandiyoti, Deniz (1999a): 'How to get it Wrong in Rural Uzbekistan: An Ethnographic Critique of Household Survey Categories', *DPR Discussion Paper 0699*, Centre for Development Policy & Research, School of Oriental and African Studies, University of London, UK.

Kandiyoti, Deniz (1999b): 'Poverty in Transition: An Ethnographic Critique of Household Surveys in Post-Soviet Central Asia', *Development and Change*, **30(3)**, 499–524.

Kapur, Ishan, and Emmanuel van der Mensbrugghe (1997): 'External Borrowing by the Baltics, Russia and Other Countries of the Former Soviet Union: Developments and Policy Issues', *IMF Working Paper WP/97/72*, International Monetary Fund, Washington DC.

Kaser, Michael, and Santosh Mehrotra (1996): 'The Central Asian Economies after Independence', in Roy Allison (ed.), *Challenges for the Former Soviet South*, Brookings Institution, Washington DC (for the Royal Institute of International Affairs, London UK), 217–305.

Keane, Michael, and Eswar Prasad (1999): 'Consumption and Income Inequality in Poland during the Economic Transition', *IMF Working Paper WP/99/14*, International Monetary Fund, Washington DC.

Khalmurzaev, Nurullo (2000): 'Small and Medium-sized Enterprises in the Transition Economy of Uzbekistan: Conditions and Perspectives', *Central Asian Survey*, **19(2)**, 281–96.

Klugman, Jeni (1997): 'Education and Equity in the Former Soviet Republics: Disruption and Opportunities in Financing and Governance', background paper for Chapter 4.3 of the MONEE Project CEE/CIS/Baltics Regional Monitoring Report No.5 *Education for All?* UNICEF International Child Development Centre, Firenze IT.

Klugman, Jeni (1998): *Wages in Transition: The Case of Uzbekistan*, PhD Thesis, Australian National University, Canberra.

Klugman, Jeni, and Jeanine Braithwaite (1998): 'Poverty in Russia during the Transition: An overview', *World Bank Research Observer*, **13**, 37–58.

Klugman, Jeni, Sheila Marnie, John Micklewright and Philip O'Keefe (1997): 'The Impact of Kindergarten Divestiture in Central Asia', in Jane Falkingham et al. (eds), *Household Welfare in Central Asia*, Macmillan, Basingstoke UK, 183–201.

Koenker, Roger, and Gilbert Bassett (1978): 'Regression Quantiles', *Econometrica*, **46(1)**, 33–50.

Koenker, Roger, and Kevin Hallock (2001): 'Quantile Regression', *Journal of Economic Perspectives*, **15(4)**, 143–56.

Konings, Jozef, Hartmut Lehmann and Mark Schaffer (1996): 'Job Creation and Job Destruction in a Transition Economy: Ownership, Firm Size, and Gross Flows in Polish Manufacturing 1988–91', *Labour Economics*, **3(3)**, 299–317.

Krueger, Alan, and Jörn-Steffen Pischke (1995): 'A Comparative Analysis of East and West German Labor Markets: Before and After Unification', in Richard Freeman and Lawrence Katz (eds), *Differences and Changes in Wage Structure*, University of Chicago Press, Chicago IL, 405.

Lanjouw, Peter (1997): 'How important is a Poverty Line in the Central Asian Context?', in Jane Falkingham et al. (eds), *Household Welfare in Central Asia*, Macmillan, Basingstoke UK, 61–77.

Lanjouw, Peter, Branko Milanovic and Stefano Paternostro (1998): 'Poverty and Economic Transition: How do Changes in Economies of Scale affect

Poverty Rates of Different Households?', *World Bank Policy Research Working Paper No. WPS 2009*, World Bank, Washington DC, November.

Lewis, W. Arthur (1954): 'Economic Development with Unlimited Supplies of Labor', *Manchester School*, **10**, 139–91.

Lubin, Nancy (1984): *Labour and Nationality in Soviet Central Asia: An Uneasy Compromise*, Princeton University Press, Princeton NJ.

Lubin, Nancy (1999): 'Energy Wealth, Development, and Stability in Turkmenistan', *NBR Analysis*, **10(3)**, 61–78 (Seattle WA: National Bureau of Asian Research).

McAuley, Alastair (1979): *Economic Welfare in the Soviet Union: Poverty, Living Standards, and Inequality*, University of Wisconsin Press, Madison WI, and George Allen and Unwin, London UK.

McAuley, Alastair (1994): 'Poverty and Anti-poverty Policy in a Quasi-developed Society: The Case of Uzbekistan', *Communist Economies and Economic Transformation*, **6(2)**, 187–201.

McMillan, John, and Christopher Woodruff (1999a): 'Interfirm Relationships and Informal Credit in Vietnam', *Quarterly Journal of Economics*, **114(4)**, 1285–1320.

McMillan, John, and Christopher Woodruff (1999b): 'Dispute Prevention without Courts in Vietnam', *Journal of Law, Economics and Organization*, **15(3)**, 637–58.

Marnie, Sheila, and John Micklewright (1997): 'Poverty in pre-reform Uzbekistan: What do official data really reveal?', *Review of Income and Wealth*, **40(4)**, 395–414.

Massell, Gregory (1975): *The Surrogate Proletariat: Moslem Women and Revolutionary Change in Soviet Central Asia 1919–1929*, Princeton University Press, Princeton NJ.

Matthews, Mervyn (1986): *Poverty in the Soviet Union: The Life-styles of the Under-privileged in Recent Years*, Cambridge University Press, Cambridge UK.

Mercer-Blackman, Valerie, and Anna Unigovskaya (2000): 'Compliance with IMF Program Indicators and Growth in Transition Economies', *IMF Working Paper WP/00/47*, International Monetary Fund, Washington DC.

Mee, Wendy (2001): *Women in the Republic of Uzbekistan*, Asian Development Bank, Manila.

Milanovic, Branko (1998): *Income, Inequality, and Poverty during the Transition from Planned to Market Economy*, World Bank, Washington DC.

Mudahar, Mohinder S. (1998): 'Kyrgyz Republic: Strategy for Rural Growth and Poverty Alleviation', *World Bank Discussion Paper No. 394*, World Bank, Washington DC.

Musaeva, Jarkinay, Kylychbek Supataev, Tenti Iskakov, Evgeny Ivanov and Bolot Joldubaev (2000): *The Kyrgyz Republic: Private Sector Development in Rural Areas*, Project report, World Bank, Bishkek.

Naughton, Barry (1995): *Growing out of the Plan: Chinese Economic Reform, 1978–1993*, Cambridge University Press, Cambridge UK.

Newell, Andrew, and Barry Reilly (1996): 'The Gender Wage Gap in Russia: Some Empirical Evidence', *Labour Economics*, **3(3)**, 337–56.

Newell, Andrew, and Barry Reilly (1999): 'Rates of Return to Educational Qualifications in the Transitional Economies,' *Education Economics*, **7(1)**, 67–84.

Newell, Andrew, and Barry Reilly (2001): 'The Gender Pay Gap in the Transition from Communism: Some Empirical Evidence', *Economic Systems*, **25(4)**, 287–304.

Noorkoiv, Rivo, Peter Orazem, Allan Puur and Milan Vodopevic (1997): 'How Estonia's Economic Transition affected Employment and Wages', *World Bank Policy Research Working Paper 1837*, World Bank, Washington DC, October.

Ochs, Michael (1997): 'Turkmenistan: The Quest for Stability and Control', in Karen Dawisha and Bruce Parrott (eds), *Conflict, Cleavage, and Change: Central Asia and the Caucasus,* Cambridge University Press, Cambridge UK, 312–59.

Ofer, Gur, and Aron Vinokur (1982): 'Earnings Differentials by Sex in the Soviet Union: A First Look' in S. Rosefield (ed.), *Economic Welfare and the Economics of Soviet Socialism*, Cambridge University Press, Cambridge, UK. Reprinted in Gur Ofer and Aron Vinokur (1992): *The Soviet Household under the Old Regime*, Cambridge University Press, Cambridge UK, 229–70.

Ogloblin, Constantin (1999): 'The Gender Earnings Differential in the Russian Transition Economy', *Industrial and Labor Relations Review*, **52(4)**, 602–27.

Olcott, Martha Brill (1996): 'Demographic Upheavals in Central Asia', *Orbis*, Fall, 537–55.

Olcott, Martha Brill (1998): *Kazakhstan: A Faint-hearted Democracy*, Carnegie Endowment for International Peace, Washington DC.

Orazem, Peter, and Milan Vodopivec (1995): 'Winners and Losers in Transition: Returns to Education, Experience and Gender in Slovenia', *World Bank Economic Review*, **9**, 201–30.

Orazem, Peter, and Milan Vodopivec (2000): 'Male-Female Differences in Labor Market Outcomes during the Early Transition to Market: The Cases of Estonia and Slovenia', *Journal of Population Economics*, **13(2)**, 283–303.

Pastor, Gonzalo, and Ron van Rooden (2000): 'Turkmenistan – The Burden of Current Agricultural Policies', *IMF Working Paper WP/00/98*, International Monetary Fund, Washington DC.

Patnaik, Ajay (1989): *Perestroika and Women Labour Force in Soviet Central Asia,* New Literature, New Delhi.

Paternosto, Stefano, and David Sahn (1999): 'Wage Determination and Gender Discrimination in a Transition Economy: The Case of Romania', *Policy Research Working Paper WPS 2113*, World Bank, Washington DC, May.

Pissarides, Francesca (1998): 'Is Lack of Funds the Main Obstacles to Growth?' *EBRD Working Paper No.33*, European Bank for Reconstruction and Development, London UK.

Pissarides, Francesca, Miroslav Singer and Jan Svejnar (2000): 'Objectives and Constraints of Entrepreneurs: Evidence from Small and Medium-sized Enterprises in Russia and Bulgaria', *EBRD Working Paper No. 59*, European Bank for Reconstruction and Development, London UK.

Pomfret, Richard (1995): *The Economies of Central Asia*, Princeton University Press, Princeton NJ.

Pomfret, Richard (1996): *Asian Economies in Transition*, Edward Elgar, Cheltenham UK.

Pomfret, Richard (1999a): 'Living Standards in Central Asia', *MOCT-MOST: Economic Policy in Transitional Economies*, **9(4)**, 395–421.

Pomfret, Richard (1999b): *Central Asia Turns South? Trade Relations in Transition*, Royal Institute of International Affairs, London UK, and The Brookings Institution, Washington DC.

Pomfret, Richard (2000a): 'Transition and Democracy in Mongolia', *Europe-Asia Studies* (formerly *Soviet Studies*), **52(1)**, 149–60.

Pomfret, Richard (2000b): 'Agrarian Reform in Uzbekistan: Why has the Chinese Model Failed to Deliver?' *Economic Development and Cultural Change*, **48(2)**, 269–84.

Pomfret, Richard (2000c): 'The Uzbek Model of Economic Development 1991–99', *Economics of Transition*, **8(3)**, 733–48.

Pomfret, Richard (2001): 'Turkmenistan: From Communism to Nationalism by Gradual Economic Reform', *MOCT-MOST: Economic Policy in Transitional Economies*, **11(2)**, 155–66.

Pomfret, Richard (2002a): 'State-Directed Diffusion of Technology: The Mechanization of Cotton-Harvesting in Soviet Central Asia', *Journal of Economic History*, **62(1)**, March.

Pomfret, Richard (2002b): *Constructing a Market Economy: Diverse Paths from Central Planning in Asia and Europe*, Edward Elgar, Cheltenham UK.

Pomfret, Richard, and Kathryn Anderson (1997): 'Uzbekistan: Welfare Impact of Slow Transition', *WIDER Working Paper 135*, United Nations University World Institute for Development Economics Research, Helsinki, Finland – revised version published in Aiguo Lu and Manuel Montes (eds) *Poverty, Income Distribution and Well-being in Asia During the Transition*, Palgrave, Basingstoke UK, 2002.

Pomfret, Richard, and Kathryn Anderson (1998): 'Transition and Poverty in Central Asia', *The Soviet and Post-Soviet Review*, **25(2)**, 149–62.

Pomfret, Richard, and Kathryn Anderson (1999): 'Poverty in Kyrgyzstan', *Asia-Pacific Development Journal*, **6(1)**, 73–88.

Pomfret, Richard, and Kathryn Anderson (2001): 'Economic Development Strategies in Central Asia since 1991', *Asian Studies Review*, **25(2)**, 185–200.

Popkin, Barry (1994): 'A Subsistence Income Level for Kyrgyzstan', unpublished paper. Carolina Population Center, University of North Carolina, Chapel Hill, NC.

Reilly, Barry (1999): 'The Gender Pay Gap in Russia during the Transition, 1992–96', *Economics of Transition*, **7(1)**, 245–64.

Research Triangle Institute (1996): *Kyrgyzstan Analysis Report, Spring 1996, Living Standard and Measurement Survey*, Center for International Development, P.O. Box 12194, Research Triangle Park, NC 27709-2194, USA.

Roberts, Bryan (1997): 'New Evidence on Household Consumption, the Shadow Economy, and Relative Prices during Transition to a Market Economy', unpublished paper, University of Miami, Coral Gables FL.

Rosenberg, Christoph, and Maarten de Zeeuw (2000): 'Welfare effects of Uzbekistan's Foreign Exchange Regime', *IMF Working Paper 00/61*, International Monetary Fund, Washington DC.

Rutkowski, Jan (1996): 'High Skills Pay Off: The Changing Wage Structure during Economic Transition in Poland', *Economics of Transition*, **4(1)**, 89–112.

Rutkowski, Jan (2001): 'Earnings Mobility during the Transition: The Case of Hungary, 1992–1997', *MOCT-MOST: Economic Policy in Transitional Economies*, **11(1)**, 69–89.

Schultz, Theodore W. (1975): 'The Value of Ability to Deal with Disequilibria', *Journal of Economic Literature*, **13**, 827–46.

Smeeding, Tim (1990): 'Economic Status of the Elderly', in R.H. Binstock and L.K. George (eds), *Handbook of Aging and the Social Sciences*, Academic Press Inc., San Diego CA, 362–81.

Smith, Craig (1995): 'An Economic Analysis of Ethnicity in Uzbekistan', *Comparative Economic Studies*, **37(2)**, 97–110.

Spechler, Martin (1999): 'Uzbekistan: The Silk Road to Nowhere?', *Contemporary Economic Policy*, **18(3)**, 295–303.

Svejnar, Jan (1999): 'Labor Markets in the Transitional Central and East European Economies', in Orley Ashenfelter and David Card (eds), *Handbook of Labor Economics*, vol. 3B, Elsevier Science, Amsterdam, 2809–57.

Swafford, Michael (1978): 'Sex Differences in Soviet Earnings', *American Sociological Review*, **43(5)**, 657–73.

Tarr, David (1994): 'How Moving to World Prices Affects the Terms of Trade of 15 Countries of the Former Soviet Union', *Journal of Comparative Economics*, **18(1)**, 1–24.

Taube, Günther, and Jeromin Zettelmeyer (1998): 'Output Decline and Recovery in Uzbekistan: Past performance and future prospects', *IMF Working Paper WP/98/132,* International Monetary Fund, Washington DC.

Tursunkhodjaev, Khasan (2000): *The Efficiency of the Privatization Process in Central Asia: The Case of Kyrgyzstan,* MA Thesis, Graduate Program in Economic Development, Vanderbilt University, Nashville TN.

Ubaidullaeva, R.A. (1982): 'The Twenty-fifth Congress of the CPSU and Current Problems of Employment of Female Labor in the Republics of Central Asia' – translated from a 1976 Russian text and reprinted in Gail Warshofsky Lapidus (ed.), *Women, Work, and Family in the Soviet Union,* M.E. Sharpe, Armonk NY, 147–55.

UNDP (1994): *Human Development Report,* United Nations Development Program, New York.

UNDP (1997a): *Human Development Report: Kyrgyz Republic,* United Nations Development Program, New York.

UNDP (1997b): *Human Development Report: Tajikistan,* United Nations Development Program, New York.

UNICEF (1999): *Women in Transition; The MONEE Project Regional Monitoring Report No.6,* United Nations Children's Fund International Child Development Centre, Florence, Italy.

Vecernik, Jiri (1995): 'Changing Earnings Distributions in the Czech Republic: Survey Evidence from 1988–1994', *Economics of Transition,* **3,** 333–53.

World Bank (1992): 'Measuring the Incomes of Economies of the Former Soviet Union', *Policy Research Working Paper WPS 1057,* World Bank, Washington DC.

World Bank (1995): *The Kyrgyz Republic: Poverty Assessment and Strategy,* Report No.14380-KG, World Bank, Washington DC.

World Bank (1996): *World Development Report 1996: From Plan to Market,* World Bank, New York.

World Bank (1997): *Transition,* **8(1),** 3.

World Bank (1997): *World Development Indicators 1997,* World Bank, Washington DC.

World Bank (1998): *World Development Indicators 1998,* World Bank, Washington DC.

World Bank (2000): *Republic of Tajikistan: Poverty Assessment,* Report No.20285-TJ, World Bank, Washington DC.

World Bank (2002): *Transition: The First Ten Years – Analysis and Lessons for Eastern Europe and the Former Soviet Union,* World Bank, Washington DC.

Zettelmeyer, Jeromin (1998): 'The Uzbek Growth Puzzle', *IMF Working Paper WP/98/133,* International Monetary Fund, Washington DC.

Index